DIGITAL COMMAND CONTROL

THE DEFINITIVE GUIDE

DIGITAL COMMAND CONTROL

THE DEFINITIVE GUIDE

Ian Morton

First published 2011

ISBN 978 0 7110 35027

Published by Ian Allan Publishing

an imprint of Ian Allan Publishing, Ltd, Hersham, Surrey KT12 4RG.

Printed in England by Ian Allan Printing Ltd, Hersham, Surrey KT12 4RG.

Visit the Ian Allan Publishing website at www.ianallanpublishing.com

Distributed in the United States of America and Canada by BookMasters Distribution Services.

Contents

Preface

This book starts from the assumption that you have already decided that DCC is for you, and that you want to get the most from it. Its aim not to provide a simple guide to the basics of DCC or sufficient information for you to decide if you should adopt it for your layout, these topics are covered in *Aspects of Modelling – Digital Command Control*. While this definitive guide covers many of the same aspects as that earlier book, it goes further into the possibilities that DCC offers and provides more detailed explanations of what is required to tame the technology.

DCC is continually evolving and new products are coming on the market all the time. What might once have seemed difficult or impossible may now be an off-the-shelf product. While I have tried to suggest here how things might develop, it is, of course, quite possible that manufacturers may go down an entirely unforeseen route.

Chapter 1

The Background

On a DCC layout, a computer can act as an extra operator, drive mainline trains while you shunt a yard, act as signalman or look after the fiddle yard. *Hornby Magazine's* Bolsover and Seven Lane Pit uses Hornby RailMaster software to manage train movements. PHOTO: MIKE WILD

The idea of command control systems has been around since the 1940s. Over the years a number of manufacturers have attempted to market them, but it was only in the 1970s that multiple-train control systems started to become commercially feasible. There were a number of false starts; equipment from competing manufacturers was not compatible, meaning that once you selected one of these expensive systems you were limited to what that particular manufacturer offered. The early systems were not very reliable either, and the limited take-up meant they disappeared from the general market.

However, the idea lived on. The National Model Railroad Association (NMRA) in America adopted a proposal for a set of standards for multiple-train control from Lenz in Germany. They believed that if all the equipment was compatible, it would benefit both manufacturers and modellers. The standards were developed; the system was named Digital Command Control (DCC) and made freely available for manufacturers to use. Today, a wide range of manufacturers offers all sorts of DCC equipment and, within certain limits, it is compatible between their various ranges.

So what is a Digital Command Control system, and what advantages does it offer over conventional model train control?

In a conventional control system, speed and direction are set at the controller to which the motor is directly connected. In a command control system, the speed and direction are set at the controller and the information is sent to a device next to the motor, which in turn controls the motor.

The information can be sent by a variety of means such as infrared beams, radio transmission or superimposing the information onto a power supply voltage. The key is that control takes place near the actual motor itself, rather than at the controller.

Even a simple branch terminus to fiddle yard layout needs a number of switches for power distribution if you use analogue (DC) control. All these switches could be eliminated by converting to DCC.

The first advantage – when you are dealing with low-voltage motors such as those fitted in model locomotives – is that the voltages and currents are not further reduced by yards of wire and rail, switch contacts, plugs and sockets. Instead, the current only has to travel along a few inches of wire, which makes for more reliability and better control.

The second advantage is that the overhead of a conventional cab control system – whereby a section of track can be connected to a specific controller – is no longer required, meaning less switches, less wires, less connectors and less that can potentially go wrong. The command control system sends the right information to the right locomotive, leaving the operator to concentrate on driving it rather than flicking block control switches.

The third advantage is that since each locomotive now has its own local controller, each one can be tailored to suit it. This is not possible with a conventional control system, as each of the controllers can operate any of the locomotives – unless the controller's characteristics can be set, and the operator sets them each time a different locomotive is used. As a bonus, the local controller can also used to control other things, such as lights.

With DCC the information is superimposed on a power supply voltage. This means that there is a constant voltage on the track which is used to power the locomotives and other accessories. This voltage is higher than would normally be used to run trains, and so the problem of lower voltages being attenuated by wires and rails is reduced. The overall effect is to improve the electrical pick-up of the locomotives on the layout. As the DCC voltage is AC rather than DC, there is no

DCC is not just for 'serious' modellers. It is ideally suited to junior layouts too, with the ability to run any train anywhere and to change track layouts without extensive rewiring.

nett electrical charge on the layout, which helps to reduce the amount of dirt that accumulates on wheels and rails.

Despite all these benefits, command control systems were not widely adopted before the advent of DCC. Many of the earlier systems were analogue rather than digital and were limited in terms of the number of locomotives that could be operated, the size of the components needed to build the controllers for the locomotives, the relatively high cost of the system and the fact that different systems were not compatible – once you chose a system you were stuck with it, particularly if it was withdrawn or the manufacturer went out of business.

Consumer technology has raced forward over the past 30 years. Many items now incorporate digital technology – the same circuitry and processing power that you find in computers. Digital circuit parts have grown smaller, cheaper and more powerful, leading to devices like mobile phones and digital cameras that would have been the stuff of science fiction only a few years ago. DCC uses digital technology and benefits from many of these advances. You can buy decoders that will fit inside small locomotives, handheld controllers with graphical screens and command stations that have more processing power than NASA used to put a man on the moon – and all at prices that many modellers can afford.

DCC is also standardised. Any locomotive or accessory decoder will work with any command station. You are not tied to the products of one manufacturer but can mix and match to suit availability and your own needs. Bernd Lenz, the pioneer of DCC, developed the standards and passed them to the American NMRA (National

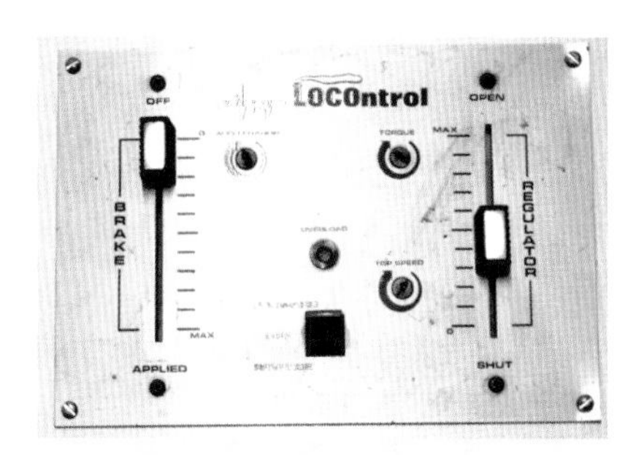

Some analogue controllers came with features to simulate the way real locomotives work. This one had a separate brake and throttle, plus controls to set the acceleration rate and momentum. The controls would be reset for each locomotive every time that you drove it. With DCC the acceleration rate is set in the decoder and applies whenever the locomotive runs, whichever controller handset is operating it.

Model Railroad Association), who in turn published and policed the standards. Any manufacturer can use them; provided their product has been tested and found

The layout gives no visible indication as to whether it is analogue (DC) or DCC operated. In fact, this Hornby T9 came with a DCC decoder already installed. Built for the Activity Media DVD *Starting on the Right Track*, it is controlled via a Hornby Select controller.

to meet the standards, it can also carry the NMRA-approved logo to show it is compatible.

The NMRA standards only apply to the information that leaves the command station and is received by the decoders. It does not apply to the various methods of linking controllers to the command station or of providing feedback from points, signals, occupancy detectors and so on. These areas remain under the control of the manufacturers. The NMRA is slow to adopt changes to its standards, but this is no bad thing. Changes must be made in such a way that older equipment will still be able to work – however appealing a new feature may be, if it involves replacing all your locomotive decoders it is unlikely to catch on. The changes must represent a worthwhile enhancement.

DCC System Components

A DCC system consists of a command station, one or more cabs and one or more boosters. Some or all of these may be in the same box, but they all perform different functions. At the other end, everything that will be controlled by the DCC system – from locomotives to points – will need to have a DCC decoder.

Cabs

Or the controller, as we British would normally call it. The cab (the word underlining DCC's American origins) is the component that tells the system what you want the locomotive to do. Cabs come in a wide variety of sizes, styles and capabilities. Even a layout operated by a single person can, at times, find a use for more than one cab. While it is simple to change which train you are operating from your cab, if you have more than one running at a time it can be easier to cope if you have more than one cab.

Some cabs are designed to be used at a traditional control panel, the standard way in which British layouts have been operated over the years. Others are handheld units that allow you to move around with your train. The latter come in two types: tethered, which have a cable that runs from the controller to the layout, and remote, which have either an infrared or a radio link.

Command Station

The brains of the system. This is a computer that takes information from the cabs and any other devices that generate commands and converts them into DCC signals. The command station will also keep track of what is going on and ensure that everything is running smoothly. For example, it will not send a command like 'Locomotive 4 turn your headlight on' once but a number of times, in case the locomotive had temporarily lost power due to some dirty track just as the message was sent.

A DCC system can have a number of cabs and boosters but will only have one command station. If you connected two command stations into your system then they would both try to process and send commands, which would at best send conflicting messages and at worst lead to your DCC system being damaged.

Boosters

The brawn to the command station's brain. These take the DCC signal, which at this point is still just data, and add it to the power supplied to the rails and DCC bus. Boosters will also monitor the layout and, if a short circuit is detected, shut down before anything can get damaged. It will notify the command station of the shutdown and, in turn, the command station will normally pass the information on to the cabs.

On a layout where there are many decoders drawing current, it may be necessary to have more than one booster. When you have more than one the outputs must be electrically isolated from each other, which will normally entail separate sections of layout.

DCC Decoders

Decoders are the local controllers that use the DCC signal to make locomotives or accessories do what you want them to.

- **Locomotive Decoders**
  Designed to be installed inside a locomotive, they control the motor's speed and direction. This requires that the motor is connected to the

Bachmann's Dynamis cab has a large graphical display which can provide more information than many cabs with one- or two-line, character-only displays.

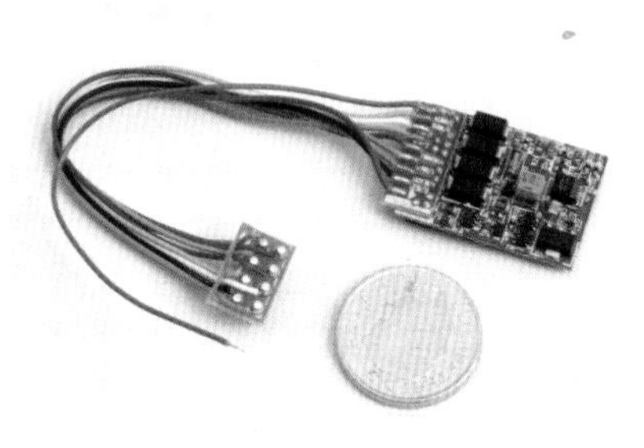

The Hornby Sapphire decoder can be used in both 8- and 21-pin, DCC-fitted locomotives.

decoder rather than to the track. One of the easiest ways to destroy a locomotive decoder is to leave one of the motor's brushes still connected to the track.

The decoder takes the DCC input and extracts the DCC signal to check if it contains information that needs to be dealt with. If the message is for another decoder, it will carry on with what it was already doing; otherwise it will read the message and perform the necessary action.

The decoder is a basic computer and can perform a number of tasks. For example, when told that the motor should now run at a certain speed, the decoder can work out whether this should be faster or slower and gently accelerate or decelerate.

Decoders often have function outputs which can be used to power accessories such as lights. These can be turned on and off by DCC commands from the command station.

Sound decoders come with loudspeakers that make locomotive sounds synchronised to the movement of the model. Again, additional functions are available to create the sound of whistles and other noises on demand.

- **Function Decoders**
  These are locomotive decoders without motor control circuitry. In fact, people often use old locomotive decoders that have been replaced by newer ones and just ignore the motor connections.

  Function decoders can be fitted in other rolling stock such as brake vans, coaches and dummy locomotives to control lights and other effects. Sometimes it is necessary to install both a locomotive decoder and a function decoder to cope with the various lights and other working gadgets that have been added.

- **Accessory Decoders**
  Sometimes called stationary decoders, these are for operating fixed objects like points and signals. Usually, one decoder will operate a number of different accessories – typically four.

Some accessory decoders have the ability to take their power from a separate supply, whilst taking the signal from the DCC supply. This is of great benefit when you are using solenoid point motors, as the large current draw when they fire can diminish the current elsewhere on the layout and lead to locomotives failing to respond to controls, as well as other problems.

Other facilities found on accessory decoders include local control (using panel switches rather than the DCC system to operate an accessory), feedback (sending information about the state of the accessory – for example, how a point is set – back to the command station) and route setting(where triggering one output causes a number of other accessory outputs to change).

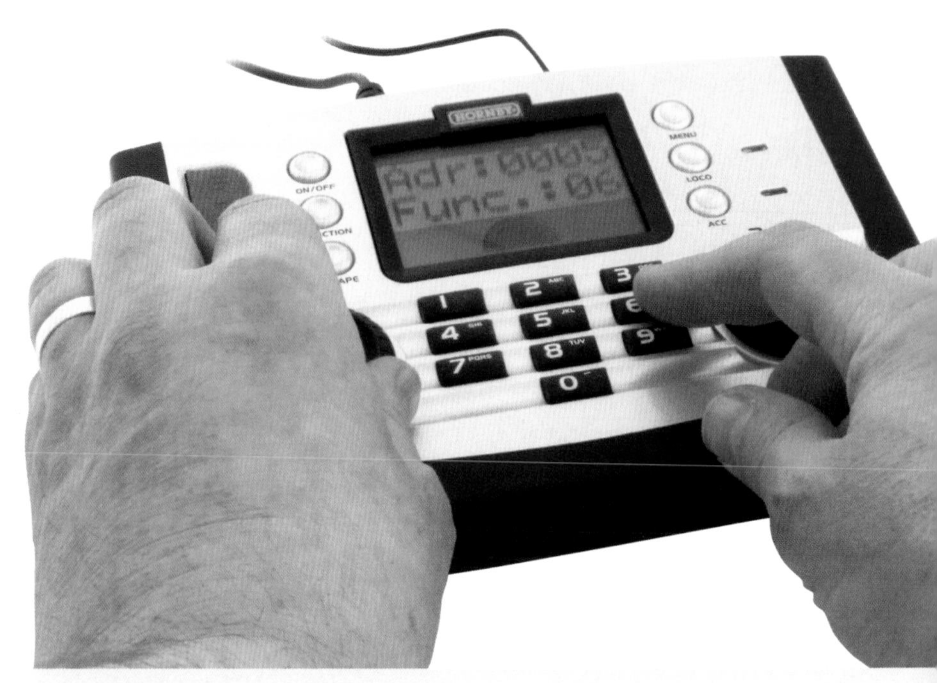

Some DCC systems, like Hornby's Elite, combine the functions of cab, command station and booster. The Elite comes with two built-in cabs – hence the two knobs – allowing the direct control of two locomotives simultaneously.

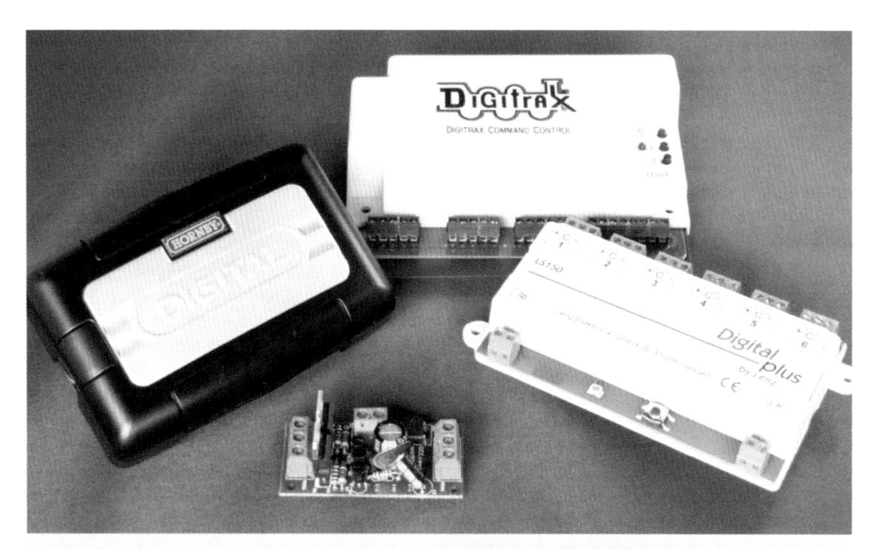

Accessory decoders are used to operate point motors, signals and other working accessories. As with locomotive decoders, different manufacturers offer different facilities. Any decoder can be used with any DCC system.

How DCC Works

While you don't need to know how DCC works in order to use it, many people are curious. If you really don't want to know how it works its magic, feel free to skip on to the next section.

An Overview

Inside each locomotive on an analogue (DC) model railway is an electric motor connected to the track. A standard model railway controller is also connected to the track. As we turn the knob on the controller from OFF to MAXIMUM, the motor in the locomotive will run faster and faster. When we turn the knob back to OFF, the motor stops. If we then change the direction switch and move the knob again, the motor runs in the opposite direction. This allows us to control the direction and speed of our model, but how does the magic actually work?

Each of the rails is connected to the controller. The wheels of the locomotive are electrically connected to the motor. With the locomotive standing on the track, the controller is connected via the rails and wheels to the motor.

The controller puts a VOLTAGE across the two rails. This is what causes the motor to run. As the voltage increases from 0 (OFF) to 12 Volts (MAXIMUM), the motor goes faster. If we change the direction switch then the voltage is applied the other way around and goes from 0 (OFF) to -12 Volts (MAXIMUM – in reverse).

If we want to have more than one locomotive on the layout then the other locomotives must be parked on lengths of track that are not connected to the controller. When we want to use a different locomotive, then the track that it is on must be connected to the controller and the other track disconnected. A track or locomotive that is disconnected from the controller is called 'isolated'.

On a simple layout you can use the points to isolate locomotives. Most commercially produced points isolate one track and power the other – the one on the direction that the point is set, but for more complex layouts or operation you will find that some lengths of track need to be isolated by means of switches on a control panel. Similarly, if you have two or more controllers so that you can have more than one locomotive moving at a time, you will find that there is a need for control panel switches to choose which

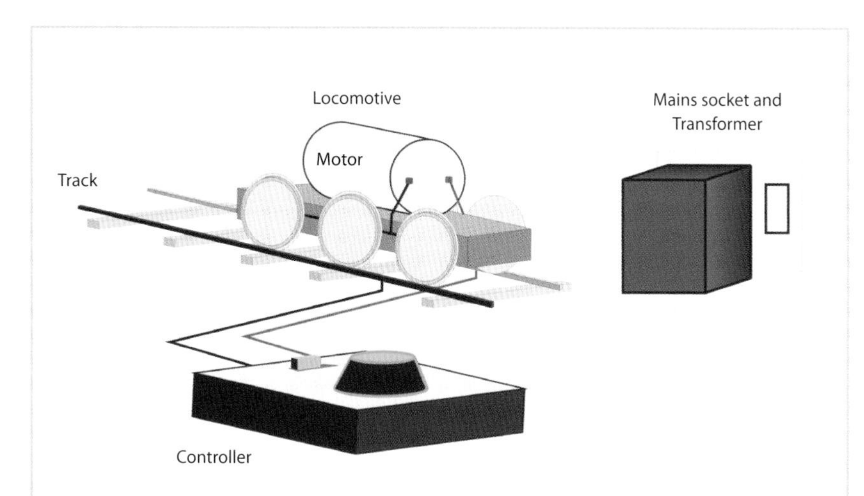

The electrical connections needed to make a model locomotive move. A transformer is plugged into a mains socket. The transformer converts the mains voltage electricity into something safer to use. The transformer powers the controller which has a knob to control the locomotive's speed and a switch to control its direction. Two wires from the controller run to the rails, one each side of the track. The locomotive has metal wheels that pick up electricity from the track and are connected in turn to the locomotive's motor.

controller is connected to a particular track.

On a medium to large layout these extra isolated sections and switches lead to a lot of wiring. While the individual circuits are simple, the sheer number of switches and wires can make the underside of a layout look like a complex jumble of cables.

A DCC system still uses the rails to carry electricity to the locomotives but works differently. DCC track not only carries the electricity but also information, in the form of electrical signals, that is used to control the locomotives. Each locomotive is fitted with an electronic circuit called a decoder that reads the signals and responds accordingly. The DCC command station supplies the power and creates the signals used to control the locomotives. With DCC you do not need to isolate spare locomotives and you can, depending on your layout and reactions, run more than one locomotive using a single controller.

With a DCC system there are two extra items, a command station and a decoder. You can plug a number of controllers into a command station and run as many locomotives as you like on the same length of track. Each locomotive needs to have its own decoder, which responds to the signals sent by the command station.

The Science Bit

The DCC system delivers both power and commands in the electrical voltage supplied to the rails. Communication from the command station to the decoder is accomplished by transmitting a series of 'bits' that convey instructions. A bit is a signal which represents one of two conditions, which are called '1' and '0'. The DCC voltage on the track is always either positive or negative; the data bits are transmitted by the length of time between the transition from negative to positive. The timing for a '1' bit is 58 ms (milliseconds) between transitions, giving 116 ms for the bit, whereas a '0' bit is at least 100 ms between transitions, giving at least 200 ms for the bit.

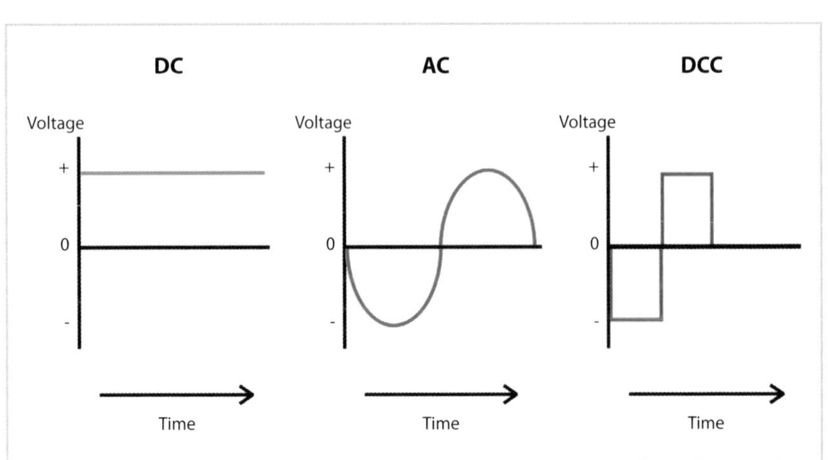

Analogue (DC) locomotives run on DC where a constant voltage is put across the tracks. Normal AC has an average zero voltage, although it is continually changing. The voltage on a DCC system is either fully negative or fully positive but, like AC, averages out to zero.

The bits are put together in groups of eight, called a byte, which can represent values between 0 and 255 in binary numbers. The bytes are put together in packets which contain a number of bytes that make up a command. A packet consists of a number of sections. The first is the preamble, which is a minimum of 10 x '1' bits and is used to synchronise the decoders with the command station. If a decoder has lost contact with the command station at some point, usually due to some dirt on the track, then the preamble allows it to work out that a new command is starting. The second is the address of the decoder that the command is being sent to. This is

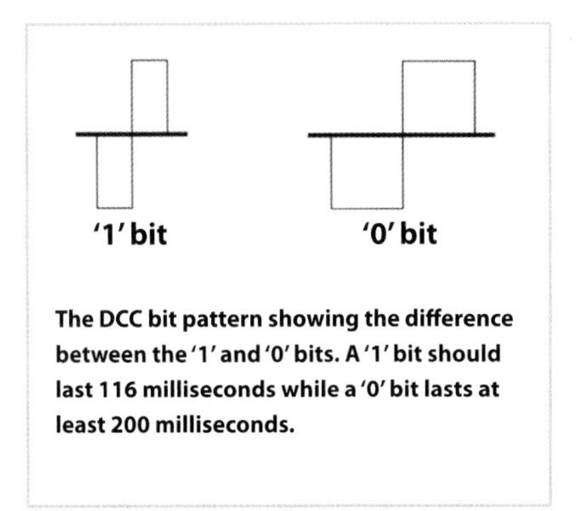

The DCC bit pattern showing the difference between the '1' and '0' bits. A '1' bit should last 116 milliseconds while a '0' bit lasts at least 200 milliseconds.

followed by the command itself and finally an error byte which the decoder uses to check that the packet has been received correctly.

All decoders receive and check each packet that the command station sends. First the error byte is checked to ensure that the packet has been received correctly, and then the address is checked to ensure that the decoder should respond. If the packet is addressed to the decoder, or is a broadcast message such as an emergency stop, the decoder will then process the command.

To enable the use of analogue (DC) locomotives, the DCC standards allow for the '0' bits to be stretched. By lengthening either the positive or negative part of the '0' bit, the overall voltage on the track can be changed. By making the overall voltage positive an analogue locomotive will move forwards, and by making it negative the locomotive will move backwards. The DCC signal and decoders are unaffected by this and continue to work normally.

Driving the Train

Manufacturers of DCC systems often promote them by saying that they let you drive the train, not the track. It makes a good slogan it is also one of the fundamental differences between DCC and conventional control. Many people who complain about the complexity of operating with DCC have failed to grasp this basic truth: with DCC, *you* are the engine driver.

You can illustrate this very simply. With conventional DC, you turn the controller up and your locomotive moves. Pick the locomotive up, turn it round and put it back on the track; to someone standing on the model's footplate, it now travels in the opposite direction. Pick it up and put it on an isolated section of track and it won't move at all. Take a locomotive from an isolated section, put it on the live track and it will start running. Everything depends on the right controller being connected to the right piece of track.

With DCC things work very differently. Start a locomotive running. Pick it up, turn it round, put it back on the track and, to someone standing on the model's footplate, it appears to travel in the same direction. Pick it up and put it somewhere else on the layout and it will continue to move in that direction. Pick a stationary locomotive up and put it anywhere on the layout and it still won't move.

This gives you great power as an operator. You can run a locomotive anywhere on your layout regardless of what the other locomotives are doing. You can park them buffer to buffer, have station pilots aiding the departure of express trains, add banking engines – in fact, just about anything that the real railway can do.

Needless to say, there are downsides too. If you have a number of operators you will need some form of signalling or train control, otherwise you may well find two trains trying to occupy the same length of track at the same time. You lose the 'turn a knob and go' simplicity that many people use when operating fiddle yards. You lose the ability to perform simple automation, like a branch line shuttle, cheaply and easily.

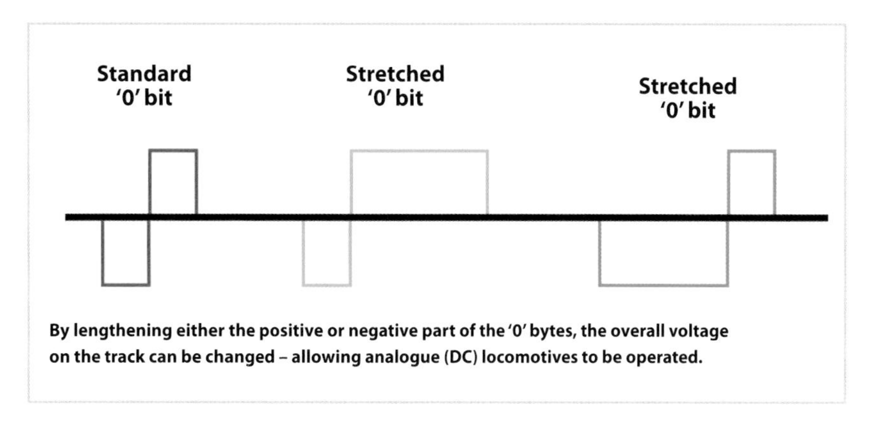

By lengthening either the positive or negative part of the '0' bytes, the overall voltage on the track can be changed – allowing analogue (DC) locomotives to be operated.

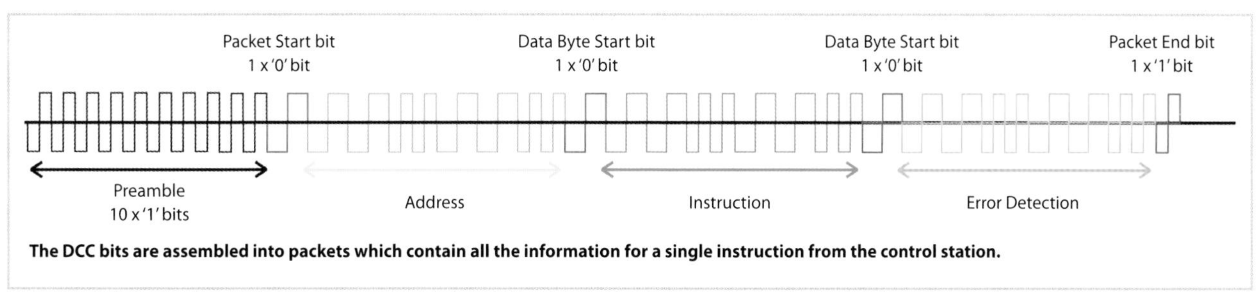

The DCC bits are assembled into packets which contain all the information for a single instruction from the control station.

DCC decoders allow you to tailor performance to get the best out of each locomotive. A model that does a lot of shunting, like this Hornby M7, can be optimised for low-speed running.

High Frequency Track Cleaners

Some analogue (DC) layouts use electronic track cleaning devices to improve running. The track cleaner is connected between the controller and the track as well as to a separate 16V AC supply. The AC supply is converted to a high-voltage, high-frequency output at a negligible current. If the resistance across the tracks suddenly increases then the high-frequency signal current increases. This will ionise any air gap or burn away any dirt film, leaving a path for the normal traction current. As soon as the traction current starts flowing again, and the motor starts turning, the high-frequency signal drops back to a negligible current.

These devices are incompatible with DCC as the high-voltage output will destroy locomotive and accessory decoders, and quite possibly the command station. Fortunately, the high-frequency DCC signal does help to keep the track clean, rendering such devices redundant anyway.

Multiple Operators

On a conventional DC layout there are a couple of ways of catering for multiple operators. They can each be responsible for the operation of trains on a part of the layout, or else some can be signalmen and others drivers. While it is easy to convert 'drivers and signalmen' to DCC operation, the 'operating area' scenario seems to be more common in the UK and is much harder to convert as it revolves around controlling the track rather than the trains.

Turn a Knob and Go

Many layouts with fiddle yards select the train to run via a road in the yard. Often people cite operating the fiddle yard as a reason for not adopting DCC, asking how they would know which locomotive address to select. On layouts which operate to some form of schedule, this isn't a problem – after all, if you know it is the down express then you should know which locomotive is hauling it. For layouts operated without a schedule this is a bigger problem, especially if the fiddle yard is out of sight, and simple manual guides such as Post-It notes or a notepad to record which locomotive is on which road are required.

Simple Automation

Over the years, modellers have developed many simple circuits to add some form of automation to their layouts. These range from a simple diode at the end of a siding, to stop locomotives running off the end, to devices that control a branch-line shuttle service. All of them work on the basis of controlling the track and the corresponding locomotives. With DCC, there is very little scope for making all trains do something particular at a certain place.

There is, however, the ability to broadcast commands to all locomotive decoders. The emergency stop is a good example: it doesn't matter where a locomotive is, what its decoder settings are or what it is doing, if the command station sends an emergency stop signal out, it stops. Unfortunately, because the signal goes out across the whole layout, it can't be used for localised control such as stopping for 30 seconds at the branch halt. Some manufacturers have produced circuits that try to do such things, but they aren't a great solution. To fit them, the area where the automation takes place needs to be isolated from the rest of the layout and connected through a special circuit. This circuit detects when a train is in section and broadcasts the necessary commands in place of the normal DCC signal. Obviously, the train needs to be entirely within the special section to stop the broadcast signal reaching the rest of the layout and stopping every train.

Given the complexity of the circuit, these units are far more expensive than the equivalent for conventional DC. Some DCC manufacturers have built automation into their systems – the Lenz Asymmetric Braking Control is one example – and CT decoders have the ability to automatically do the 'shuffle' needed to uncouple Kadee couplers. Use of these features does limit your choice of decoders, which needs to be weighed against the benefits.

Traditionally, British layouts have tended to be run from control panels where all the necessary controls are grouped together. DCC was developed for the US market, where it is more common to have handheld controllers so that you can move with your train. It is plain to see that the US style of operation – centred on

A high-frequency track cleaner produced by Gaugemaster. Any devices like this need to be removed from your layout when you convert to DCC, as they will destroy locomotive and accessory decoders.

the train rather than the place – easily adapts to DCC by simply replacing the DC circuitry powering the track. Everything else can stay the same.

British modellers who are used to controlling everything from a panel have a tendency to assume that, because the train is controlled from their handset, everything else should be too. DCC can be used to control points and anything from animated swing bridges to container cranes, but it is not necessarily the best way to do it. This may come as a shock if you have invested several hundred pounds in a DCC system, but DCC is at its best in controlling trains. Anything else is a bonus.

Let's look at a typical US walkaround layout and see how it is operated. When such layouts are operated by a group of friends, these sessions are perhaps fortnightly or even monthly; for the rest of the time, the owner runs trains on his own. With a walkaround controller he can always be near his train, so that he can see what he is doing. As a result, the points need to be controlled from somewhere

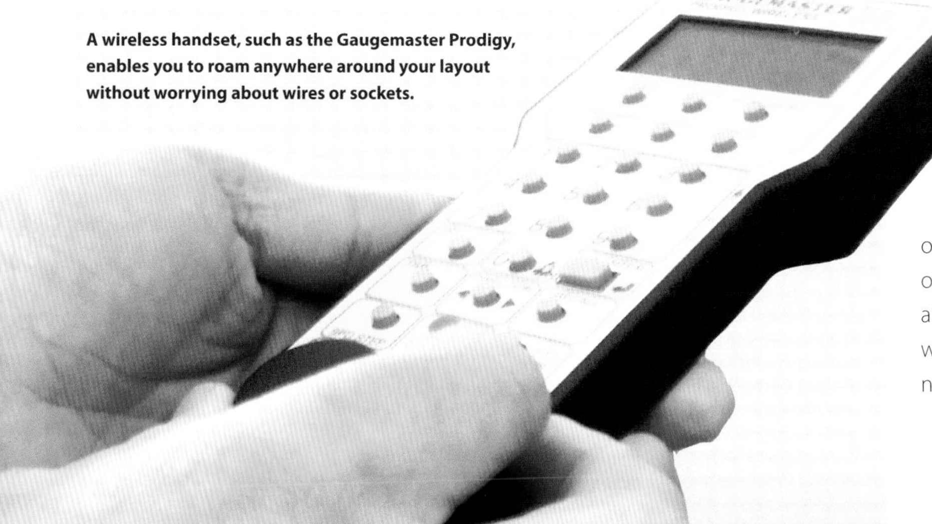

A wireless handset, such as the Gaugemaster Prodigy, enables you to roam anywhere around your layout without worrying about wires or sockets.

For years, modellers have used simple circuits to automate operations. A typical example is a train that shuttles backwards and forwards between a branch terminus and the bay platform at the junction station.

close at hand. With DC, this can be achieved with a small local panel controlling the points in the station, or even at one end of the station, or alternatively by throwing the points by hand. You can still do exactly the same with DCC but, as a bonus, also have the option of controlling the points from your DCC handset. This removes the need for the local panel altogether, although a small track diagram showing the DCC address for each of the points is very helpful. Even route control – where one button sets a number of points – has a use because, like us, US modellers have fiddle yards (they call them staging yards) and route control allows them to set all the points for a particular road in the yard on one DCC address.

Compare this to a typical UK layout. Normally they are operated by one person from a central control panel, which does everything except make the tea. Trying to shoehorn all these functions into something that you can hold in your hand is a difficult task, especially if you want to

The Lenz LH100 handset is a typical walkaround controller. Not only can it run locomotives, it can also program the decoders and operate points and other accessories.

Many layouts in the UK are operated by a single person via a large panel that controls it in its entirety.

run more than one train at a time. If you are firmly wedded to this style of operation then your options are to leave the other controls alone, to just convert the train control or to use a different controller for the points. Where you have more than one person setting points there is always the possibility of conflicting routes being set up, or of a point being changed in front of (or even underneath) another operator's train. With the US method an operator will only be changing the points in sight of his train, not on the other side of the layout.

Signals are another issue that muddies the DCC waters. Most UK layouts don't have them – or if they do they are purely cosmetic, not actually for controlling trains. This is in no small part due to the trade which, over the years, has not managed to solve the problem of making operating signals that are not excessively expensive, delicate or unrealistic.

This is a shame because, if you have people driving trains, they need some form of signalling to stop them from crashing into each other. The UK rail system goes to great lengths to ensure that points are correctly set and a route is signalled before a train is allowed to move. While that move is taking place, the points are locked and conflicting moves cannot be signalled. If you have ever tried to use a mechanical lever frame you will know that, not only do you have to pull all the right levers for a given movement, but they have to be pulled in the right order too – you cannot clear the signal until the points are set, you cannot move the points until the facing point locks are released, and so on. DCC on its own cannot match this kind of complex functioning. It cannot replicate colour-light, multiple-aspect signalling, where the signal aspect varies depending on how far ahead the line is occupied. In both cases, you need extra hardware to make it all work. You may choose to use DCC as the link between the control system and the points and signals – or you may choose something else altogether.

47 035

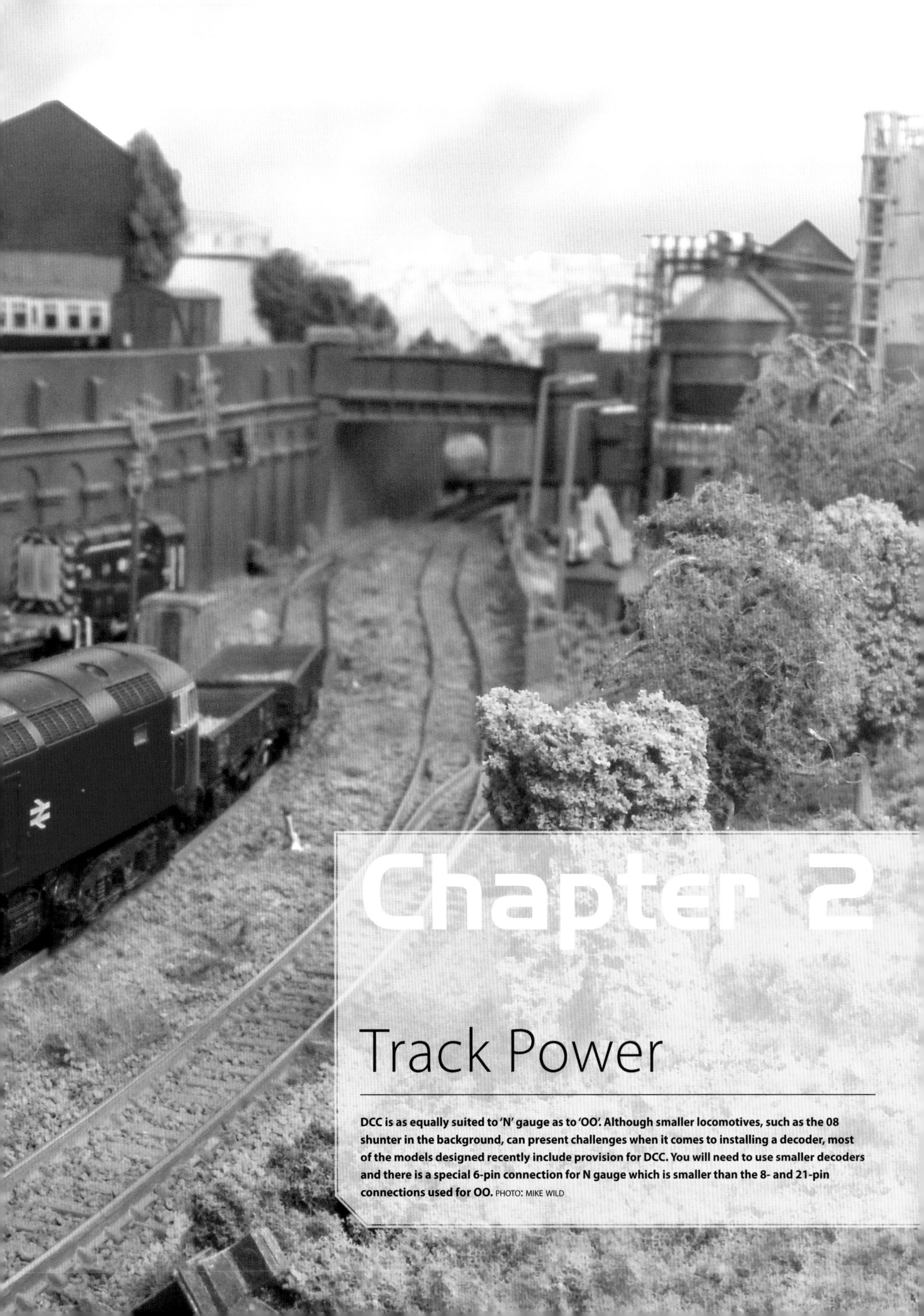

Chapter 2

Track Power

DCC is as equally suited to 'N' gauge as to 'OO'. Although smaller locomotives, such as the 08 shunter in the background, can present challenges when it comes to installing a decoder, most of the models designed recently include provision for DCC. You will need to use smaller decoders and there is a special 6-pin connection for N gauge which is smaller than the 8- and 21-pin connections used for OO. PHOTO: MIKE WILD

Choosing a DCC System

There are DCC systems to suit most requirements, from a child's train set through to a complex multi-operator empire. Selecting a suitable system is a matter of matching the facilities offered to your requirements and budget. Whilst you can operate any DCC decoder with any DCC command station, the cabs, command stations and boosters are not necessarily compatible between manufacturers.

By and large, the more flexibility and functionality that you require from your DCC system, the more you will have to pay. Fortunately, in many cases it is possible to add extra units to a basic system to expand it, without having to discard your original items.

At the bottom end of the range of prices and functions are the basic systems, such as the Bachmann E-Z Command which has limited capability but is exceedingly simple to install and operate. At the top end of the range are systems which allow more cabs and boosters than you are ever likely to need; these can be interfaced to a computer as well as operating many functions and accessories. In between these extremes are some mid-range systems that have sufficient functions and flexibility for most British layouts.

Many of the DCC manufacturers and retailers have displays at the major model railway exhibitions. If you are considering an expensive system then you would be well advised to go along and try it out for yourself. However good a system appears on paper, there are a number of questions that can only be answered when you see it reality:

- If it is a walkaround, does the cab fit comfortably in your hand?
- Is the speed control easy to operate?
- Are the buttons large enough for you to operate comfortably?
- Can you read the display?

When trying to shortlist a DCC system, the key questions that you need to ask yourself are as follows:

- How many locomotives am I likely to have?
- How many locomotives will be running at once?
- Will I be using carriage lighting?
- How many cabs do I need?
- Do I want walkaround control?
- Is there a cab bus?
- Do I want to operate points and signals?
- Do I want a computer interface?
- Is there a means of updating the command station's program?
- Do I have any special track formations?
- How many functions do I need on my locomotives?
- Can I install it all at once or do I want to do it in stages?
- How much can I afford?
- How technically minded am I?

How many locomotives am I likely to have?

If you only have room for two locomotives on your layout, then you can get by with a system that has 9 locomotive addresses. If you are installing DCC on a club layout with a vast pool of locomotives, then you may need to be able to use over 1000 addresses. Most people will find themselves somewhere between the two extremes; as most of the DCC systems currently available are able to address 9999 decoders, there should be no problem. Do be careful of 'bargain' second-hand systems like the Lenz Compact which have older, poorer specifications.

Many DCC systems have the ability to name locomotives rather than use an address. How much use this is to you will depend on your locomotive fleet, your handset and you. If you have a narrow gauge layout where every locomotive has a name, then it will be far easier to scroll through the list of names to select *Mountaineer* than to try and remember its number. If you have a large fleet of Class

The Hornby Elite combines the cab, command station and booster into a single unit. There are two control knobs which allow you to control two trains at the same time.

25 diesels, then typing in the number on the cab will be quicker than scrolling through a list of similar numbers.

If your handset does not let you name locomotives, then you will need to devise a scheme to make your addresses easy to work out. Since the 1970s, UK locomotives have carried TOPS computer numbers which run to five digits, a two-digit class number followed by three digits to identify the specific locomotive – for example, 66 503. Many modellers use the first and last two digits of the number as the locomotive's address – 6603 in this case. Multiple units have a three-digit class number and so need a different system; my personal preference is to use three class digits and the final digit of the number, thus 323 024 would be 3234.

Prior to the implementation of TOPS, locomotives could have numbers of anything from one to six digits long, so you need to devise a system best suited to your own locomotive stud. If all else fails, then a simple list of locomotives and their addresses is an invaluable thing to have to hand when operating the layout.

Using names or addresses is one thing, but the number of locomotives that the system will remember is quite another. Most systems have a limited memory and can only cope with a number of locomotives at once. Remember that details like the locomotive name, unlike the address or acceleration rate, are stored in the command station or controller handset rather than the locomotive decoder. The Bachmann Dynamis is perfectly happy with four-digit addresses but can only remember the names and details of a maximum 40 locomotives at once; add a 41st and it has to forget one of the others. The Lenz 90 handset will only allow you to scroll through the last 8 addresses entered, if you want to use a different locomotive you will have to enter the address, which can take around 20 key presses.

Running Analogue Locomotives with DCC

Many DCC systems allow you to run a standard analogue locomotive. While this can be very useful you should be aware that analogue locomotives should not be left standing on a DCC powered track.

Any such locomotive left standing will seem to buzz. This is due to the track continuously veering between a positive voltage of around 14 V to a negative one and back again. While the average voltage seen by the motor is zero and thus the motor doesn't run, the constant changes of voltage do cause the motor to buzz and heat up. If the locomotive is left in this state for more than a few minutes, the heat can cause the motor windings to melt and the motor to expire with a wisp of smoke. To avoid this, you need to ensure any analogue locomotive not in motion or temporarily stopped is either removed from the layout or parked on an isolated track. Bear in mind that some DCC systems can be configured to provide up to 22V AC on the tracks, and this could destroy a model motor very quickly.

To run analogue locomotives, the DCC system stretches some of the pulses, either on the positive or negative cycle, depending on the direction of travel required. This changes the overall average voltage seen by the locomotive without affecting DCC operation. This means that the DC voltage seen by an analogue locomotive is pulsed rather than smooth DC. While this can elicit better slow-speed performance from some locomotives, the rapid pulsing will destroy high-quality coreless motors, such as the Escap range. These are normally only found in kit-built locomotives, but if you are in any doubt, DO NOT run an analogue locomotive on DCC until you have checked that it is not fitted with a coreless motor.

I would strongly advise that you should not run an analogue locomotive on a DCC layout at all. Instead, make alternative arrangements for testing and running-in locomotives under analogue control, such as using a DC controller and a rolling road.

How many locomotives will be running at once?

The more locomotives that are running at once, the more power you need. Don't forget that with DCC you can operate several locomotives at once. For example, you could have 2 trains looping the main line, 1 double-headed, while you shunt the yard. That would be 4 locomotives just on one cab.

The more locomotives that are running, the more likely it is that one of them will get into trouble. This will either result in a short circuit or the need to press the emergency stop button. On a basic system, either of these will result in everything stopping and, if you have DCC-powered accessories, not being able to change the points either. On a home layout, this is irritating; on an exhibition layout it is a big problem, especially when the power is restored and each locomotive has to be restarted individually. More advanced systems offer a staged emergency stop where a quick press of the button only stops the locomotive controlled by that handset and holding the button down will, after a couple of seconds, stop everything.

Splitting the layout into separate power districts, either with their own booster or circuit breaker, will avoid a short in one area stopping everything else on the layout. Even on a simple layout, if you have points operated from an accessory decoder you should ensure

If you wire coach lighting direct to the rails, it will remain on all the time. If you install a DCC decoder as well, then you can turn it on and off at will.

that the latter is on its own bus. One of the most common causes of a short is driving a locomotive onto a point that is set against it. Unless your track and accessory power are on separate districts, you can't reverse the train because the track power is cut off and you can't change the point because the accessory power is cut off.

Will I be using carriage lighting?

The constant voltage on the track makes it easy to install things like carriage lighting – but all those lights take current. This needs to be added onto your power requirement and, if you want to be able to turn the lights on and off, then you will need a decoder in the coach which, of course, adds to the number of addresses that you will need to use.

Bear in mind that the function outputs from a decoder will only provide a limited current and you will not be able to run the lights for a six-coach rake from a single decoder. Whilst each decoder in the rake can have the same address, they will all draw power.

Of course, once you have a decoder installed you can consider using it to do other things, like remote uncoupling.

How many cabs do I need?

Each operator will need their own cab. You may also want some extras to save switching between different locomotives in use at the same time. Digitrax produce a cab that has two speed controls, allowing you to control two locomotives at the same time, which is ideal not only for the solo operator but for those whose layouts feature trains being banked up a hill.

The cab is the part of the system that you will use the most and so it must be something that you are happy with. Excessive button pushing, meaningless displays or an uncomfortable shape are all things that will get irritating very quickly and changing them will usually mean a completely new DCC system.

With most systems you can have different styles of cab for different uses. For programming, you will probably want a fully-featured handset with a clear display and sufficient buttons to make it easy. For an operator who just needs to run a train, then a simpler cab will be sufficient. In extreme cases, the extra cabs can be extremely limited – Hornby's Elite allows you to name locomotives and use addresses up to 9999 – but the Select controller used as extra cabs doesn't allow naming and only accepts addresses up to 59.

Do I want walkaround control?

Many DCC systems have both fixed and walkaround cabs available. In the past, most UK layouts have used fixed control systems where the operator sits in one location with all the necessary controls to hand.

With walkaround cabs, the operators can move around with their trains. Obviously this means that any controls must be situated near to where they are used but, as DCC removes the need for block and power switches, you only need to consider controls for points, signals and other accessories. Of course, if you use DCC to control these items as well, then everything can be operated from the walkaround cab. It is, of course, possible to have a combination of fixed and walkaround cabs if you wish.

Walkaround cabs come in two varieties, tethered and remote control. Tethered cabs are connected to the layout by a long cable. You plug these into sockets placed around the layout; you can unplug the cab and move it to a different socket without having to stop the train. Remote control cabs use radio or infrared signals to link to a receiver situated under or over the layout. These are more expensive and less common than the tethered variety.

With controllers of this type there is a trade-off between number of controls and functionality. If there are a few buttons then it is easy to perform simple operations, but it can be difficult, or even impossible, to achieve more complex tasks. If there are a lot of buttons then it requires fewer key presses, but it is easier to hit the wrong button when you are watching the train rather than looking at the controller.

Is there a cab bus?

Many DCC systems have a system that allows extra cabs, boosters and other accessories to be connected together easily. This is normally called a cab (or control) bus. Where a common standard is in use, equipment such as cabs from different manufacturers can be used together.

Two examples of common cab buses are the Lenz XpressNet (also called XBus III) and the Digitrax Loconet. The two systems are not compatible with each other, but any XpressNet-compatible item can, in theory, be plugged into an XpressNet bus regardless of the manufacturer. Similarly, any LocoNet-compatible item can be used on a LocoNet bus. If the manufacturer of your chosen DCC system has their own type of cab bus, then you will be restricted to using only their cabs, boosters and accessories.

Digitrax's LocoNet differs significantly from other manufacturers' offerings, in that it also carries feedback from other devices and signals for accessory decoders. In fact, it isn't really a cab bus at all but a network connecting various input and output devices that happen to include the DCC system's cabs – it is even possible to run it as a stand-alone network for accessory decoders and feedback devices (like track occupancy detectors) without having a Digitrax command station.

Feedback from devices – to indicate that sections are occupied, points have been thrown or similar crucial information – needs its own bus if you are not using LocoNet. Lenz has its RS bus, for which a limited number of devices are available, and in mainland Europe the S88 bus, from non-DCC manufacturers, is the system of choice. The main reason for using a feedback bus is to provide some form of full or partial automation; if you don't need to automate anything then you probably won't need to go to the trouble and expense of setting up a feedback bus.

Do I want to operate points and signals?

You can use DCC to run locomotives whilst sticking to conventional systems to operate points and signals – or you can use DCC for those too. You can even use DCC for the points and conventional control for the locomotives if you wish, probably as an interim measure whilst fitting your locomotives with decoders.

DCC does not eliminate wiring – though it reduces it considerably. Point motors need to be connected to accessory decoders and tracks to the DCC bus. All those wires have short runs to the decoder or bus – only the bus wires run for long distances. DCC makes the traditional control panel obsolete as everything cab be operated from the controller.

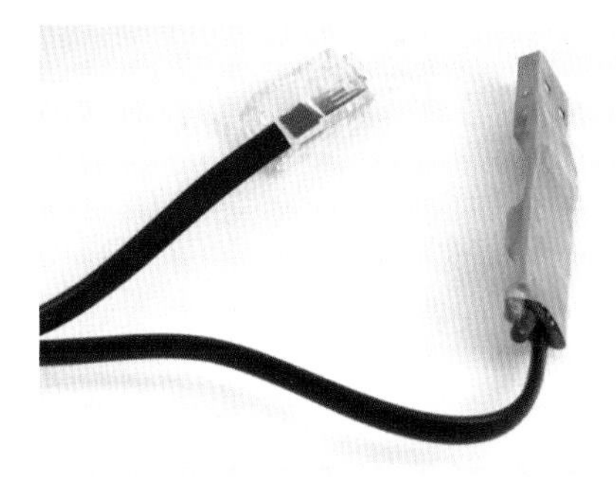

If you buy a computer interface for your DCC system, it may not seem that you get much for your money – as with this interface for the Gaugemaster Prodigy. But they do contain specialised electronic circuitry to connect the computer and the DCC controller, and to ensure that neither can damage the other.

Operating points from your handset is great if you have a walkaround layout with small stations or shunting locations. As you reach each location you can throw one or two points, perform your shunt and then carry on to the next. For complex layouts or main lines where there are other trains likely to be operating alongside you, the larger number of button pushes and possibility of conflicting moves make this less desirable.

Some accessory decoders, like those in the Digitrax range, allow you to combine local panel and DCC operation of points. Panel mounted pushbuttons can operate a point (or route) when you are standing nearby; entering the point's DCC address on the handset can do the same when you are on the other side of the room.

Route control is another useful feature offered by some control stations, or even some accessory decoders. Selecting a given address will cause all the points for a given route to be set. An example of where this might be used is in a fiddle yard, where each track in the yard is given an address and, by entering that address, all points needed to access the track are set. Many systems allow you to configure a delay between each point being operated, so that if you use solenoid point motors the accessory decoder has a chance to recharge before firing the next one in the sequence. One thing that the systems do not do is prevent you selecting a conflicting route. If one operator selects fiddle yard road 3 and another selects road 5, it is quite possible that neither road will be selected.

Do I want a computer interface?

A computer can drive trains whilst you act as signalman, it can act as signalman whilst you drive trains or it can drive trains at the same time that you do, providing other traffic for you to work around.

If that doesn't appeal, then the computer can provide a control panel for your points and signals – allowing you to select routes, warning you if you try to set up a conflicting route and automatically clearing the signals for you. If you add train detection circuits to your track, the computer can also track the trains' progress and operate the signalling automatically.

Unfortunately, not all computer interfaces are equal. The MRC/Gaugemaster Prodigy only works with its own special program, which is limited to on-screen cabs and reading/writing decoder CVs. Hornby's Elite has the ability to update the command station's program, but is very slow to pass information from the computer to the command station and back. Make sure that the system you choose is capable of doing what you want, or think that you might want in the future.

Is there a means of updating the command station's program?

Some systems have a facility to download updated software from the internet, some of them by replacing one of the integrated circuits inside the controller; others require that the unit be returned to the manufacturer for upgrading while the rest have no upgrade path.

An upgraded program may be needed to solve problems with the command station or to provide new facilities, such as the ability to operate more functions. Downloaded updates are the cheapest and easiest way to upgrade your system, entailing no extra cost, no time when the system is out of service and no need to open the command station up. It is possible for an upgrade to fail, which can result in the system needing to be returned to the manufacturer after all, but this is very unusual.

Replacing one of the integrated circuits sounds frightening, but is really no worse than installing a locomotive decoder. You need to open the command station up, identify the component to be replaced, gently lever it out and replace it with the new one. Check that the new component is the right way round, none of the legs have got bent and are all in their sockets. The old component is then usually returned to the manufacturer. In rare cases, the same procedure can apply to handsets which need an upgrade.

Returning a unit to the manufacturer or distributor is the least convenient method of upgrade. The unit needs to be posted via a service that guarantees delivery and carries sufficient insurance to provide a replacement in case of loss or damage, typically by Royal Mail Special Delivery. You are then without a DCC system until it is returned. While this is not important on the wider scale of things, being unable to operate any trains for a fortnight or so can be extremely frustrating.

Do I have any special track formations?

Wyes, reversing loops and turntables all need special treatment. Do you want to operate the voltage changeover manually or automatically? Some systems, such as Bachmann's Dynamis, have such sensitive overload cut-outs that none of the automatic reversing units will work with them. If you don't have any of these track formations, then it isn't a problem. If you do, then you struggle to remember to switch the polarity manually, since you don't need to throw any other track-power switches. Of course, you may be able to arrange the polarity to be switched automatically by the contacts on a point, but you do need to take this into account.

How many functions do I need on my locomotives?

Modern light systems can take up four decoder outputs – then there is sound, remote uncoupling, smoke generators...

If your layout is 'N' gauge, then you will have less scope for functions; most models are limited to head and tail lights, but a modern, sound-equipped, 4mm-scale diesel locomotive can use over a dozen functions. The more keys that you have to press to operate a function, the less you will use it. It makes sense to ensure that your handset can easily access the highest number function that you are likely to use regularly.

Can I install it all at once or do I want to do it in stages?

Features like a computer interface or automatically operated reversing loops can be added later. Point and signal operation can be converted to DCC once the locomotive conversion is complete.

How much can I afford?

Be realistic. It is easy to get carried away with features that you may never need or use. Don't be tempted by features that you don't really want, or won't be able to work out how to use – they only push the price up without any benefit to you, the buyer.

How technically-minded am I?

Let's face it: if the clock on your car dashboard is an hour out for half the year because you can't adjust it for British Summer Time, you're unlikely to be able to master the more advanced facilities in a DCC system's repertoire.

On the other hand, if you love gadgets and can make your mobile phone do things that even the designer didn't realise it could do, you will outgrow a basic system very quickly.

Configuring Your Command Station

Most command stations offer a range of settings that can be configured by the operator. These are usually hidden away in the documentation and remain unknown to many owners. As an example, the Lenz LZV100 has an AUTO and a MANUAL mode. In AUTO mode, when you turn it on the system carries on with what it was doing when it was shut down; so locomotives that were moving then will immediately start moving again and functions that were turned on then will be turned on again. In MANUAL mode, the system starts up with all locomotives stationary and functions turned off. You can also set the track voltage to a value between 11 and 22 Volts in 0.5 Volt steps.

More Than One Train, More Than One Operator

Given that DCC provides the ability to run more than one locomotive at a time on a layout, the systems need to cater for more than one operator. In fact, most DCC systems allow for a number of operators, each of which can control a number of trains.

Once you have a number of trains and a number of operators, sooner or later you will reach a point where two operators are trying to control the same train. This may happen by mistake – for example, when someone incorrectly enters the locomotive address – or by design, when a train is being passed from one operator to another.

If you have extra functions available on a decoder, it is a good idea to separate the front and rear lights. When hauling a train, the locomotive's taillights should be off.

First, let's look at how one operator can control more than one locomotive. You select the first locomotive as normal and set it running. Its decoder will carry on running the locomotive at the set speed until it either receives a command to do something different, loses all contact with the command station or loses power; so it can be left to run around a circuit without any operator intervention. If the operator now selects a second locomotive, they have direct control of that locomotive while the first one carries on running. Depending on the DCC system in use, a single cab can operate a number of locomotives at a time with the ability to quickly switch between them.

Obviously, the more locomotives that you are running at once, the harder it is to keep track of them and the quicker you need to be able to switch from one to another to avert potential crises. Some cabs, like the Lenz 90, provide a method to scroll through the locomotives that have recently been controlled by the handset; some others, like Bachmann's Dynamis, scroll through all the locomotives that the handset knows about, while others still require you to enter the locomotive's address each time.

The locomotive's decoder responds to commands from the command station, but it doesn't care where the command originated; so if two cabs are sending instructions for the same locomotive, it is up to the command station to sort it out. The simplest method is to process both sets of commands and pass them through to the locomotive. This will result in the locomotive obeying the last command it received. There are two other commonly implemented ways of dealing with the situation: one is to let the most recent cab take control and tell the other cab that the locomotive has been 'stolen'; the other is to ask the operator who's trying to take control if they wish to 'steal' the locomotive. The second option is preferable, as it requires positive confirmation that the operator knows what they are doing and avoids, as far as possible, taking over a locomotive in error.

Accidentally taking over a locomotive results in two perplexed operators: one who can't understand why his locomotive won't move, no matter how much he fiddles with his cab, and another who can't understand why his locomotive has gone berserk!

Boosters

These are the things that power your layout. You need to have sufficient capacity to run all the locomotives and accessories you are likely to need. Many boosters have a 5 Amp capacity which – when compared to the typical 1 or 2 Amp supply of a conventional DC controller – seems somewhat excessive. However, because DCC allows you to do more, you do tend to use that greater capacity, as the booster has to supply all the power that might have been provided by two or more conventional DC controllers.

Imagine that you have two operators, each driving a locomotive, plus another locomotive running around the main line and a couple of sound-equipped locomotives idling in some sidings. That could easily consume 2 Amps. Now add in coach lighting, say a couple of 5-coach trains with each coach having five LEDs drawing 20 mA – that's 100 mA per coach, 500 mA (or 0.5A) per train and 1 Amp for the coaches. We're up to 3 Amps.

Now throw a point operated by a solenoid point motor – which could draw 3A for the time that it takes to fire – and the layout's needs have gone up to 6 Amps.

Multiple Boosters

There are a number of different ways of connecting boosters to a layout. If you have a lot of solenoid point motors that need to be thrown, then a booster supplying the accessory decoders can ensure that switching points doesn't drain power from the track.

If you have areas on the layout where there is a high power draw – perhaps in the engine shed, where sound-equipped locomotives are left idling, or at the main station where there are usually rakes of lighted coaches at the platforms – then these can be connected to a booster separate from the rest of the layout.

When connecting two or more boosters to the track, you need to electrically isolate the areas fed by each booster with insulated rail joiners in both rails. Make sure that you wire the boosters to the track so that the 'red' and 'black' rails are connected the same way, otherwise one or both of your boosters will shut down when a locomotive crosses between the sections.

Transformers for Boosters

Of course, if you don't need 5 Amps for your shunting layout there is the temptation to save a bit of money by using an old transformer. Unfortunately, this is a very bad idea. The booster will only recognise a current that is over its limit as a short circuit. If you use a transformer that, for example, can only supply 2 Amps at most, then the booster will never see a 5 Amp current and therefore never recognise a short circuit. As a result, when something does cause a short on the layout, instead of the booster shutting down virtually instantaneously, the current continues to flow – causing damage to the models, hte electronics and possibly worse.

Always use the correct transformer for your booster.

Power Districts

Once you start using DCC, you will quickly find that short circuits seem to happen more often than they did when you used DC, and that when they happen they shut the whole system down. As a result, many people believe that DCC is unreliable. So what causes this and what can be done to avoid it?

With DCC, all the track is live all the time. With DC, the track is only live when a locomotive is actually moving and when you put a locomotive on the track the controller is off. With DCC , it is easy to short the rails together as you put a locomotive on the same track. Similarly, if your locomotive wheels are not set to the correct gauge (not uncommon with ready-to-run stock), they can cause a short as they run through points.

DC controllers tend to have slow-acting thermal overload cut-outs to protect them from short circuits, so a momentary short – such as a locomotive crossing a point – does not trip the cut-out and the locomotive's momentum carries it across the point, clearing the short. The observer may see a spark, or the locomotive stutter, but will not register it as a short circuit. With DCC, the electronic cut-out responds to a short very quickly and shuts down the power to the whole layout, bringing not only the locomotive but everything else to a halt. You can minimise the problem of short circuits with DCC by checking that the metal wheels on locomotives and the rolling stock are set to the correct gauge and do not foul your points.

The other main cause of the system shutting down is driving a locomotive into a point that is set against it. Whilst the simple answer is that real locomotive drivers don't do it, and so therefore neither should you, mistakes do happen. The easy way to solve the problem is to change the point, but if you are operating your points by DCC you can't do that until the short is cleared. What you need is a separate DCC circuit for the points.

Enter the power district – the electrical area of the layout which has an independent cut-out and, in some cases, its own power supply. Taking a simple station to the fiddle-yard layout, as an example, this can be divided into three power districts: one for the station plus the connecting line, one for the fiddle yard and one for the points, signals and other accessories. This would mean that a derailment or problem in the fiddle yard will not stop operations in the station. No matter what happens above the baseboard, the points and signals will still work.

A power district does not need to be physically linked; for example, on a double-track oval with a fiddle yard to the rear, station to the front, locomotive yard on one side of the station and goods yard to the other, the power districts could be set up as:

1. Fiddle yard
2. Main lines and platforms
3. Goods yard and locomotive yard.

You can purchase special units that divide the output from your DCC controller up into power districts. The units provide a number of outputs, each with its own electronic cut-out that will operate before the cut-out on the DCC controller, thus limiting the effect of a short circuit or overload to the district in which the problem has occurred.

One such unit is the NCE EB1 Circuit Breaker. The EB1 provides short circuit protection for a single power district. The trip current and time can be set individually for each EB1. This can be very useful if you are operating sound-equipped locomotives, as they tend to draw more current when they power up and a crowded diesel depot would benefit from some extra time or current when you turn your DCC system on. The EB1 has an LED that indicates that all is well, or unwell, with the district. Screw connectors are provided so that you can run wires to an extra LED mounted on

The NCE EB1 circuit breaker allows you to divide your layout into power districts, so that a short circuit or other problem in one area won't affect operation in another.

your control panel. The EB1 can be used with any manufacturer's DCC system.

The EB1 comes with screw terminals for the wires to and from the controller and track, so no soldering is necessary in order to install it. Using the small plastic connectors supplied, you can limit the current to between 2.5 to 8 Amps. To adjust the time before a power district shuts down when a short is encountered, you need a DCC system that can program locomotives on the main line. The response time can be varied for each power district from 1⁄100th of a second up to half a second. As supplied the unit is set at 1⁄10th of a second.

Installation is simple and the unit can be mounted under the baseboard. The board has four mounting holes. The manufacturers recommend using no. 4 x ¾" (19mm) round-head wood screws with no.4 flat washers. Do not over-tighten the screws. Lightly snug the screws up just enough to keep the circuit board in place without bending it. Bending the circuit board can fracture the fragile electronic components. Cover the washers with adhesive tape to ensure that they do not accidentally bridge any contacts on the circuit board. Connect up the input wires to your DCC controller and the output wires to the track (don't forget to isolate your power districts from each other, either by cutting gaps in both rails or fitting insulating rail joiners) and you are ready to go. You can test the unit is working correctly by shorting the track in the power district – put a coin across the rails. If everything is connected up correctly, your DCC controller should still be operational and the LED on the EB1 will flash.

One thing to watch for if you are installing power districts is to ensure that you are consistent with connecting the red and black bus wires in each section. The easiest way to check that you have done this correctly is to use a meter set to its AC Volt scale and connect it to the 'red' rail in two different sections. If the meter reads 0V then both rails really are 'red'. If it reads the full DCC voltage (around 14V), then one rail is 'red' and the other 'black'. Swap the connections over in one of the sections and try again.

If you operate point motors and other accessories using DCC, you may wish to have a separate bus for them to avoid their current draw affecting the trains. Another possibility is to use point motor decoders that have their own capacitor discharge unit (CDU) which will provide the large kick that solenoid point motors need to operate without leaving the rest of the layout short of power.

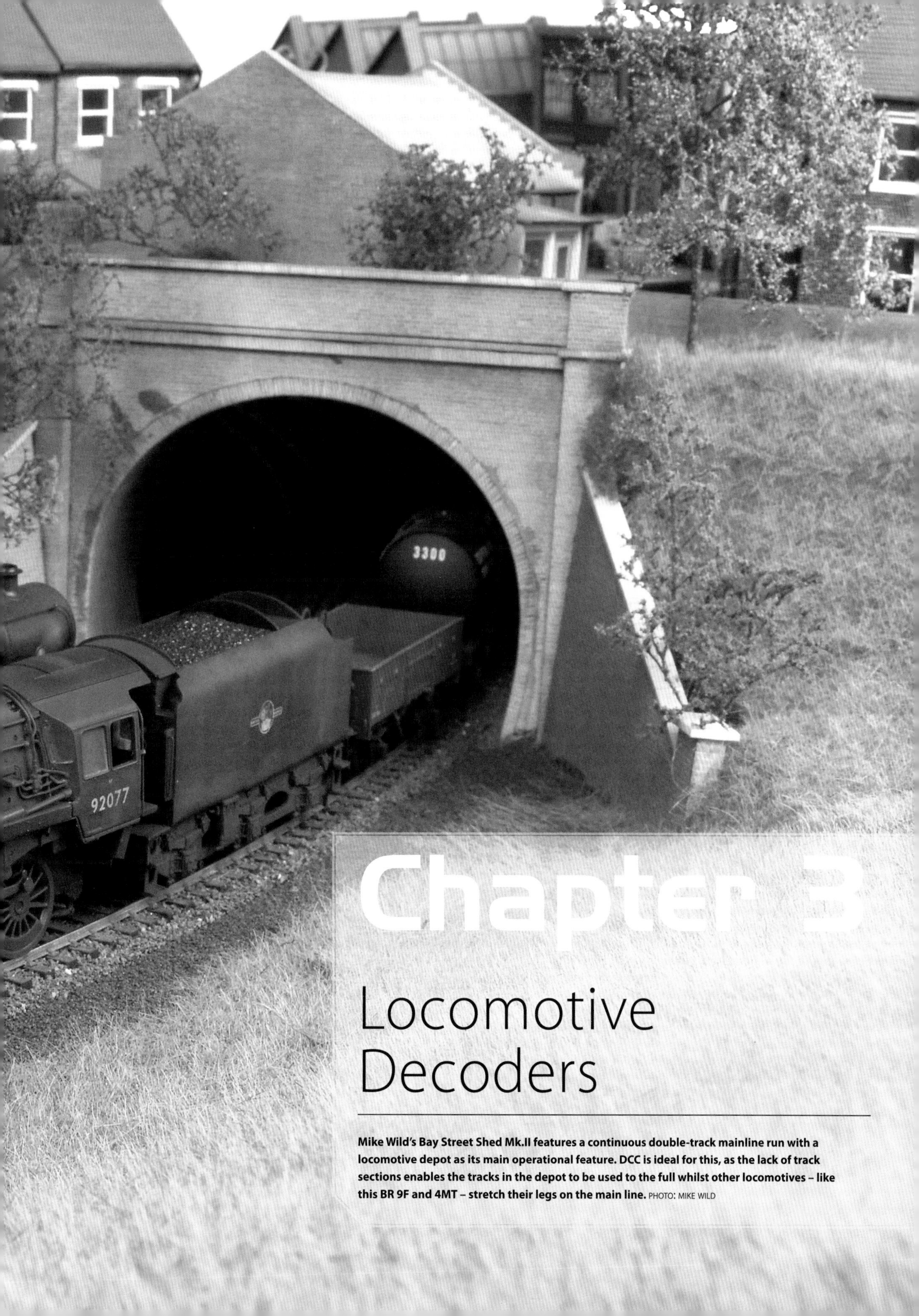

Chapter 3

Locomotive Decoders

Mike Wild's Bay Street Shed Mk.II features a continuous double-track mainline run with a locomotive depot as its main operational feature. DCC is ideal for this, as the lack of track sections enables the tracks in the depot to be used to the full whilst other locomotives – like this BR 9F and 4MT – stretch their legs on the main line. PHOTO: MIKE WILD

Locomotive decoders have evolved over the years – from large units built from individual electronic components with limited functionality to today's devices, which incorporate small computers and components that are difficult to see without a magnifier. The fact that they all look much the same tends to make people think that there isn't much difference between them, but this is far from the case.

The heart of the modern decoder is a microcontroller, a basic computer given input and output circuitry to connect it to your model locomotive. Depending on the skill of the programmer, the complexity of the microcontroller and the nature of the input/output circuitry, the performance of the decoder can vary from poor to exceptional.

All decoders need to be able to read the DCC signal reliably. If a decoder has been tested and meets the NMRA standards, then it should carry an NMRA-compliant logo to certify this. If it hasn't been tested, then it's best to give it a good leaving alone. Some decoders have been reported as interfering with the DCC signal, causing other decoders to misbehave as a result.

Motor control is another area where decoders vary greatly. Until recently, a number of decoders had difficulty coping with the capacitors installed in model locomotives to suppress TV interference caused by the motor. Many articles in the model railway press and on the internet recommend removing any capacitors as a matter of course. However, most modern decoders are designed to cope with them and, as a result, you should leave them in place unless the decoder refuses to behave normally after it has been installed. I personally haven't yet had to remove any capacitors when installing a decoder. Expensive motors require better decoders than those fitted to ready-to-run stock; they are happiest on pure DC and the pulsed output from a decoder can cause them to overheat or run roughly. They need a decoder designed to provide a suitable output for their delicate needs.

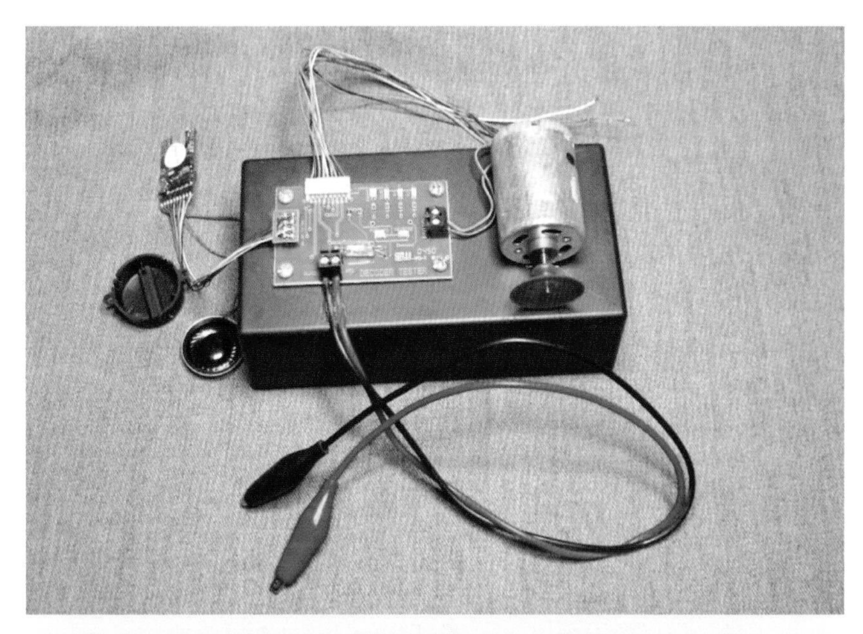

DCC decoders almost always work straight from the packet and tend to carry on working. However, if you are a cautious type you may wish to test your decoders before you install them. A decoder tester is simple to build using LEDs, a motor and some crocodile clips. The clips connect to the track; the decoder plugs into an 8-pin socket, croc clips or similar; the red-and-black power wires are connected to the track. The tester is run via your DCC controller. PHOTO: MAX WRIGHT

You should always remember that the DCC decoder in your locomotive is the equivalent of the controller in a conventional DC system. It provides the power for the motor and, on all but the most basic decoders, processes feedback to keep the locomotive moving at the chosen speed. Buying a poorly specified decoder is like buying a poorly specified DC controller – it will still run your trains but you can't expect to get high-end performance.

In the early days of DCC, decoders had to be hard-wired into the locomotive. Later, a standard 8-pin plug and socket was devised for HO-scale locomotives. While it is possible to put the plug in the socket the wrong way around, the clever pin alignment means that if you do the motor is still connected to the pickups (it is just the lights that don't work). Many decoders now have an extra function, F2, which means that there is an extra purple wire from the decoder which needs to be connected to whatever it operates – not quite as 'plug-and-play' as the original standard. Sound decoders have a further two brown wires which connect to the loudspeakers.

Later standards were introduced for large scale (G scale), with its higher current requirements, and 'N' gauge, with its smaller size decoder fitting.

It's an apparent mystery as to how the 6-pin 'N' gauge decoders work, as there is no function common (blue wire) connection. In fact, what happens is that the function outputs are run to one of the track pickups and, as a result, only receive half-wave voltage. This means that bulbs and LEDs will not shine as brightly as

A 21-pin decoder fitted to a Bachmann Class 47 chassis. The decoder is the small blue circuit board in the middle.

they would with a normal decoder. The manufacturers take this into account by installing lower value resistors in the lighting circuits, where a 6-pin socket is fitted. If you decide to wire in a standard decoder instead of using a 6-pin one, you should be aware of this and fit extra (or replacement) resistors to stop the LEDs and bulbs from being too bright and possibly burning out.

With the increasing number of functions needed on the current generation of ready-to-run HO and OO scale locomotives, there was much discussion among the NMRA regarding a larger number of decoder connections. The discussions took a long time without reaching a conclusion, so Bachmann – with ready-to-run ranges in the US, UK, mainland Europe and China – broke ranks and introduced a 21-pin standard across its various ranges.

If you were designing from a blank sheet of paper then 21 pins would give you a staggering number of functions available at the connection; strangely, for a mainstream manufacturer, Bachmann chose to support a large number of legacy system connections, with the result that only five functions (F0 to F4) are catered for. A number of decoder manufacturers now supply 21-pin decoders.

For those who wish to exploit DCC to the full, one problem with 21-pin decoders is that, as there are no wires, it is difficult to access a function output, whether in order to re-route it or install an extra accessory. If you wish to use an extra function – for example, to operate a smoke unit – then you need to find a suitable point to connect to the function output on the locomotive's circuit board.

Things to Consider

There are a number of things to consider when choosing the decoder for your model:

Plugs and Sockets

Some models are supplied 'DCC ready' and come with a standard socket that a decoder can be plugged into. If you have such a model then you need a decoder with a plug. Other models need one which ends in wires. You can, of course, convert an 8-pin plug-fitted decoder to a wire connection one by cutting the plug off – but, as you will probably have paid extra for it in the first place, you won't want to make a habit of it.

The Bachmann website (*www.bachman.co.uk*) includes a list of locomotives currently in their range that are fitted with a DCC socket. The socket blanking plug is also illustrated on the exploded diagram included with each locomotive, so you don't need to take the body off to establish if a socket is fitted. All Heljan locomotives are fitted with a DCC socket. For Hornby locomotives, you can download service sheets from the Hornby website (*www.hornby.co.uk*) – which include an exploded diagram showing the DCC blanking plug, part number X9255, on locos fitted with a DCC socket. Recent 'N' gauge locomotives produced by Dapol have a 6-pin socket, but earlier ones do not and can be difficult to fit decoders to. Models in the Graham Farish range vary in their levels of DCC-friendliness: some have 6-pin sockets, some need decoders to be soldered into them and others need some conversion work.

Most decoders that have a plug fitted come with an NMRA 8-pin plug that

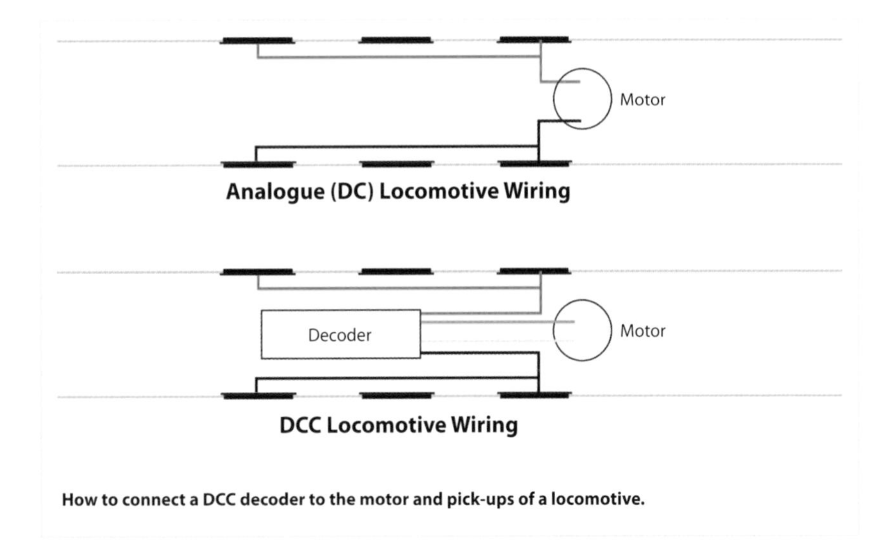

How to connect a DCC decoder to the motor and pick-ups of a locomotive.

matches the socket in most OO and HO-scale, DCC-ready locomotives. Large-scale models and their corresponding decoders come with a 4-pin version designed for carrying higher currents, while there is also a rarer 6-pin version intended for 'N' scale and the new 21-pin version for OO and HO scales..

For 8-pin decoders, some manufacturers mark pin number 1 on the socket, usually with a small triangle. If you can't work out which is pin 1, don't worry – the connections have been specified so that it will not harm the locomotive or decoder if you plug it in the wrong way round. If you do plug the decoder in incorrectly, the locomotive may run but the lights won't work. Just unplug the decoder and plug it in the other way around.

It isn't possible to plug a 21-pin decoder in the wrong way round – but, if you are sufficiently heavy-handed, you can fit it upside down. If you need to force it, you are fitting it the wrong way. You need to be fairly gentle when removing the blanking plate and installing the new decoder. I have heard of people managing to pull some of the pins off the locomotive's circuit board when removing the blanking plate, or bending them when pushing the decoder on.

Standard DCC plug/socket wiring (2 rows of 4 pins)

PIN	WIRE COLOUR	FUNCTION
1	Orange	Motor +ve
2	Yellow	Rear Light (F0)
3	Green	F1
4	Black	Track pick up (left rail)
5	Grey	Motor –ve
6	White	Front light (F0)
7	Blue	Light/function common
8	Red	Track pick up (right rail)

By the way, if you buy a DCC fitted locomotive with a 21-pin decoder installed and wonder what the decoder-like item in the box is, it is a blanking plug for use if you wish to remove the decoder. The 6-pin decoder can be fitted the wrong way around, but if you do nothing will work.

If you are installing a DCC decoder with wires rather than a plug, then the diagram above shows how it is connected between the track pickups and the motor. The red decoder wire goes to the right rail (facing forwards) and the black one to the left rail. The orange wire goes to the motor terminal connected to the right rail and the grey wire to the other motor terminal. If you get the red and the black swapped around, or the grey and the orange, all

Large scale DCC plug/socket wiring (2 rows of 2 pins)

PIN	WIRE COLOUR	FUNCTION
1	Grey	Motor –ve
2	Orange	Motor +ve
3	Black	Track pick up (left rail)
4	Red	Track pick up (right rail)

Small DCC plug/socket wiring (1 row of 6 pins)

PIN	WIRE COLOUR	FUNCTION
1	Orange	Motor +ve
2	Grey	Motor –ve
3	Red	Track pick up (right rail)
4	Black	Track pick up (left rail)
5	White	Front light (F0)
6	Yellow	Rear Light (F0)

21-pin DCC plug/socket wiring (2 rows of 11 pins) DCC connections only

PIN NUMBER	FUNCTION
1	
2	
3	
4	F4
5	
6	
7	F0 Reverse (Rear light)
8	F0 Forward (Headlight)
9	Loudspeaker A
10	Loudspeaker B
11	Index – pin not present, blanked
12	
13	F3
14	F2
15	F1
16	Function common
17	
18	Motor – ve
19	Motor + ve
20	
21	Left rail power (black)
22	Right rail power (red)

that will happen is that the locomotive will go backwards instead of forwards. However, you must be careful not to mix up red and orange or grey and black, as this will damage your decoder.

Size

Obvious really, but if it is too big to fit into whatever hidey hole is available in the locomotive then it just won't do. Some 8-pin and all 6- and 21-pin decoders have their plugs built into the circuit board, so they just sit above the DCC socket. Other decoders have separate plugs with connecting wires and must be located somewhere within the model.

Check the dimensions of the decoder that you intend to use. If you don't have one, make a mock-up from cardboard and see if it will fit. Don't forget that you will need space for the wires as well.

In some models, finding space can be a big problem and it may be necessary to cut away parts of weights or the chassis. Don't forget useful hidey holes such as the fuel tanks underneath diesel locomotives or steam-engine cabs and tenders.

Power Rating

Can the decoder provide enough power for the motor and anything else that it will be called on to operate, such as lights and smoke units? In general, most Z or 'N' gauge models draw 0.75A or less. Modern OO or HO models typically draw less than 1A, with older ones needing up to 1.5A. O gauge and larger models can draw as much as 4A. If you fit a decoder intended for an 'N' gauge model in your O gauge class 47, it will have a pretty short lifespan.

You will often read that it is necessary to know, or determine, the stall current of a locomotive before you fit a decoder. To establish the stall current you will need to connect a meter between a conventional DC power pack and the track and set it to a suitable Amp scale, then hold the locomotive so that the wheels cannot rotate and give it a burst of full power. This is a fairly risky process as you may damage the model or its motor. In truth, there is no need to precisely measure the stall current as decoders come with a limited range of current capacities. For an electric locomotive to be drawing the stall current, it would need to either have something wedged in the gears or wheels in order to bring it to a complete halt. Even the worst derailment will normally leave the wheels free to rotate, so a complete stop is a fairly unlikely eventuality. It is far more important that your chosen decoder can provide the current needed for normal continuous running. By and large, models built in the past few years have a lower current consumption than those built years ago.

Sometimes the only way to get a decoder to fit is by brute force. Here, a rotary tool is being used to mill away some of the metal from an 'N' gauge Pannier tank to make room for a decoder. This is a posed photo – in reality, the body should be held in a vice to reduce the risk of milling your fingers instead of the model.

Addresses

Some decoders only support locomotive addresses up to 99 (called 2-digit addressing), while others go up to 9999 (4-digit addressing). If your DCC system only supports 2-digit addressing, then you can buy either type. If you never intend to use more than 99 locomotives, or to use your locomotives on another layout which might, then you can use 2-digit decoders. If your DCC system offers 4-digit addressing, then it is probably better to only use 4-digit decoders.

Functions

How many accessories do you want to operate? For most UK outline models, this is usually limited to lights and two functions (F0 forward, F0 reverse) will cope with normal directional lighting.

The function outputs can do all sorts of things – provided that the model is equipped to use them. Lighting is a favourite feature and to correctly replicate modern UK practice you need four function outputs. Other features that are suitable for function control include horns or whistles, remote control uncoupling and smoke generators.

Whilst some new locomotives produced for the UK market now include factory fitted lights, many still do not. If you wish to install lighting, Express Models supply kits for many diesel classes and oil-type head and tail lamps for steam outline models.

Motor Control

More expensive decoders tend to offer facilities to improve the control of the locomotive's motor (similar to DC feedback controllers), shunting modes and high-frequency operation for high-quality coreless motors.

Shunting mode, usually operated by pressing a function key on your cab, reduces the maximum speed of the model, thus giving you a greater range of control. This is useful for fine control when inching up to a train. Normally, the acceleration and deceleration rates set in the decoder's CVs (configuration variables) are turned off as well, giving direct control of the locomotive.

Sound

The range of sounds available for UK models is increasing slowly. While sound-equipped decoders are expensive, they are also very impressive, especially as the sound is automatically matched to the motion of the model.

One problem with sound-equipped decoders is finding room for the larger sized decoder and accompanying speaker. In 4mm-scale diesel locomotives, the fuel tank between the bogies is one possible place for hiding the speaker. As technology advances the units become smaller, and it is now possible to obtain decoders and speakers to fit into N-scale locomotives. Another problem is that the range of UK locomotive sounds available is limited at the moment, but it is expanding all the time.

When installing a sound equipped decoder, you should always try to fit the largest speaker that the locomotive can accommodate, as this will give better sound quality and volume. In addition, rectangular speakers, where available, usually have a better frequency response and are preferable to circular ones.

Never fit a sound system to a noisy locomotive, as the mechanical noise will drown out the expensive sound. Similarly, you should not fit sound systems to locomotives fitted with old open-frame motors as these can often generate radio frequency interference, which may be picked up by the decoder circuitry. If possible, you should always try to use locomotives fitted with high-quality 'can' motors for this type of installation.

Coreless Motors – A Warning

High quality coreless motors, such as those produced by Escap, need special consideration. Due to their design, they are unsuited to the pulsed DC provided by standard DCC locomotive decoders. This causes them to heat up rapidly and they can burn out very quickly. This type of motor needs pure DC, or something close to it.

If you have locomotives fitted with coreless motors, then you need to install high-quality decoders with a 'silent' or 'high frequency' drive and, ideally, **adjustable back EMF**. Suitable decoders include the ESU LokPilot, the Lenz Gold series and the Zimo range.

You should never run a locomotive fitted with a coreless motor as an analogue locomotive on a DCC system. Again, the pulsed DC power will cause the motor to heat up and burn out.

How do you know if you've got coreless motors? If you need to ask then you probably haven't. They are expensive motors, normally fitted to kit builds or conversions.

If you have a small layout, then you could opt to install the sound-equipped decoder underneath it rather than in a locomotive. It would need to be wired into the track bus and could be used in conjunction with any suitable locomotive. To operate it ,you would simply use the DCC consist facility that enables a number of locomotives to be operated as a set. This would mean that the decoder's sounds would reflect the locomotive's operation. Mounting the decoder under the layout would also allow the use of a much larger speaker with a corresponding improvement in sound quality. You could, of course, install a number of decoders in this way, so that you could have a number of different locomotives apparently producing sound at the same time and match the type of sound to the type of locomotive.

Sound-equipped decoders for UK outline models are available from a number of suppliers, mainly using ESU LokSound decoders. In addition, Bachmann and Hornby market ready-to-run locomotives equipped with DCC decoders and sound.

One last warning: sound-equipped decoders are very easily damaged, so make sure that you read and follow the instructions supplied with them.

Special Features and Extra Functions

Some decoders have special features such as automatic braking, auxiliary power supplies and bi-directional communications. If you want to use facilities such as these, then you will probably be very restricted in your choice of decoder. In addition, some decoder ranges have special features that match their manufacturers' command stations. If you wish to use these features then you are tied to specific decoders.

One of the things that many newcomers to DCC find mystifying is the

Before you install a DCC decoder, you need to ensure that your locomotive runs well on DC. DCC will not cure mechanical problems. If you don't have a continuous run, then a rolling road is useful for running in the mechanism.

wide variation in prices for locomotive decoders. This difference is largely due to the features that are included. Some decoders only support a limited number of CVs, which limits their flexibility. Others may have extra power, a smaller size or more function outputs. Many of the more expensive decoders have sophisticated systems for getting the best performance out of your locomotives, including feedback (back-EMF monitoring) and other techniques for different types of motor.

People keep on finding extra uses for the function outputs of decoders. Express Models supply lighting kits for modern diesel locomotives that use 8 functions just for the lights. These are: (1) forward marker lights; (2) reverse marker lights; (3) forward tail lights; (4) reverse tail lights; (5) forward white headlight; (6) reverse white headlight; (7) forward cab interior light; (8) reverse cab interior light. Add sound, operating fans, remote uncoupling and a smoke unit, and that's one heck of a lot of functions.

If you need more functions than are available on a standard decoder, then it is possible to install a second 'function only' decoder, such as the Lenz LX100F in the locomotive. This type of decoder has function outputs but no motor control circuitry. You can also install a function-only decoder by itself in a piece of rolling stock that does not need motor control, such as the trailing power car in a multiple unit set.

If you install multiple decoders in the same locomotive, you will have to make sure that you can program the decoders independently and you might have to carry out the programming before installation. If you are using decoders in different vehicles of a set, such as a multiple unit, then each decoder can be programmed individually by placing each vehicle on the programming track in turn. In both cases, all the decoders should be set to the same locomotive address.

Support and Availability

Good support – such as a 'no questions asked' replacement policy – or ready availability from the shelves of your local model shop may also be important to you. Where should you buy DCC decoders from? Anywhere that can offer you the item you need, at a price you can afford and with service that you are happy with. This can be a mail order or internet retailer, model shop or eBay auction – whichever you feel happy with.

Sometimes, you will find that a better specified decoder is available for less than the one that you would normally choose. For example, on one installation I used a TCS M3, where normally I would have used an M1 as I don't need the extra function outputs, but, given the vagaries of exchange rate movements and stock levels, the M3 was actually cheaper. It is always worth comparing prices when you buy a decoder; it is surprising how much they can vary.

Tools of the Trade

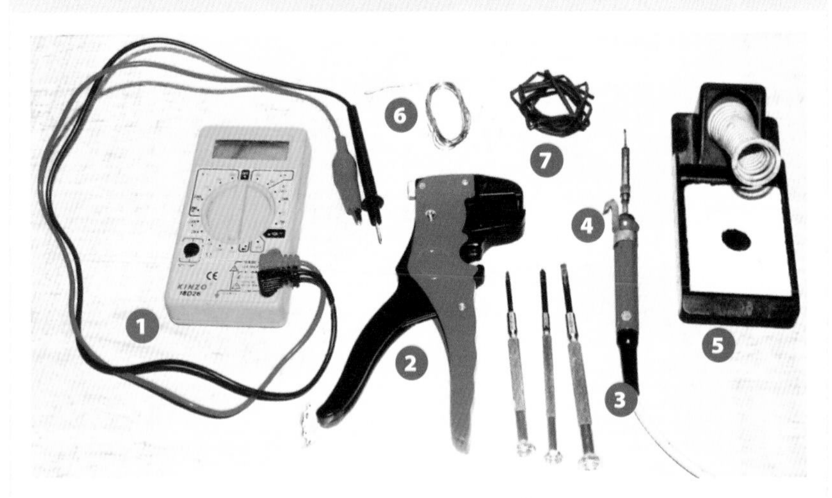

With a toolkit like this, you can tackle most DCC decoder installations.

You will need a small selection of tools and materials to install decoders in your locomotives:

1. **Electrical meter.** This can give a resistance (Ohm) reading and will normally also offer other measurements, typically AC and DC voltage (Volts) and current (Amps). A simple one priced at around £10 or less is perfectly adequate for the job and invaluable for solving electrical problems on any model railway.
2. **Wire strippers.** Proper wire strippers are far superior to attempting to strip the insulation with a knife. They ensure that the insulation is removed cleanly and leave all the wire strands intact. There is also no danger of the knife slipping and cutting your finger.
3. **Small screwdrivers.** For removing locomotive bodies and other assorted parts.
4. **Soldering iron.** An electrical iron with a small bit is needed for making electrical connections. If you also need to solder white-metal kits you should use a different bit (or even a different iron), as electrical and white-metal solders do not mix well.
5. **Soldering iron stand.** You should have somewhere safe to put your iron when you are not actually using it. A purpose-designed stand means there is less chance of accident. *(As an aside, never try to catch a falling soldering iron. The power cable will tend to make it fall with the hot bit uppermost, which is where you will be most likely to grab it, leading to badly burnt fingers. The alternative tactic of catching the lead will cause the iron to swing in an arc and burn you somewhere else. Let it drop and then retrieve it quickly.)*
6. **Solder.** Electrical solder has the flux incorporated in it.
7. **Heat shrink tubing.** Used to cover bare wires and stop accidental short circuits. Obtained from suppliers such as Maplin Electronics or Rapid Electronics.

Installation

Many guides to decoder installation suggest you should remove the suppression devices – such as chokes and capacitors – from locomotives as part of the process. These components are there to stop the models generating electromagnetic radiation that can interfere with electrical and electronic items, ranging from televisions and computers through to police radios and pacemakers. These components have been installed in order for the locomotive to comply with current EU legislation.

Chokes should always be left in place, as they do not affect the operation of the decoder. With some installations, the capacitors can cause poor or erratic running. Some modern decoders contain RF suppression components which allow the locomotive's capacitors to be removed. Others do not, and in such cases the locomotive's capacitors should be retained. You should refer to the decoder manufacturer's instructions to find out the specific recommendation for each decoder. The best approach appears to be to leave the capacitors in place and only remove them if the locomotive's performance under DCC is poor, or erratic, compared to its performance prior to conversion.

Before you begin any installation work, you should ensure that the locomotive that you are converting to DCC operates well under conventional DC. Putting a decoder in will not cure a bad motor, binding gears or bent valve gear. Old locomotives should be cleaned and serviced before conversion. Ideally, new locomotives should be run in – remember that, in some cases, installing a DCC decoder will invalidate the manufacturer's warranty, so make sure that the locomotive is not faulty in any way before you start.

New locomotives need running in and should either be driven on DC around a

Joining two wires

To make a good electrical and mechanical connection between two wires is a simple process. First you strip about a centimetre of insulation from each of the wires to be joined.

Cut a length of heat-shrink tubing a little longer than the longest of the bare sections of wire and thread it on to one of the lengths of wire. Now twist the two bare wires together.

Put the hot soldering iron on the twisted wires and let them heat up. With the soldering iron still in place, touch the twisted wires (not the soldering iron) with the end of the solder. The solder will melt and flow around the wires. Remove the solder and the iron and allow the joint to cool.

Bend the soldered joint so that it runs parallel to one of the wires. Slide the heat-shrink tubing along until it completely covers the soldered joint. Now hold your soldering iron alongside the tubing which will shrink and encase the soldered joint.

You now have a connection that will conduct electricity, resist being pulled apart and not be susceptible to short circuits if it comes into contact with other connections.

The details of modern models can cause difficulties when installing decoders. One example is the Hornby OO gauge Britannia, from which you need to remove the bolt that connects the speedo cable to the connecting rod; otherwise you will break the cable when you remove the chassis. If you don't have a set of small spanners then fine-nosed pliers will do the job.

continuous run or, if your layout doesn't permit that, on a rolling road. Rolling roads of various designs are available to suit virtually all scales. That in the illustration on page 37 is produced by Bachrus. It picks up power from a length of track and the locomotive wheels rest on bearings that allow them to run. Special parts are available to support non-powered bogie wheels and tenders. Running in a new locomotive allows the mechanism to bed in, improving the performance at slow speeds and the overall smoothness of operation.

It is a good idea to keep a record of what type of decoder you have fitted in each locomotive and what your CV settings are. This will enable you to reset the CV settings if they get changed by accident. A sample DCC locomotive record sheet is provided later in this chapter.

While some locomotives can be converted to DCC easily, others can be challenging. An increasing number of model shops and individuals are offering DCC conversion services; if you are nervous about converting a particular model then you may wish to use such a service. While this does push the cost of the conversion up, it does guarantee that you will get a working DCC locomotive.

It is imperative that decoders are insulated from the chassis, pickups and motor, but it is not advisable to cover them with heat-shrink tubing or insulating tape. Many decoders generate heat and, if it cannot escape into the air, they may overheat and cease to work. Some manufacturers supply decoders wrapped in a plastic coating; these are fine if they have been designed that way, but if your chosen decoder is not wrapped then leave it like that.

Fitting Decoders with Plugs

Fitting a locomotive decoder with a plug should be a straightforward exercise. You dismantle part of the locomotive to gain access to the socket, remove the blanking plate, plug the decoder in, test that it works, secure it in place and then put the locomotive back together.

Needless to say, things are not always that easy. Many locomotives are difficult to dismantle without damage to the finer details that today's modeller demands. Things like speedometer cables and lubricators need to be disconnected

Once the body of an older Bachmann Class 24 has been removed, the circuit board where a DCC decoder can be plugged in is easily visible. Remember to check which way the body fits, so that the number one end (with the roof fan) ends up at the front when going forwards. The underneath of the socket can be pushed down onto the chassis block when pressing the plug in, which will cause a short circuit that will destroy your decoder. A layer of self-adhesive tape on the top of the chassis block will avoid any unpleasant surprises.

or gently guided into place whilst you separate the body and chassis of a steam locomotive.

Even on an apparently straightforward fit – such as the older versions of Bachmann's OO gauge Class 24 and 25 diesels – fitting plugs can hold pitfalls for the unwary. On these models it was possible for the locomotive's circuit board to be pushed down onto the chassis block, resulting in a decoder-killing short circuit when power was applied. The cure is to cover the top of the chassis block under the circuit board with some self-adhesive tape, to give an insulating layer between the two.

Some Bachmann-Graham Farish 'N' gauge diesels have a design whereby the connection from the circuit board to the motor can short against the chassis block. While this can cause mysterious short circuits under DC operation, under DCC such a short will destroy the locomotive's decoder. It is imperative to sort this problem out before continuing with the installation.

To remove the circuit board, you need to unscrew the two small crosshead screws at opposite corners of the board, using a small jeweller's screwdriver. Put them somewhere safe and then slide the two lighting boards out of their guides at each end of the chassis. Now lift the main circuit board out and put it to one side.

To insulate the chassis block, I used brown parcel tape (the self-adhesive variety, not the sort that you need to lick). This is thin, flexible and has strong adhesive. I cut a small piece, pushed it in place with a cocktail stick, folded it back along the chassis side, cut the free section of tape down the fold and then pushed the two tabs down onto the top of the chassis. I did this for all four faces of the central well, being careful to keep the drive shaft and motor tags free of tape.

Once the tape was in place I reinstalled the circuit board, but not the body, and checked that the model still worked on DC, just to be sure that I hadn't impeded the drive train or disrupted the electrical contacts

Having got the model dismantled, located the socket and sorted out any potential short circuits, the next question is where to put the decoder. Normally this isn't a problem, as the manufacturer will have left plenty of space – but again, with some models things are harder.

The Hornby OO gauge Class 31 is a case in point. In a large model like this there should be plenty of space for a decoder, especially as it was designed from the outset to be DCC-ready. In fact, the decoder location is situated underneath the circuit board in the locomotive, so this needs to be unscrewed as well. It is held in place by two small crosshead screws at either corner of the board. Keep these in a safe place.

Gently lift the circuit board and you will see that there is not much space available, so you will need to use a small decoder. Suitable candidates include the Lenz Gold and TCS M1. Hornby supply a sleeve to put over the decoder to insulate it from the chassis. Do not use it. Decoders that come without a wrapper are designed to be left unwrapped to dissipate the heat that they produce. Wrapping them can cause the decoder to fail. Decoders that come with a pre-fitted wrapper are designed to work that way and are therefore a better choice in this situation.

Attach the decoder to the underside of the circuit board with a sticky pad and then route the wires as shown in the photo. Screw the circuit board in place and plug the cable into the socket, making sure that pin 1 (the orange wire) on the plug aligns with pin 1 as marked on the circuit board.

Bachmann's OO scale Ivatt 4MT is another example of hidden decoder locations. The body is secured by two

Some Graham Farish 'N' gauge models have a potential short circuit problem if the motor contact arms touch the chassis block. Fixing the potential short is a few minutes' work with some parcel tape. The black tape underneath the circuit board is factory-fitted to stop the board shorting on the chassis block.

Some older locomotives came fitted with directional lighting using bulbs. You can convert this type of lighting to DCC, but it is usually better to replace the bulbs with LEDs.

The decoder location in Hornby's OO gauge Class 31 diesel is hidden away under the circuit board. Be careful when you lift the circuit board, otherwise you may disconnect some of the wires. The decoder compartment is small and enclosed.

The decoder's wires need to come up through an opening in the circuit board and then plug into the socket.

Once you have got into Bachmann's Ivatt 4MT the DCC socket is easy to find, but where does the decoder go?

Inside the boiler. You need to remove a weight to do this, which does reduce the model's hauling capacity. Fortunately, most layouts cannot accommodate trains that would seriously challenge the model in this respect.

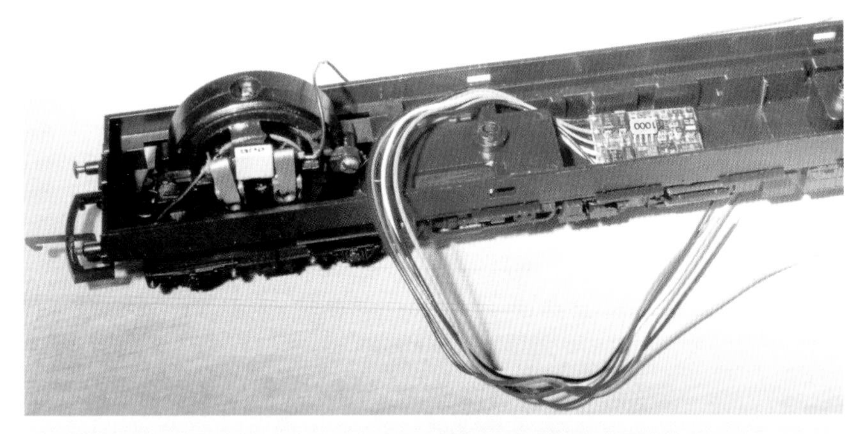

The belly tanks on diesel models often provide an ideal home for larger decoders, which is especially useful if you want to equip your locomotive with sound. The motor bogie was a standard design, so these notes apply to virtually any Lima model.

screws. Once these have been removed you can gently ease the body off to reveal the DCC plug on a circuit board under the chimney. This is actually harder than it sounds, as the two screws that secure the chassis are underneath some of the plastic brake gear which must be gently eased to one side. The body is a stiff fit and some of the pipework below the cab on the right-hand side of the engine is attached to the body, the rest to the chassis.

You can now remove the blanking plug and put it somewhere safe, then plug in the decoder. Put the chassis on the programming track and check that the decoder responds correctly. Make sure that the decoder does not touch any metal parts of the chassis, motor or track, whilst you do this.

To make room for the decoder, you need to remove the weight from the boiler. This is secured by a small screw. Again, put them somewhere safe in case you ever want to convert the model back to analogue operation. Tuck the decoder into the smoke box and you are now ready to put the body back on. Once again this is a difficult process, with the pipework at the side of the cab being difficult to get back into position.

Fitting Decoders without Plugs

Fitting a decoder without a plug is known as hard-wiring and is usually regarded as harder than fitting one with a plug. This may or may not be the case, depending on the model. Simple installations, such as those on models produced by Lima, may often be less hassle than one of the more awkward DCC ready models. At the other end of the scale, models like the early Dapol 'N' gauge Class 66s are so awkward that it is easier to sell them and buy a newer DCC-ready version.

Lima OO Gauge Models

While the Lima range is no longer in production, there are many thousands of locomotives produced by them which are still around. Most UK outline models produced by Lima used the same design of motor bogie, so these instructions apply equally well to virtually all Lima models. The only difference is in locating a suitable place to install the decoder.

Incidentally, the Lima motor is not highly regarded due to its lack of controllability and reliability. You may wish to replace the motor with a different unit, such as the Black Beetle powered bogie available from Branch Lines.

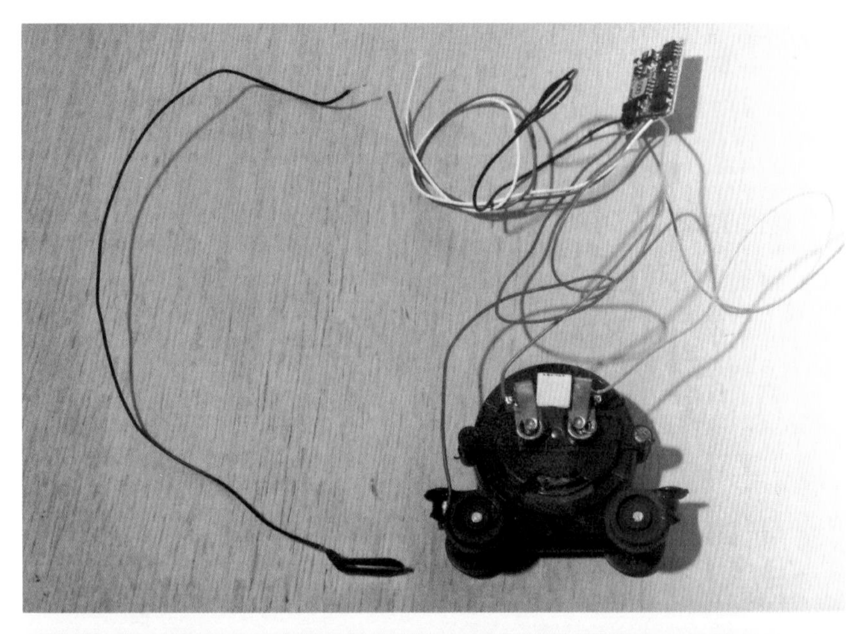

Even simple installations can display spaghetti-like tendencies. The 2-rail wiring has been removed (except for the suppression capacitor between the motor terminals) and the DCC wiring has been soldered to the Lima motor bogie. The orange and grey wires are connected to the motor terminals and the red wire to the pickup. All that remains is to connect the black decoder wire to the pickup from the other bogie and insulate the blue and white function wires to stop them causing any trouble.

This version of the Ringfield motor bogie, without the screws at the top of the brush holders, is the easier version to convert to DCC operation.

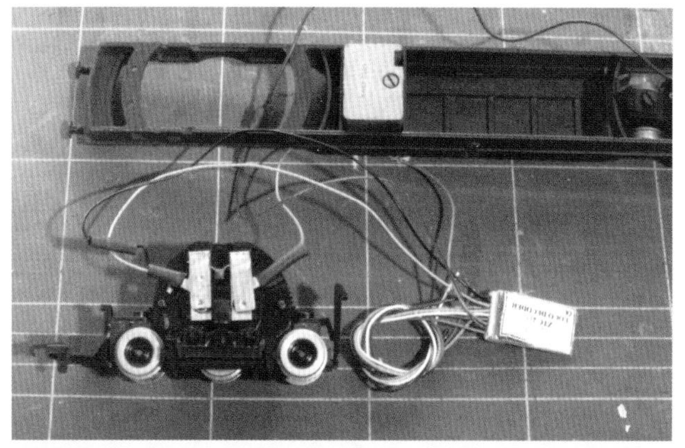

Disconnect two wires, solder the four from the decoder in place and the conversion is ready for testing.

There is also a kit available from the Australian company ModelTorque, which converts the existing Lima motor into a much higher specification item ideal for those who do not wish to make structural changes to the model's chassis. The kit is available direct from the manufacturer or from The Engine Shed and Inter-City Models in the UK. The bodies tend to be clipped rather than screwed in place. To release them, you need to use a small screwdriver to release each clip in turn until you can lift the body off the chassis.

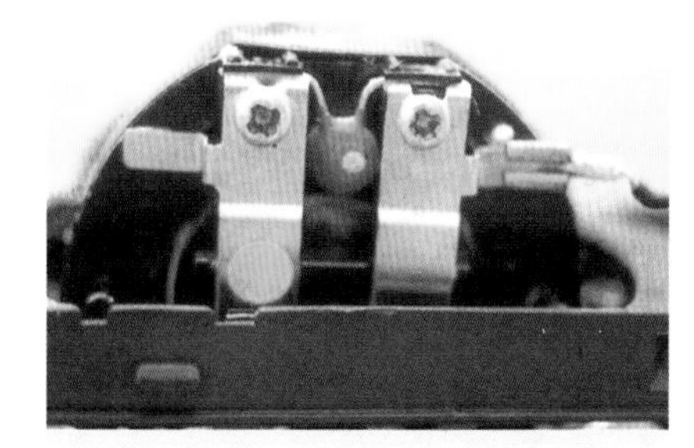

This type of motor bogie, with the two screws at the top of the brush holder, involves some extra work.

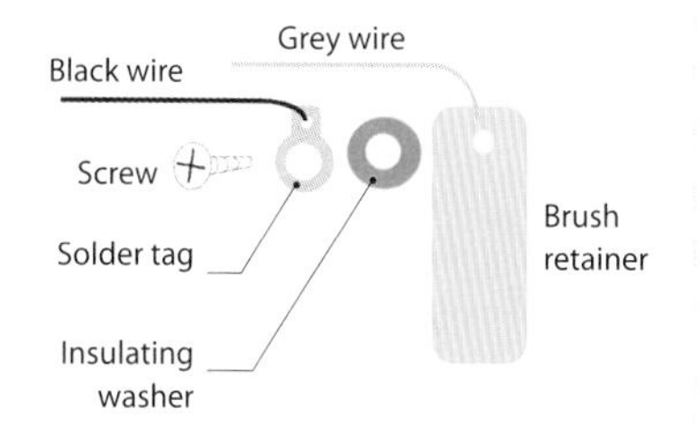

This diagram shows how the connections for the black and grey wires need to be made and to be isolated from each other.

The Lima Class 117 DMU is still the only ready-to-run model of a first generation high density DMU in OO gauge, so despite its many faults they can still be found pottering around many layouts. With the interior visible through the coach windows, there appears to be limited space to conceal a decoder. The bulkhead between the guard's section and passenger sections provides a suitable place to secure a decoder. Alternatively, as with many diesel models the belly tanks provide a large space where a decoder can be completely concealed, even a large one with sound and a speaker. Once you have decided where the decoder is going, you can disconnect the feed from the front bogie (it just pulls off the central pivot) and remove the motor bogie by unscrewing the outer frame.

The short wire connecting the motor bogie pick up to one motor terminal should be unsoldered and discarded. The black pickup wire from the other bogie should be unsoldered and retained. You can now solder the DCC decoder's motor wires to the motor terminals and the decoder's track wires to the motor bogie pickup and the black pickup wire. Any function wires should be insulated with heat-shrink sleeving to stop them causing any problems later.

The motor bogie can now be temporarily reconnected to the pickup bogie and the installation tested on the programming track. If there are no problems, the decoder can be fixed in place and the model reassembled.

Hornby OO Gauge Ringfield Motor

Many older Hornby models are powered by a Ringfield motor. These can be found in diesel motor bogies, tank engines and steam engine tenders. They are all to a similar pattern and have been part of the hobby for more years than most people care to remember. The Ringfield motor bogie comes in at least two versions, which require slightly different treatment. The first step (after you have made sure that the model is working on standard

DC) is to dismantle it and see what you are dealing with.

If your motor bogie does not have screws at the top of the brush holders, like the one above, then fitting the decoder is a simple matter.

Disconnect the two wires from the motor, attach them to the red and black decoder wires and solder the orange and grey wires to the tags on the motor. You can then test the installation, stick the decoder down and reassemble the model.

Motor bogies that have two screws at the top of the brush holders need more extensive work. Some motors have two connections to pickups, others only have one. In both cases there is a hidden connection that enables the motor to collect power from one side of the motor bogie. If you fail to disconnect this then your decoder will be destroyed the first time that you try to use it.

Looking at the motor bogie above, there are two screws which keep the brush holders in place. The one on the right is perfectly normal, but the one on the left is longer and connects the brush holder to the chassis and thence to the track.

First you must remove the left hand screw. You need a solder tag and insulating washer to fit. Connect the solder tag to the decoder's black wire (track pickup). If the left-hand brush retainer is also connected to a wire, then that wire needs to be unsoldered and connected to the decoder's black wire. Now unsolder the other pickup from the right-hand brush holder and connect to the decoder's red wire.

The grey wire can now be soldered to the left-hand brush holder and the orange wire to the right-hand one. Place the solder tag on the screw, followed by the insulating washer, and then replace the screw. Make sure that the solder tag does not make contact with the brush holder or the chassis.

You can either make your own solder tags from brass strip or purchase them from Maplin Electronics, Rapid Electronics or Squires Model & Craft Tools. Similarly, plastic sheeting can be used to make suitable insulating washers by shaping to ensure the solder tag does not touch the motor; or else you can purchase them from Rapid Electronics or Squires Model & Craft Tools.

Bachmann and Mainline OO Gauge Split-Chassis

There are some models that are nothing less than challenging when it comes to fitting a DCC decoder. Among these are some of the older Bachmann and Mainline models that have a split chassis, divided into two electrically live halves separated by insulating spacers. In theory, there is no difference in fitting a DCC decoder to a split-chassis locomotive than any other, but in practice it involves virtually complete disassembly of the model.

The procedure is similar for all the split-frame models in the Bachmann and Mainline ranges: the A4, B1, V2, V1/3, J72, J39, Lord Nelson, Manor, 43xx/53xx/93xx/47xx, Hall, original Jubilee, Scot and Patriot, Ivatt 2-6-2T, 4MT and 04 diesel shunter. Fortunately, Bachmann are gradually working through their range, replacing the split-frame models with conventional chassis that are DCC ready. The split-chassis locomotives tend to be short on space within the body, so most decoder-fitting services actually remove some of the chassis block to make room. If you don't have access to a milling machine, you may find it easier to install

Using a foam cradle helps to stop the chassis moving about whilst you are working on it and reduces the risk of damage.

With the keeper plate removed from this model you can see the two halves of the chassis, two of the plastic spacers and all those valve components that we don't want to disturb.

a small decoder in the locomotive's cab or run wires to a decoder sited in the tender.

One of the problems with fitting DCC decoders is that it is very easy to damage the locomotive whilst you are doing it. A foam cradle will help keep the locomotive still and safe while you tinker with its chassis. The model illustrated is made by Peco and is available in most model shops.

Disassembly varies from model to model, but they all follow the same pattern. First remove the screws securing the body, remove the body itself and put it somewhere safe. (I use an old ice cream tub to keep all the bits in whilst work is in progress. This ensures that no vital parts get lost.) Leading and trailing pony trucks or bogies are unscrewed next, watching out for any springs or washers that might make a bid for freedom. Remove any plastic brake rigging, if fitted, and then unscrew the keeper plate from the bottom of the chassis.

This decoder has been hidden away in the cab of the locomotive in preference to removing some of the chassis casting that fills the boiler.

To remove the wheels, you will first of all need to pull the cylinders off the chassis. Be gentle and take your time; the valve gear is delicate and easily damaged. If you cannot get them off then it is still possible to remove the wheels, but getting the valve gear back in place when you reassemble the model will be much harder. Once you have done that, you can lift the wheels out of the chassis block.

Taking the chassis block out of the cradle, you can lay it on its side and undo the screws that join the two halves. The two halves are separated by small plastic spacers; be very careful not to lose them when you separate them. You will probably have to resort to more gentle persuasion from a screwdriver to get the two parts to separate.

This is the two halves of a B1 chassis, showing how the motor terminals fit against it.

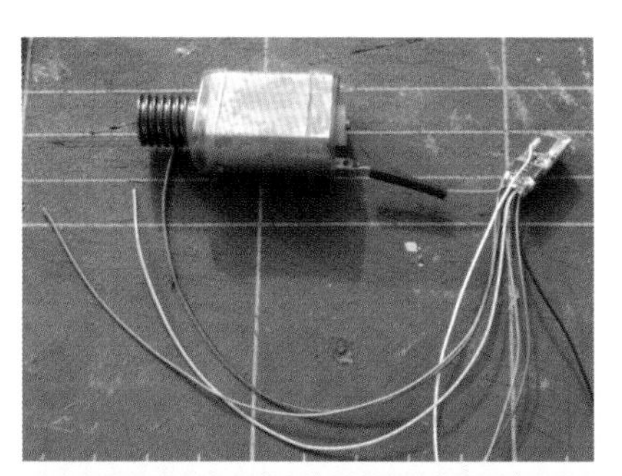

Don't forget to slide the heat-shrink tubing onto the decoder wires before you solder them to the motor terminals. Once the wires have been soldered, you should then cover all the exposed wire and tag with the tubing, shrinking it by heating with the edge of the soldering iron.

There are two springs which provide electrical connections to the motor. Don't worry if these spring out when you separate the chassis – they are the only bits that you won't need to put back. Before you lift the motor out, make a note of which way up it goes and which tag is connected to the right-hand side of the chassis. (This is usually marked with a red dot; if it's not, it might be a good time to do so with a felt-tip pen.)

The orange wire from the decoder will be connected to the terminal with the red dot, the grey one will go to the other terminal. To insulate them from the chassis you will need to use a length of heat-shrink tubing. Don't forget to slide this onto the wire before you connect it to the motor. The wires should be cut to length; the

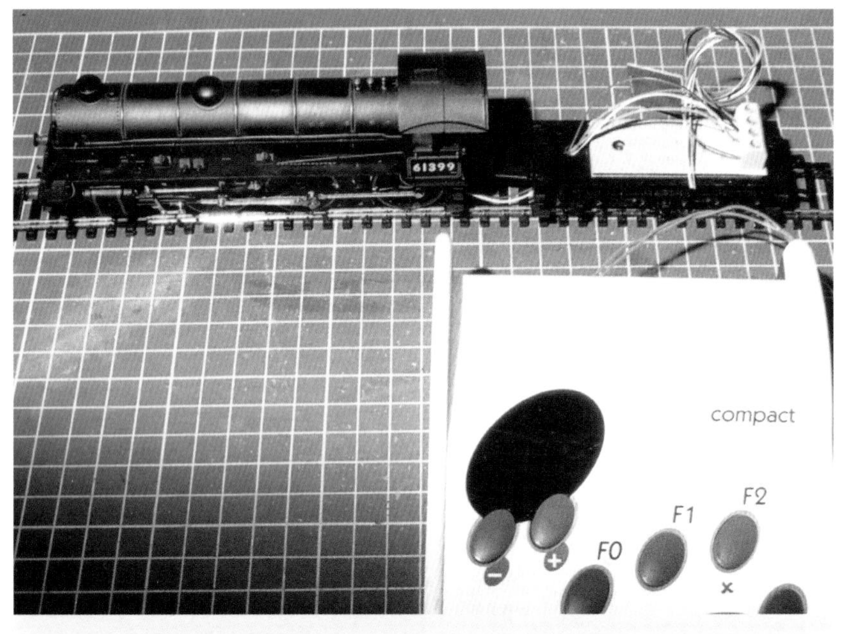

With a tender locomotive, the cab is often too visible an area to hide a decoder, so on this B1 I ran wires to the tender which had plenty of space inside.

length will vary depending on where you have decided to fit the decoder. Solder the wires in place, slide the heat-shrink tubing over so that it covers the whole tag and connection. It is vital that there is no bare wire, tag or solder, as this will cause a short that will destroy your decoder.

Before you replace the motor, check that you have removed the two small springs that connect it to the chassis; while you are at it, remove any grot or fluff from the worm and gear.

With the motor in place you can start to rebuild the locomotive. Check that the motor is the same way up as it was when you started and that the worm and gear mesh nicely. You can now put the two halves of the chassis together and replace the screws.

The next step is the trickiest part of the whole exercise, getting the wheels back in and the valve gear in place. If you have a digital camera then you might find it worthwhile to take a picture of both sides of the locomotivebefore you start – there are a surprising number of rods and they all need to be correctly aligned if you want the locomotiveto run when you have finished. Once everything is back in place, put the cylinders on and reattach the keeper plate and pony trucks.

The black and red wires need to be fixed to the opposite sides of the chassis. You can drill a hole for a small bolt, sandwich some PCB between the chassis halves or find something to connect to. Scrape the black coating off the chassis where you want to make your connection and fix the wires in place. The red wire goes on the right-hand side of the chassis, looking forwards, and the black wire on the left. Now is the time for a test run before the body goes back on.

You can cut the function wires off if you don't want to install lighting. If you wish to keep your options open, then trim them back a bit to make them easier to conceal. Fix the decoder in place and, if necessary, disguise any visible wires with some black paint.

Graham Farish 'N' gauge

Many Graham Farish models use a system where one or both of the motor brushes are built into the live chassis. A brass 'top hat' houses the motor brush and is held in place by a clip which makes the electrical connection between the brush and the chassis. With the older diesel models both brushes are directly connected to the chassis, while on steam locomotives it is the bottom brush that is connected to the chassis, the top one being connected with a wire.

The easiest way to convert this type of model is to use a specially-made, insulated top hat and to cover the arms of the clip with an insulated sleeve. Various other methods have been tried, but this is without doubt the quickest and easiest. The parts are available from DCC Supplies (*www.dccsupplies.com*) and go under the name of the 'Digi-Hat'.

Once you have confirmed that the locomotive works well on DC, you can remove the body and then undo the screws that hold the keeper plate in position. Remove the wheels, and possibly the couplings, and then undo the nut and bolt that hold the top wire in place. Unsolder the brass tag from this wire; it will be fitted to one of the decoder leads later.

Gently lever the bottom copper clip from the chassis. Use a small screwdriver to lever the brass top hat out and then tap the model on the bench to get the spring and carbon brush out. Fit the DigiHat, replace the brush and then the spring. A small screwdriver is a useful tool for positioning the DigiHat and spring. Slip the new clip over the chassis and test the motor by connecting it to a DC (analogue) controller. Check that the motor wires are both insulated from the chassis and then connect them to the motor output (orange and grey wires) of your DCC decoder.

While the more recent chassis designs of Graham Farish models are DCC-ready, the older designs – like this 0-6-0 tank engine chassis – are not. The lower motor brush is directly connected to the chassis.

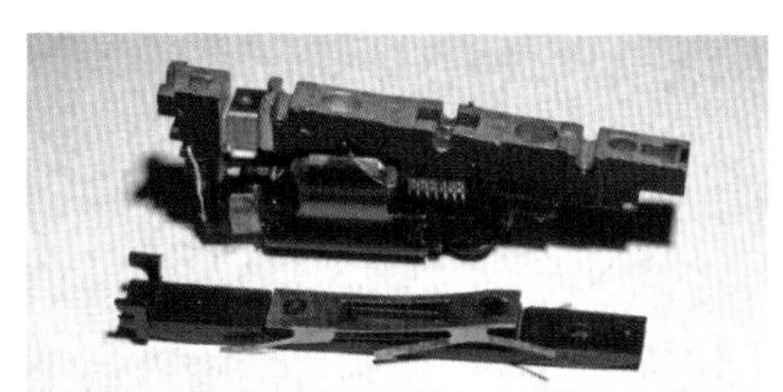

When you disassemble the chassis, note which way round the components go for reassembly. The bottom keeper plate houses the pickups. The copper strip goes against the chassis, making a live connection to one rail. The other pickups are connected via a bolt to a tag atop the chassis, linked by wire to the top motor brush. Two copper clips hold the motor brushes in place and feed them electricity. One clip (atop the motor) is isolated from the chassis.

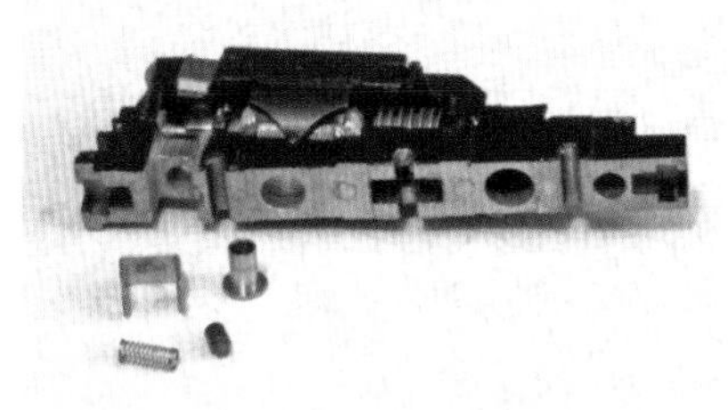

These are the components from the bottom motor brush. The clip, the brass top hat, the brush spring and the carbon brush itself. The clip and the top hat need to be modified or replaced to isolate the brush from the chassis.

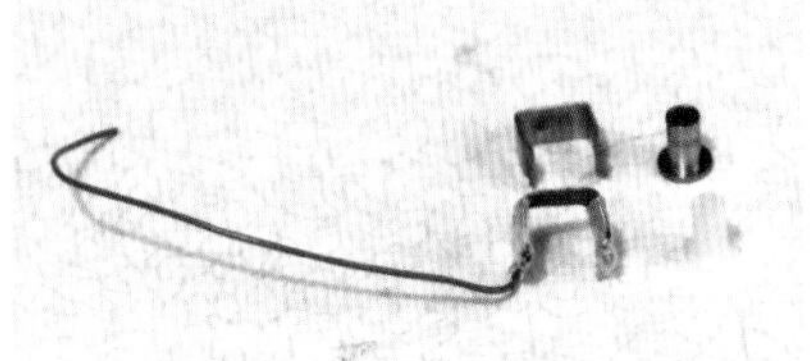

DCC Supplies provide an insulated top hat called a DigiHat and a replacement clip with insulated sleeves on the sides. Alternatively, they can supply the sleeving for you to fit to your existing clip.

With the DigiHat in place, you can replace the brush and then the spring. A small screwdriver makes a useful tool for positioning the DigiHat and spring in the hole.

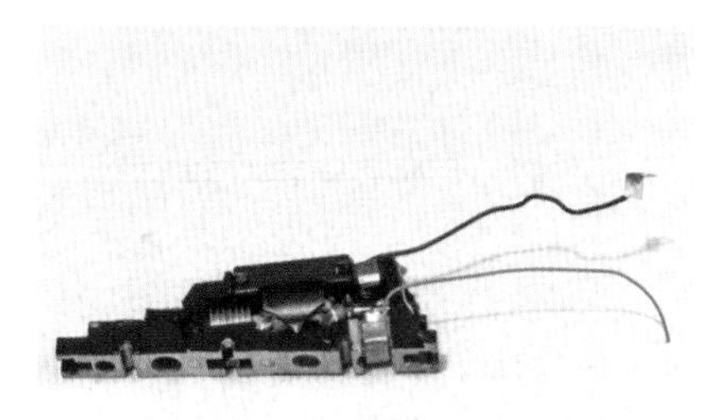

The replacement clip holds the brush assembly in place when you connect the wires to a DC (analogue) controller to test that the motor still works. Afterwards, use a meter to check that both motor wires are isolated from the chassis.

Once you are happy that the motor is isolated and working, its wires can be connected to the grey and orange wires of a DCC decoder. Don't forget to slip some heat-shrink tube on the wires before you join them. The red and black wires can then be connected – one by soldering to the tag that goes on the bolt, the other to the chassis itself. I removed the capacitor from this model and used the place where that fitted for the black wire. (The twisted black wire on the left is holding the keeper plate in position.) The function wires can now be trimmed right back, unless you are planning to add lighting.

At first glance it would appear that there will be plenty of room to fit a DCC decoder in this Graham Farish multiple unit. The motor is in the centre coach of the 3-car unit.

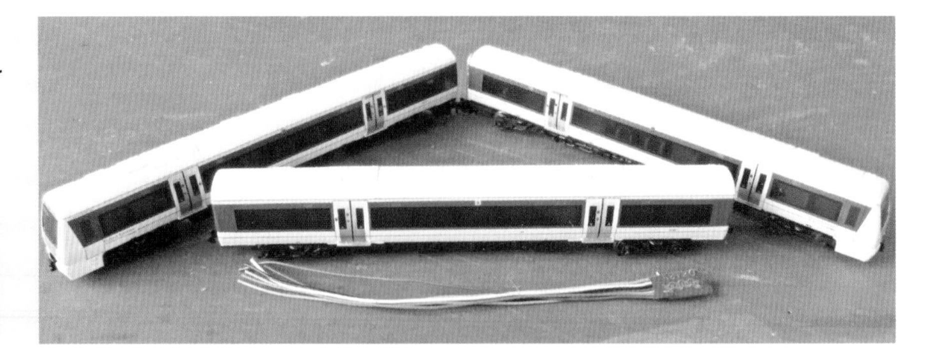

With the body removed, you can see the split chassis construction. This design of chassis is used for units with differing wheelbases and bogie centres, so it is important to get the bogie mounts the right way around (note which way the little dot faces) and sitting in the right set of locating slots.

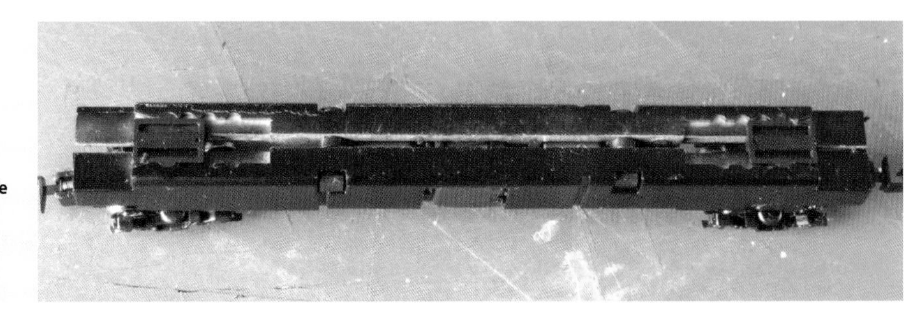

With the two halves separated, you can see how the motor contacts press against the chassis sides (as do the bogie pickups), providing a direct electrical path from one to the other.

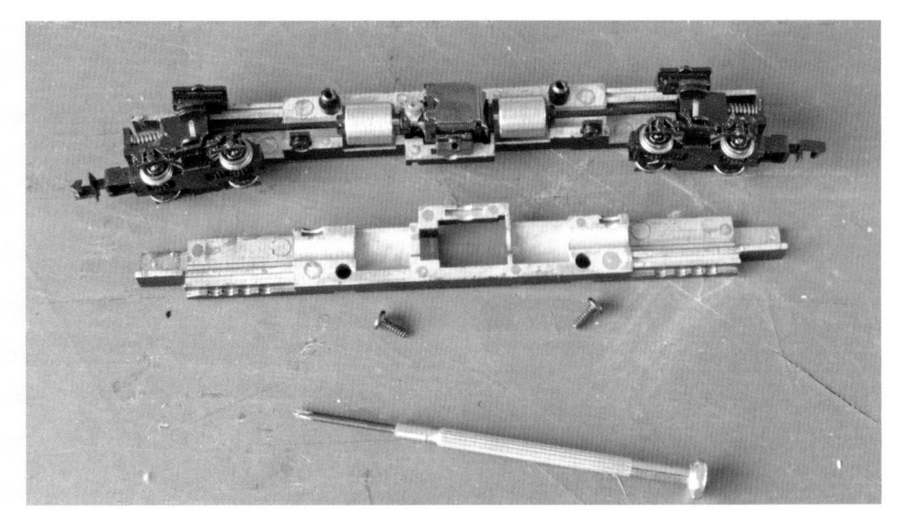

The area of the chassis around the motor contacts needs to be filed away, isolating the motor from the chassis. Fortunately, this only takes a few minutes with a small file. The top section shows the chassis before filing while the bottom section shows it afterward.

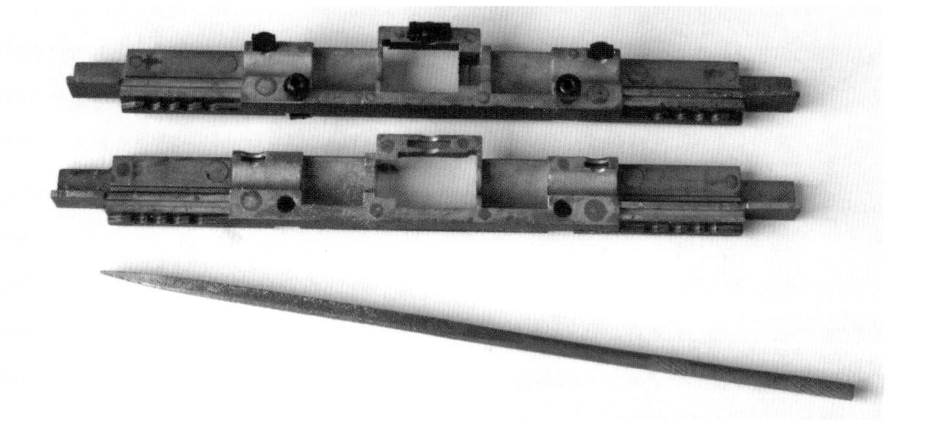

Put the two halves of the chassis back together and use a meter to check that the motor is electrically isolated.

You will probably have to file in a groove for the motor wires to pass up the side of the chassis block to reach the decoder.

The orange and grey decoder wires should be soldered directly to the motor contacts. The black and red wires can be stripped and secured against the chassis, using the screws that hold the two parts together. Getting everything back together is a tricky job, so it helps to use Blu-Tack or a similar product to hold things in position.

Either the red or black decoder wire should be soldered to the tag, and the tag replaced on the bolt. The other wire needs to be soldered to the chassis. If you remove the suppression capacitor from the model then you will be able to use the furrow that the capacitor wire fitted into.

A number of the Graham Farish multiple-unit models use a split chassis system, where the chassis is divided along the middle and each half is live to one rail. The motor is electrically connected to both halves of the chassis while plastic spacers keep them from touching each other. The only way to convert these models to DCC is to completely isolate the motor from the chassis. If you are installing a decoder that doesn't have an insulating cover, you also need to be careful not to let it touch either side of the chassis.

When taking a chassis like this to bits, it is a good idea to use a digital camera to take photographs as you go along – it is very easy to forget how all the parts fit together. These particular components are used for multiple units with various wheelbases and bogie centres. If you put the bogie pivots back in the wrong position, or the opposite way around, they may well fit but won't match the model's bodywork.

Separate the two halves of the chassis and then file away the area that touches the motor contacts. This is a relatively quick job using a small file. Keep the motor somewhere safe, as getting metal filings in it could seriously shorten its working life. Put the motor in place and the two halves of the chassis back together, checking that the motor is isolated from the chassis. You will probably have to file a groove in the chassis block for the motor wire to run up it to the decoder. Depending on the model, you may also have to file a depression in the top of the chassis block for the decoder to sit in, or cut away part of the false roof in the body shell.

Special Decoder Features

Asymmetrical DCC

Lenz pioneered a system called ABC (Automatic Brake Control) that allows some measure of automatic control to be applied to DCC-fitted locomotives without the need for computers. The concept is very simple. The standard DCC track voltage is made up of positive and negative voltage pulses of the same size. If the size of either the positive or negative pulse is reduced slightly, this can be detected by the decoder without impairing its performance. This is called Asymmetrical DCC.

In its simplest form, the reduction in voltage can be achieved through the use of standard diodes. These are electronic components that pass current in one direction only and drop a small amount of voltage.

You can build a simple unit to make trains slow and stop at red signals using

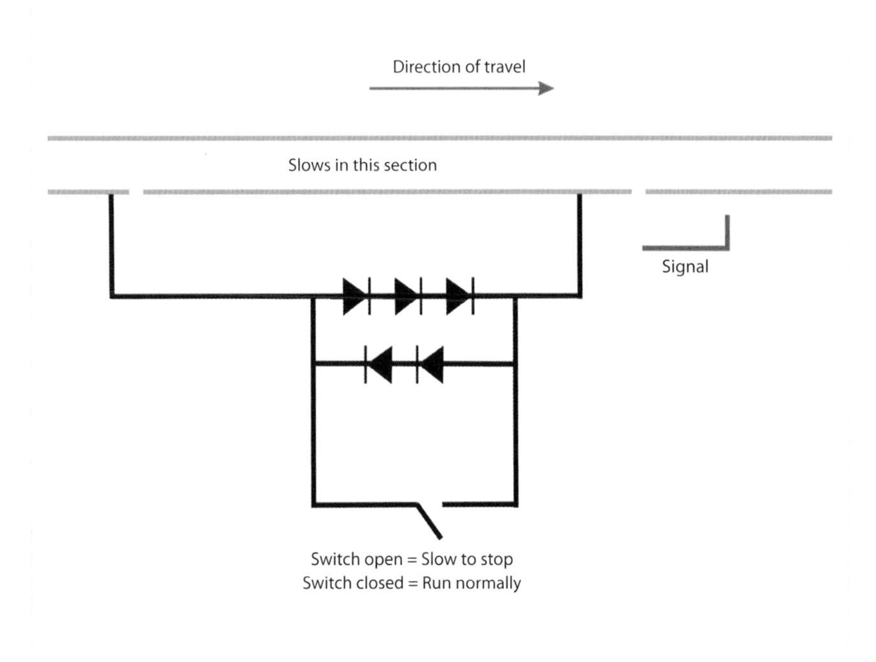

If your locomotive decoders can detect asymmetrical DCC, then it is possible to create simple devices to automatically slow and stop trains at red signals.

5 diodes and a switch. (The switch should, of course, be linked in some way to the signal.) With the switch open, the diodes create a lower DCC voltage on the right rail than on the left. The decoder detects this and slows the locomotive to a stop. If the switch is then closed, the locomotive will accelerate back to its previous speed. If the switch is closed before the locomotive has stopped, it will carry on running and accelerate back to normal speed. If the switch is closed before the train enters the braking section, the unit will have no effect. It also has no effect on trains running in the opposite direction

Lenz have three asymmetrical DCC modules in their range which provide functions for slow-to-stop and slow-down-but-keep-running, and one which allows you to create signal-controlled blocks. To utilise this system, your decoders must not only support Asymmetrical DCC but also have the appropriate CV set to enable the braking operation.

Most decoders that support ABC also have the ability to slow to a stop in a given distance. This makes automatically stopping in the right place very simple. For example, if your locomotives are set to slow to a stop in one foot then, whatever speed they are doing when the enter the ABC section, they will stop one foot into it.

Railcom

It may come as a surprise to you to learn that DCC, as described so far, is a one-way system; the command station sends commands to the decoders but gets no information back from them. It will normally issue a command several times in order to be sure that a decoder has received it, but gets no response to confirm this.

The exception to this is on the programming track. Here the command station plays a sort of electronic version of 20 Questions to establish the current decoder settings. It sends a series of queries such as, 'Is CV1 set to 1?', 'Is CV1 set to 2?', 'Is CV1 set to 3?', etc, until the decoder sends a brief pulse to the locomotive's motor. This is picked up by the command station which then knows what the CV setting is. This type of feedback cannot be used when programming 'on the main', so the command station cannot know what the CV settings of any decoder are when in use on the layout.

Apart from the obvious desirability of being able to check a CV before amending it by programming on the main, there are a number of other situations where it would be useful to know the value of a CV. Some newer decoders and command stations now provide for bi-directional communication where the decoder can be asked for information, or even broadcasts it itself.

Railcom is the standard for bi-directional communication between the decoder and the control system. When used with a Railcom capable control system, these decoders will provide information about speed, locomotive identification and other operating parameters. These decoders will also work normally with non-Railcom control systems, but will not be able to transmit information. Similarly, non-Railcom decoders will happily work on a Railcom-equipped layout, but will not transmit any information.

To take advantage of the bi-directional features in RailCom, it is not necessary for the locomotive to be at a precise point on your layout to transmit information. All information is transmitted via the normal track connections.

To enable the bi-directional features of RailCom, you need three components:

One possible use of Railcom would be to communicate the amount of fuel and water consumed by the locomotive. You would have to replenish both at suitable points to avoid grinding to a halt on the main line.

1. A decoder that transmits the information. Railcom-equipped decoders include the Hornby Sapphire, Zimo, some TCS, ESU and the Lenz Standard Plus, Silver+ and Gold+.
2. A detector that can receive these transmissions.
3. A cut-out device that conditions the track for the transmission. This is normally built into your command station or booster.

Currently, there is limited support of Railcom and take-up is limited. If there were more Railcom-fitted decoders there would be a market for more Railcom devices; conversely, if there were more Railcom devices there would be a greater demand for suitable decoders.

The one mainstream device that is available is the Lenz LRC120. This can identify the address of the locomotive on a given section of track. It can be useful in a number of locations such as hidden sidings and locomotivesheds – you don't actually have to be able to see the locomotive to identify it, just read the address from the LRC120 and enter it on your cab.

Of course, you need to have an isolated section of track for the LRC120 to work, otherwise it will pick up a locomotive anywhere on the layout. At over £40 each, you won't want to install too many of them either. It would be possible to connect one LRC120 to a number of sections and switch the display according to which section you are interested in – but then you will end up running a number of wires to and from the LRC120, so you won't want to place it too far away.

Taking the concept further, the system can be used to provide a simulation of fuel use. The decoder is 'refuelled' at the engine shed and then the fuel is used up –

Is this the future? The Lenz LRC120 will display the address of a Railcom-equipped locomotive that is in the section of track it monitors.

dependent on how hard the locomotive is worked and how well it is driven – with an indication of the amount of fuel remaining on the operator's cab. Running out of fuel on the main could even bring the locomotive to a grinding halt. This simulation facility is already included in some decoders, such as the Hornby Sapphire, but at present there is no way for the locomotive to notify the driver of how much fuel and water is left.

Transponding

Transponding is Digitrax's version of bi-directional communications. It has the advantage of being able to work alongside older equipment and not interfering with the DCC signal. Only Digitrax supplies decoders equipped to generate the transponding signal, although transponder-equipped, function-only decoders are supplied for installation in locomotives with other decoders and rolling stock.

The transponder superimposes a small signal onto the DCC power on the rails, which is picked up by a special sensor attached to a Digitrax block detector. The transponder information – along with the block details – is then broadcast across the Digitrax LocoNet, where it can be picked up by other devices.

Using this system, a computer program can display details of which locomotive is where, hidden storage yards can be automated so that a given train always returns to its own line and CVs can be read when using programming on the main.

Soundtraxx have produced an under-layout surround sound system, Surroundtraxx, which reads the transponding data so that the sound follows a train as it moves around the layout. The advantage of this is that the under-baseboard speakers are large enough to give a far more realistic sound than the tiny ones that can be mounted inside a model locomotive.

Lenz Power 1

An optional accessory for the Lenz Gold decoders is their Power 1 module. This not only provides backup power for the decoder but also continues to receive DCC commands when the power is interrupted. It allows the locomotive to continue to run and respond to the command station whilst running over dirty track and dead frogs. The system also detects when the DCC signal is not present, so that it does not keep the locomotive running after an emergency stop or derailment.

The Power 1 connects to the Gold decoder with three wires that have to be soldered in place. The connection pads on the decoder are small, so you need a fine-tipped soldering iron, thin solder and good light. I fitted my Power 1 unit in the cab of a Bachmann 08 diesel shunter, cutting away the moulded control desk to make

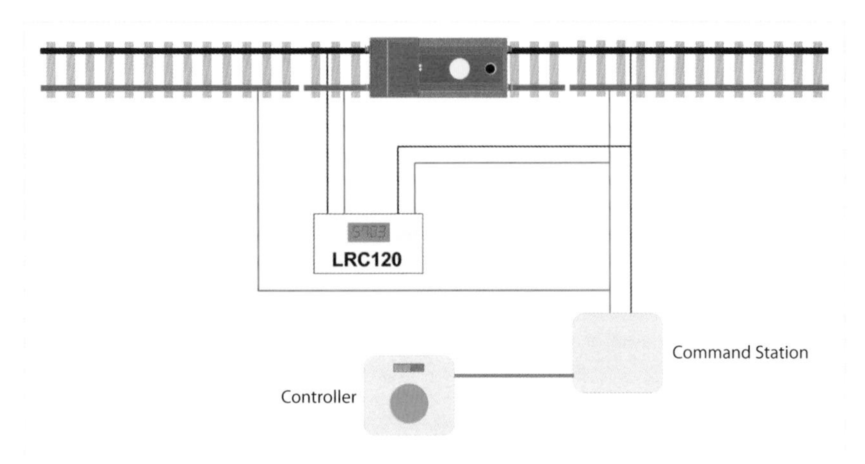

The LRC120 needs an isolated section of track to work. The locomotive on the isolated section transmits its DCC address to the unit, which then displays it.

The 08 in action on the author's Charmouth layout. With the Lenz Power 1 fitted, it can crawl over the dead frog points.

room for it. I needed to extend the wires to reach the decoder, which was situated vertically at the front of the chassis.

The result is a locomotive that can crawl without hesitation over a string of dead frog points, either running light or hauling a load. In normal operation it always responds to controller and is completely reliable. The down side is the cost. Both the Gold decoder and the Power 1 cost me more than the locomotive to which they are fitted.

For a layout that relies on one or two short wheelbase locomotives to do the shunting and is fitted with dead frog points, the Gold and Power 1 combination is excellent. Larger locomotives with more electrical pick-ups would see less benefit from the Power 1, as would a layout with live frog points. Apart from the price, the other downside to the Power 1 is its size – the small locomotives that would benefit the most area also the trickiest to install it in. Overall, the Power 1 measures 0.9" x 0.55" x 0.39" (22 x 13.3 x 9.4 mm). It will fit in a cab or possibly a bunker, but only if there is nothing else occupying the space.

CV Directory

All sorts of information which controls the way a locomotive performs are held in the Configuration Variables (CV) in the decoder. These can be set to suit your needs.

Not all CVs are implemented in all decoders. Basic decoders will only have limited functionality. The CVs that should be available in all decoders are indicated by an M in the 'Status' column of the table overleaf.

The NMRA recommends that a number of CVs are implemented in all decoders, but they are not mandatory. These are

The leads on the Power 1 are not long enough to reach from the cab to the front of the locomotive. I soldered some extra lengths of wire to the decoder, which were then soldered to the Power 1 leads and insulated with heat-shrink sleeving.

The Power 1 is held in place with a sticky pad.

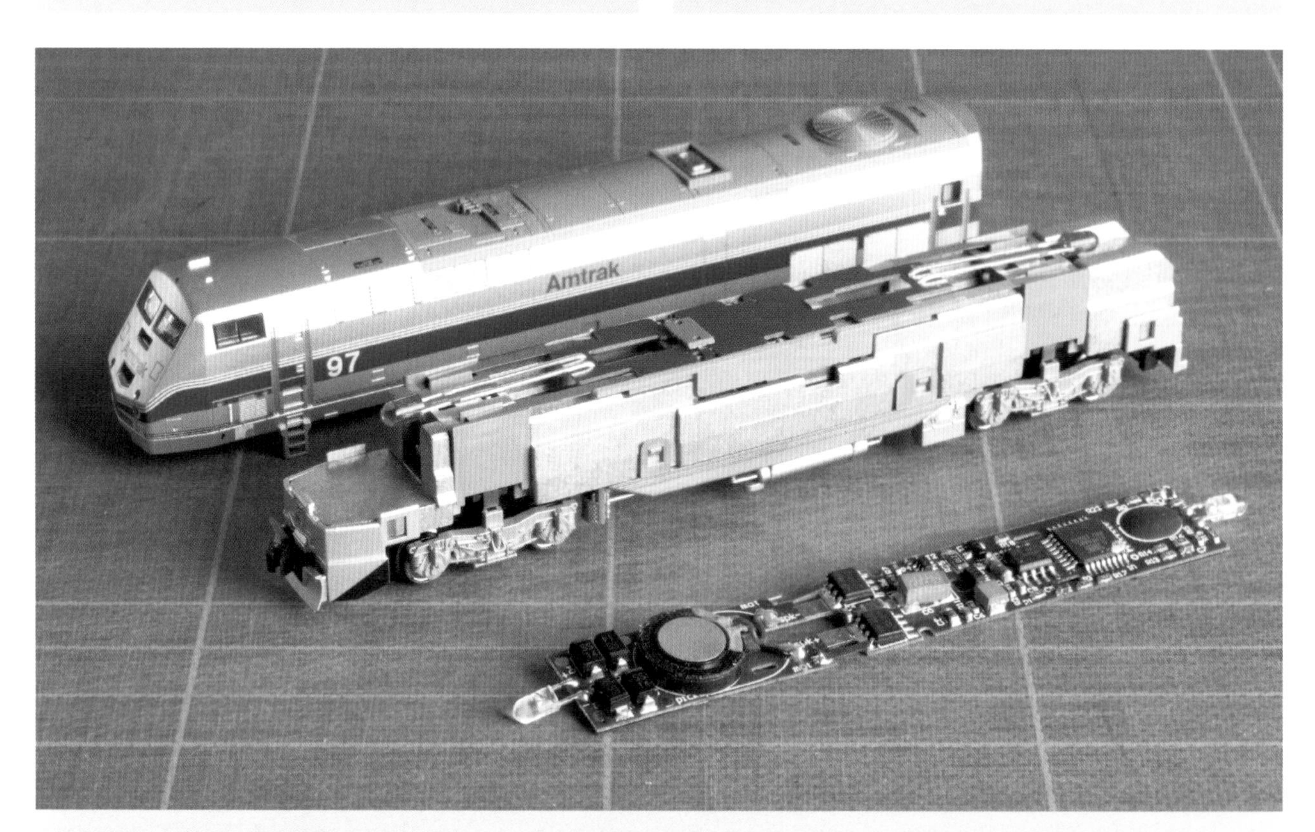

In the US, some locomotive decoders come in the form of replacement PCB boards. This is not the case in the UK, as locomotives are produced in smaller numbers which make the cost of producing the boards unrealistic. This photo shows an MRC sound decoder on a replacement board, ready for fitting to a Kato 'N' gauge locomotive.

indicated by an R in the 'Status' column. All other CVs are optional and are indicated by an O.

Not all the available CVs have been allocated a purpose. The NMRA have reserved some for future expansion of the standards, while others are reserved for manufacturers' own specific functions. Thus some of your decoders may have features using CVs that are not listed in the table below. (An explanation of what each CV does, and how it is used, is provided in Appendix B – 'CVs and What They Do'.)

Entering and Configuring CVs

Every DCC system has a slightly different way of selecting and entering CVs; however, there are some things that are common to all of them. Firstly, it is important to understand the difference between programming on a programming track and on the main. All except the most basic DCC systems have two track outputs, one for the layout and one for the programming track. The programming track is a separate length of track, electrically isolated from the layout, which is used solely for programming CVs; this is called *Service Mode programming*. The DCC system has special circuitry built in to limit the current that can be drawn on the programming track, in order to protect incorrectly installed decoders. You cannot run a locomotive whilst it is on the programming track; if you wish to test your CV changes, then you must move the locomotive to the layout and run it there. Your system should also be able to read back CV values from a locomotive that is on the programming track, which is useful to check a value before you change it.

Most systems also support Operations Mode Programming, which is also known as Programming on the Main or POM. This enables you to change the value of a CV when a locomotive is on the layout, even whilst it is in motion. A few of the simplest

CV Directory

CV NUMBER	STATUS	DESCRIPTION	DEFAULT
1	M	Primary Locomotive Address	3
2	R	Start Voltage	0
3	R	Acceleration Rate	0
4	R	Braking Rate	0
5	0	Top Speed	255
6	0	Speed Curve Modifier	0
7	M	Manufacturer Version Number	n/a
8	M	Manufacturer ID Number	n/a
9	0	Total PWM Period	n/a
10	0	EMF Feedback Cutout	0
11	R	Packet Time-Out	
12	0	Power Source Conversion	
13-14	0	Alternate Mode Fuction Status	
15-16	0	Not Currently Used	
17-18	0	Extended Address	
19	0	Consist Address	
20	0	Not Currently Used	
21-22	0	Consist Address Active for Functions	
23	0	Acceleration Adjustment	
24	0	Braking Adjustment	
25	0	Speed Table	
26	0	Not Currently Used	
27	0	Automatic Stopping	
28	0	Bi-directional Communication	
29	M	Basic Configuration Register	n/a
30	0	Error Information	n/a
31	0	Decoder Sub-address	
32	0	Decoder Sub-address Flags	
33-46	0	Function Output Locations	
47-64	0	Not Currently Used	
65	0	Kick Start	
66	0	Forward Trim	
67-94	0	Special Speed Table	
95	0	Reverse Trim	
96-104	0	Not Currently Used	
105-6	0	User Identification	
107-11	0	Not Currently Used	
112-28	0	Use specified by manufacturers	

Older steam locomotives with tender-drive mechanisms are easily converted to DCC. There is usually plenty of spare space in the tender for the decoder and no problem with squeezing things in.

systems use the layout as a programming track – typically for setting the locomotive's address and direction of travel. With these systems, it is necessary to remove all the locomotives and other decoder fitted stock from the layout, except the one being programmed; otherwise, you will find that all your locomotives have been allocated the same address.

Using your controller to set and read CVs is made more complicated than it should be by the limited display and controls. Systems with bigger graphical screens, such as ECoS, have more scope for making things easy to understand, but handset displays can get quite cryptic. The difficulty in making sense of these displays is probably why most people never venture further into the world of CVs than setting the locomotive's address.

Useful CVs

Some CVs are more useful than others and some you will never use. The most useful is, of course, the decoder's address. This is the number that identifies it to the command station. Even the most basic DCC command stations allow you to set this. Virtually all the decoders currently on the market will allow you to use any address from 1 to 9999, although not all command stations will go that high.

CV 29, the basic configuration register, is also very useful but causes a lot of confusion as it controls a lot of things:

- Direction of travel – changes which way is forwards for the locomotive.
- Analogue mode – allows the locomotive to run on an analogue (DC) layout.
- Address system – selects 2- or 4-digit decoder addressing
- Speed table – allows a special speed table to be used.
- Bi-directional communications – turns Railcom on if supported by the decoder and command station.
- Speed steps – for use with older command stations that can only support 14 speed steps.

Tenders are great places for hiding decoders. Some modern steam locomotives locate the DCC socket there.

Of these, the first two are the ones that you may wish to change; the others will normally be set by the command station if required. The difficulty with CV29 is that each bit of information relates to a different setting rather than the CV as a whole relating to one setting, like acceleration rate.

Some command stations allow you to set the values individually; others require you to enter a number. This is how to calculate the number:

- Start with a value of 0.
- Does the locomotive need to run backwards when the cab is set to forward? If it does, then add 1 to your number.
- Is your command station using 28 or 128 speed steps? If it is, then add 2 to your number.
- Do you want to be able to run the locomotive on analogue layouts? If you do, then add 4 to your number.
- If your decoder and command station both support bi-directional communications (Railcom), do you wish to use them? If you do, add 8 to your number.
- If your decoder supports special speed tables, do you wish to use one? If you do, add 16 and don't forget to set the speed table up.
- Is the locomotive's address higher than 127? If it is, add 32.

The number that you end up with is the value that should be written to CV 29.

The locomotive's top speed is set by CV 5. The CV uses a range from 0 to 255. Reducing the value by 10 will reduce the voltage reaching the motor at top speed by about 0.5V. If you have a command station that allows you to program CVs whilst the locomotive is running on the layout, you will find it a far more convenient way of setting this value than by using the programming track.

The locomotive's start voltage is set by CV 2. This should be set so that the locomotive just starts to move at speed step 1. Again, the values run from 0 to 255 and setting the CV is best achieved whilst running the locomotive on the layout.

If you have a layout that allows you to run trains, rather than shunting up and down a short length of track, then you may want to set the acceleration and deceleration rates. On analogue (DC) controllers, this effect is usually called Inertia or Momentum and mimics the slow response of real trains to changes in the power setting. Both values run from 0 to 255, with 0 being an immediate response to the controller. The ideal setting will vary depending on your layout and the type of locomotive.

If you have a locomotive that needs a jolt of power to make the motor start turning, this can be specified using CV 65 which gives an extra burst of power between speed steps 0 and 1. This is useful for older types of motor which have more mechanical resistance than modern types.

Binary/Hexadecimal/Decimal Conversion

Where a number of variables are combined in one CV, the DCC system uses a binary number system. Depending on which system you use, you may need to enter the values as binary, hexadecimal or decimal numbers. There is a full conversion table in Appendix C at the back of this book.

Speed Profiling

Having set the maximum and start speeds of your locomotive using CV 5 and CV 2, the decoder will divide the difference

Linear Speed Curve

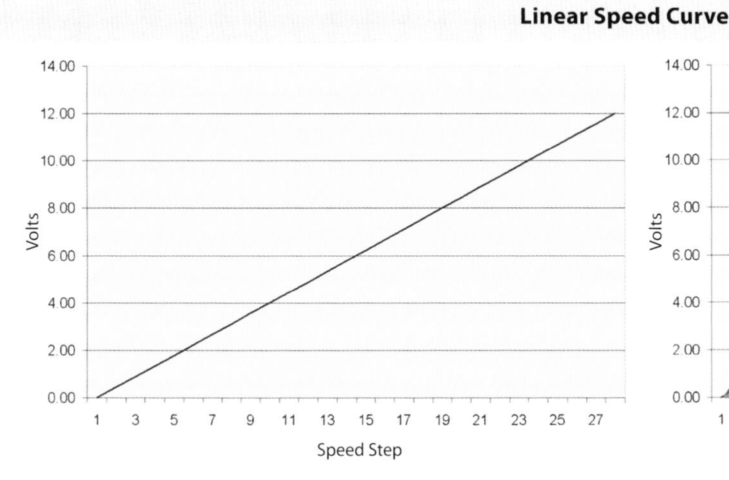

A linear speed curve. This is how a decoder will work by default, but your locomotive's speed may respond differently due to the mechanical characteristics of the motor and gears.

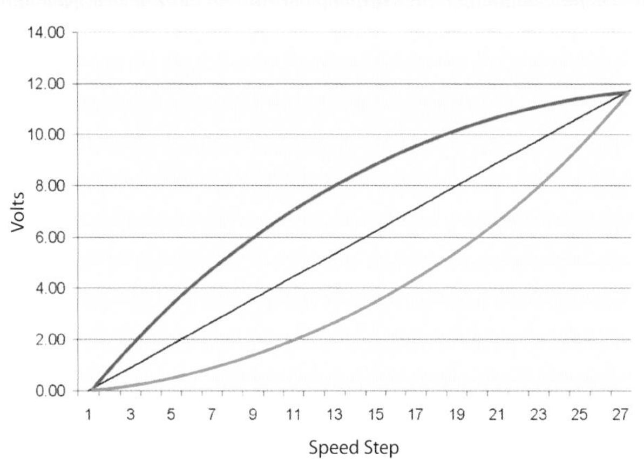

Changing the midpoint of the speed curve changes the way that the decoder responds to the speed steps. The red line shows what happens when the midpoint is increased; the blue line shows what happens when it is decreased.

If the computer can't go to the layout, then a simple programming track can come to the computer. DecoderPro will run on most home computers and a SPROG DCC controller (from www.sprog-dcc.co.uk) can be built into a small portable programming/test track, making a self-contained unit. This is Max Wright's programming track, connected to a laptop computer.
PHOTO: MAX WRIGHT

between the maximum and minimum voltages up evenly between the speed steps. If the minimum voltage is set to 1.0 and the maximum to 9.1V, then each of the 27 speed steps will increase the voltage to the motor by about 0.3V (27 x 0.3 = 8.1). This is called a linear speed curve and, on a graph, it's a straight line.

This doesn't necessarily suit all locomotive mechanisms or operating styles. You may wish to have more control at slower speeds or maybe you have a locomotive that gets less responsive to changes as the power is increased. You can change the decoder's settings to accommodate this sort of thing either by changing the mid-point on the graph, using CV6, or by using a speed table that you have defined.

Increasing the value of the midpoint means that there is a bigger difference in voltage between the lower speed steps and a smaller difference in the higher ones. Decreasing the value gives a smaller value between the lower speed steps and a larger value between the higher ones.

Using a speed table allows you to tailor the voltage at each speed step, but setting one up using a DCC command station is usually a tedious exercise. If you wish to do it, I would suggest that you need a more powerful means of setting CVs, such as DecoderPro.

DecoderPro

As anyone who has used a DCC system to program decoder CVs knows, most DCC controllers have a terrible user interface when it comes to this task. The fact is that they are limited by their displays and inputs. The home computer's 'point and click' style of presentation is far superior to anything that you can accomplish with a couple of lines of text and an array of buttons. So imagine a program that runs on your computer, has understandable screens tailored to the specific decoder that you are programming and will remember the settings so that the decoder can be reprogrammed if there is a problem. Now imagine if that program was available free of charge.

Well, such a program exists. It is called DecoderPro and is part of the JMRI suite. JMRI is a project run by a large group of modellers who have made their work freely available. It consists of a library of Java program code and some programs that work with it. You don't need to know anything about Java to use the programs; on the other hand, if you do then you can use the code to do things specific to your layout.

DecoderPro comes with the JMRI package that can be downloaded from *http://jmri.sourceforge.net/* and is available for Windows™, MacOS X and Linux operating systems. JMRI supports most DCC systems that have a computer interface, and you specify which system you are using when you start DecoderPro for the first time. JMRI is covered in chapter 7, 'Computers and DCC', but I will cover DecoderPro here. Provided that your DCC system supports a programming track, DecoderPro can program locomotives either on the programming track or on the main.

When you start DecoderPro you are offered the choice of Service Mode or Operations Mode programming. If you select Service Mode then you will be offered a screen with a selection of decoder types. If your locomotive already has a roster entry, then you can select it from the drop down list. If you think it has an entry but can't find it (or you have a number of locomotives that you can't tell apart), then pressing the 'Ident' button will search the roster for an entry that matches your locomotive. If it is a new locomotive, then you can either select the decoder type manually or press the 'Read type from decoder ' button, which will attempt to

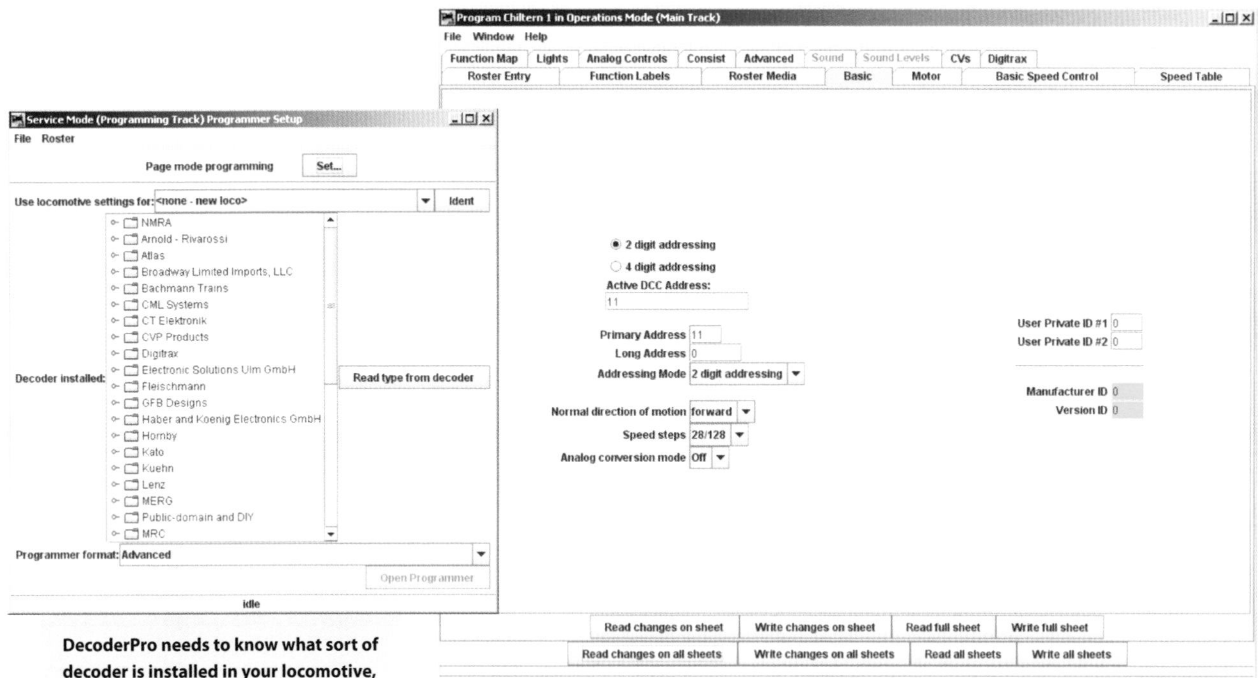

DecoderPro needs to know what sort of decoder is installed in your locomotive, so that it can tailor the screens that it displays. When you start the programmer up, it gives you the opportunity to recall saved information, select a decoder type or get the program to identify it.

The 'Basic' properties tab allows you to set the locomotive's address and other basic information easily and quickly. You simply make your changes on the screen and then press the 'Write Changes on Sheet' button to send them to the decoder.

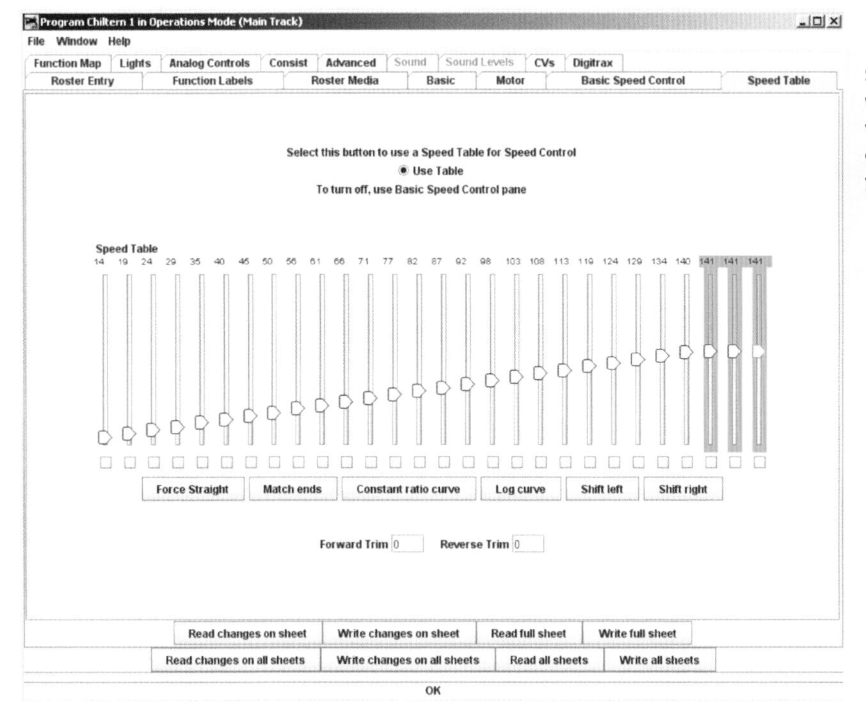

Setting the speed profile is quick and easy with DecoderPro. The program highlights values that have changed in a different colour, making it easy to keep track of what you have done.

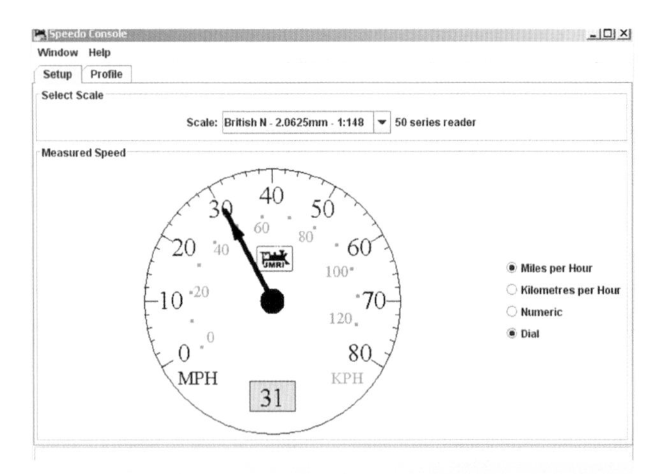

If you have a Bachrus rolling road, you can get a speedometer unit which interfaces with DecoderPro and gives you an accurate figure for the model's scale speed. You can use this information to tune the locomotive's speed profile.

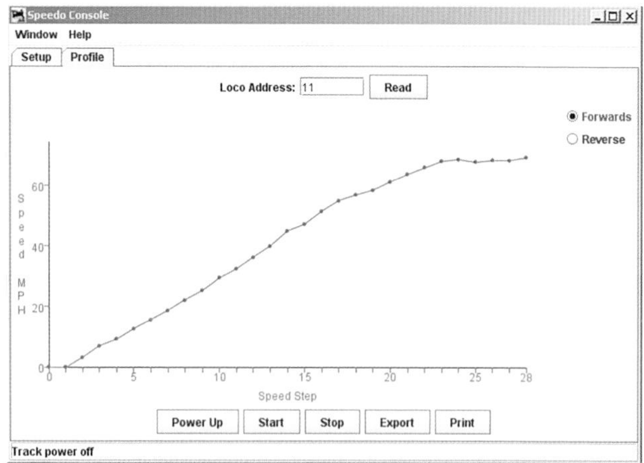

When combined with the Bachrus Speedometer, DecoderPro can chart the scale speed of a locomotive at each speed step.

This locomotive is set so that speed step 20 is a scale of 50mph; as long as the controller is set at 20 or less, the driver will not get in trouble for exceeding the speed limit.

identify it for you. This is particularly useful for identifying decoders in locomotives acquired second-hand. If you select Operations Mode then you are only allowed to select an existing locomotive from the dropdown list.

Once you have made your selection, the programmer shows a selection of tabs, each of which has options tailored to the decoder that is installed in the locomotive. The 'Basic' tab includes the locomotive's address, in both 2 and 4 digit forms. It also allows you to set the values in the Configuration Register CV29 easily.

Other tabs deal with other areas, like function mapping (covered in the next chapter), speed profiling and advanced consisting. The 'CVs' tab gives you direct access to all the CVs and the 'Roster' tabs allow you to store notes for your own reference.

DecoderPro makes setting the speed profile for a locomotive very easy. Set the locomotive running at full speed and then pull the right-hand slider down a bit and press 'Write Changes on Sheet'. You will notice that the locomotive slows down a little. Repeat this cycle until you are happy with the locomotive's top speed. Now set the controller to speed step 1. Lift the left-hand slider a little, press 'Write Changes on Sheet' and repeat until the locomotive starts to move. You will now have a strange-looking pattern on the sliders, so press 'Match Ends' and the sliders will all line up neatly. Press 'Write Changes on Sheet' again and that's it. The locomotive will now start to move at the first controller step and run at a sensible maximum speed, with the controller at maximum. Set the acceleration and deceleration rates (on the 'Motor' tab) to zero before you set the speed profile and reset them as they were after you have finished.

If you use a Bachrus rolling road to run your locomotives in, then you may be interested to know that you can buy a speedometer unit that interfaces with DecoderPro. This gives you an accurate measurement of the model's scale speed and, when combined with the speed-profiling tab, enables you to fine-tune your locomotive so that it travels at given prototype speed at certain speed steps. When you are operating, you will be able to observe signed speed limits on your layout.

Locomotive Record Cards

It is well worth keeping a record of your CV settings. This helps if you need to set up a similar locomotive, want to play with the settings or just cannot remember a locomotive's address. A sample is shown here and you can find a blank copy in Appendix D at the back of this book.

It is also worth making a 'cheat sheet' giving the address of each of your locomotives, which is a useful quick reference while operating. This can be as simple as the example below through to one with pictures of the locomotives.

DCC Addresses

Jinty	– 1
Black 5	– 2
Jubilee	– 4
Pug	– 5

DCC Locomotive Record Card

Locomotive type:	Class 24 - Blue
Number:	5087
DCC address:	2487
Type of decoder:	Lenz Silver Direct

CV	Value	Comments:
3	10	Acceleration
4	10	Deceleration
29	8	Analogue enabled

Notes:	Fitted Jan 06 No lighting.

Consisting and Double Heading

Another of the oft-quoted benefits of DCC is the ease with which double-heading can be performed. Double-heading is where two locomotives are used to haul a train, as has happened for a number of reasons on real railways. The primary reason is quite simply that the train was too heavy for one locomotive to move; the railways had far more small and medium-sized locomotives than large ones, so it was often necessary to use two smaller locomotives instead of a big one. Also, a number of lines could not take the weight of a large freight or express locomotive, so a pair of smaller locomotives would be used instead.

Sometimes it was operational needs that resulted in double-heading. A locomotive on its way to or from works attention could be added to a train, rather than running a light engine on a busy line. Similarly, a failing or failed engine could be assisted by another. Where a train is diverted or routed over lines which the crew is not familiar with, a pilot locomotive could be attached to the front driven by a local crew. For modellers, there is rarely any need to double-head our trains. powerful motors and free-running rolling stock make it unnecessary. However, we do like to replicate prototype practice, and anyway – a double-headed train looks good.

DCC offers at least three ways to double-head trains. The first is simply to set the decoders in both locomotives to the same address. The second is called universal consisting, which is where the DCC controller sends the same control signals to two different locomotives. The

Class 20 diesels usually operated in pairs, so it is easiest to set both locomotives to the same address. One of the pair needs to have CV29 set to reverse its travelling direction.

third is advanced consisting, where the locomotive decoder responds to both its own address and a second consist address.

(The terms 'consist' and 'consisting' come from the US, and refer to running a number of locomotives in multiple. In the US trains are regularly hauled by four or more locomotives – in the UK, it is very rare to need more than two.)

The way that consisting is implemented varies with different DCC controllers and decoders, not all features are available in all systems and those that are may behave differently from each other. The first port of call is the user manual, usually followed by a healthy dose of experimentation.

Simple Consisting

This is a term to describe setting two (or more) locomotive decoders to the same address. It is very simple to set up but not very flexible, best suited to locomotives that will always work together as a pair – such as a pair of class 20 diesels. By placing the locomotives on the programming track individually, the decoder settings can be modified as necessary – for example, to set one locomotive to run backwards and the other forwards. It is not possible to operate the locomotives individually, but this method will work with any DCC controller or locomotive decoder.

Universal Consisting

In universal consisting, the donkey work is performed by the DCC controller. A locomotive address is allocated to the consist as a whole and, when that address is selected, the commands are sent to all the locomotives that are part of it.

Using the controller, you can add and remove locomotives from the consist so that it is possible to run the locomotives individually when you need to. This allows you to run a train headed by a single locomotive, pull into a station where a second locomotive is added to the front and then the train can depart double-headed.

Universal consisting is controlled entirely from the DCC controller. Some simple controllers, such as the Bachmann E-Z, do not support it while others have limited functionality. Usually, the controller will have a limit to the number of consists and locomotives in each consist that it can handle, although this is not likely to be a problem on a British-outline layout.

As the consist information is in the controller, rather than the locomotive decoders, if you move the locomotives to a different layout or connect a different controller, then the consist information will need to be re-entered on the new controller.

Depending on the way that universal consisting has been implemented on your controller, you may find that the consist can be controlled by both its own address and also the individual locomotive addresses, or just the consist address.

Advanced Consisting

Holding the consist information in the locomotive decoders tends to be a feature of newer and more expensive designs. Some controllers directly support setting up advanced consists, while on others you have to set the necessary CVs yourself.

With advanced consisting, the DCC controller sends commands to the consist address and these are picked up and actioned by all the locomotives in the consist. As the consist information is stored in the locomotive decoders, the locomotives will still work together if they are moved to a different layout or a different controller is connected.

The locomotives in an advanced consist will not respond to speed or direction commands sent to their own address – only the consist address. Decoder functions, such as lighting and sound, are a more complex area and it is possible to change their behaviour using CV settings. Normally, the functions will only respond to instructions sent to the locomotive's address and not the consist address.

Matching Locomotives Up

Normally, any two locomotives will behave differently. This is especially true given the way that DCC allows you to tailor the top speed, acceleration rate and other characteristics of each locomotive. For successful double-heading, both locomotives need to be travelling at about the same speed at all times.

The easiest way to do this, for locomotives that will regularly work together in a consist, is to match the speeds of the locomotives that you are going to use by adjusting CVs 2 (Start Voltage), 5 (Top Speed) and 6 (Mid-Range Speed) whilst running them around a circuit.

However, if you don't wish to make a permanent change to the decoder settings, there are two CVs – CV 66 Forward Trim and CV 95 Reverse Trim – that allow you to make a temporary change to a locomotive's speed table. Both work the same way – they specify a factor to be applied to the voltage level when the locomotive is moving forwards or backwards. This is used to make the locomotive travel faster (or slower) than it would normally for any given speed step. If the value is 0 then no forward trim is applied. For values between 1 and 255, the adjustment is calculated as Normal Speed (CV value -128). So a value of 128 would cause the forward and normal speeds to be the same. A value less than 128 would cause the forward speed to be less than the normal speed and a value greater than 128 would cause the forward speed to be greater than the normal speed. Obviously, the modified speed cannot exceed the maximum possible for the decoder. This adjustment allows you to speed a locomotive up, or slow it down, to match another.

You won't want to find the value by experimentation every time that you make up a consist, so it is best to establish any trim values in advance and make a note of them for when you need to use them. The trim values can be set using programming on the main at the same time as you make up the consist and reset when you break it up.

With universal and advanced consisting, your DCC controller will normally have a means of selecting the direction of travel for each locomotive within a consist – so that, no matter which way is normally forwards for each locomotive, they travel the same way when working as a pair. The usual method is to ensure that they are set to travel in the same direction when they are put in the consist.

Back-EMF

Also known as feedback, this is a system used by a number of locomotive decoders to make locomotives run smoothly. In simple terms, it checks the motor's speed, compares it to what it is supposed to be and adjusts the power to the motor accordingly. This keeps a locomotive at a constant speed whether it is going around a curve, straight and level, up or down hill. However, different decoder manufacturers implement it in different ways. If the locomotives in your consist use decoders from different manufacturers, you may find that you have to turn the Back-EMF option off to get them to work together reliably. This is also true if one decoder has Back-EMF and the other does not.

Decoder Installation – A Step by Step guide

This sequence of photos gives a step-by-step illustrated guide to converting two models that can be obtained on the secondhand market. They are typical of models that have survived from childhood train sets.

Fitting a decoder to a Lima Class 87 locomotive

1 Lima produced a huge variety of OO gauge models throughout the 1970s, 80s and 90s. They all used the same motor and the DCC conversion process is therefore the same for them all. This Class 87 locomotive serves as an example.

2 Before dismantling the model, make a note of how it fits together. With diesel and electric models it is easy to put the body back the wrong way around if you are not careful!

3 A foam cradle is really useful to have as it holds models safely without the risk of damage. This one is from Peco and can be used for both OO and 'N' gauge models.

4 The body is secured to the chassis with two screws. Undo these to start the conversion.

5 Keep the parts that you remove somewhere safe, such as the polystyrene tray from the model's box.

6 The pantograph on this model is wired for electrical pickup. This is a bad idea on DCC, so we will just use the wheels.

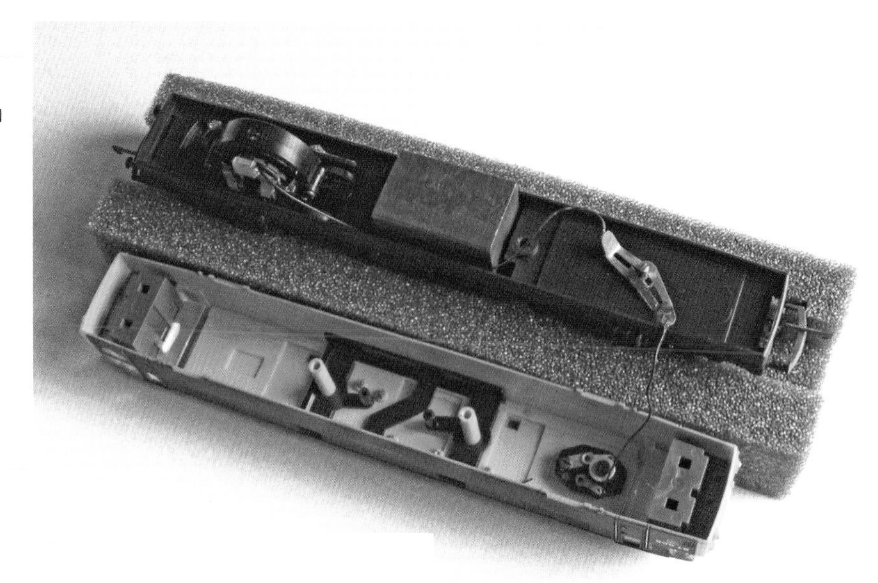

7 The connector just pulls off the brass pin above one of the bogies. Cut the wire off as close to the pantograph as you can and discard it.

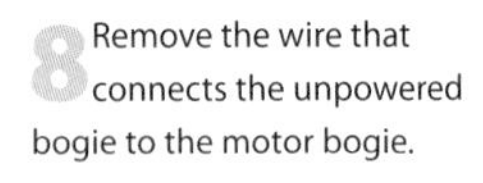

8 Remove the wire that connects the unpowered bogie to the motor bogie.

9 The unpowered bogie is now free to drop out.

10 Lift the chassis away and the unpowered bogie is left behind, to be placed in storage.

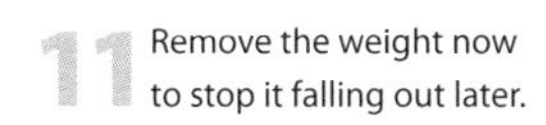

11 Remove the weight now to stop it falling out later.

12 Now we turn our attention to the motor bogie.

13 Remove the frame and coupling by unscrewing it.

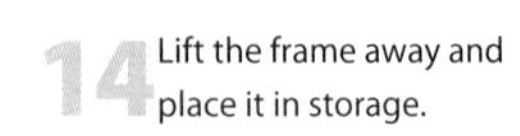

14 Lift the frame away and place it in storage.

15 Lift the chassis away, leaving the motor bogie.

16 The motor bogie – stripped of all the other parts.

18 With both the brushes and springs removed, if you wish you can remove the capacitor – that white lump between the two brush holders, which is there to stop television and radio interference. Some older decoders are not compatible with them, but most currently available decoders work happily with them in place.

17 Lift the brass flaps that hold the brushes and springs in place and tip them out. If your model has done a few miles, then the carbon brush will be worn and it will not look like this one. Replace it with a new one – Hornby's X8466 is suitable.

19 For this installation I used a Hornby R8248 decoder.

20 Cut the DCC plug off – this model does not have a DCC socket.

21 Wrap the purple, blue, white, yellow and green function wires in a piece of insulation tape. They are not needed now, but you may want to install lighting in the future.

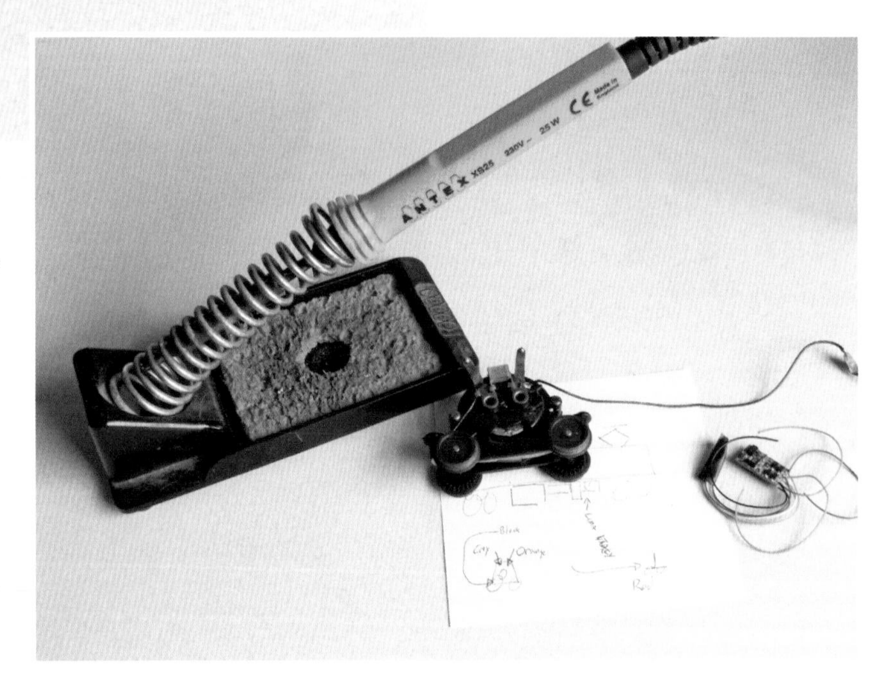

22 Before you start soldering, make a note of which colour wire goes where to avoid mistakes or confusion later.

23 Disconnect the wire from the unpowered bogie by heating it with a soldering iron.

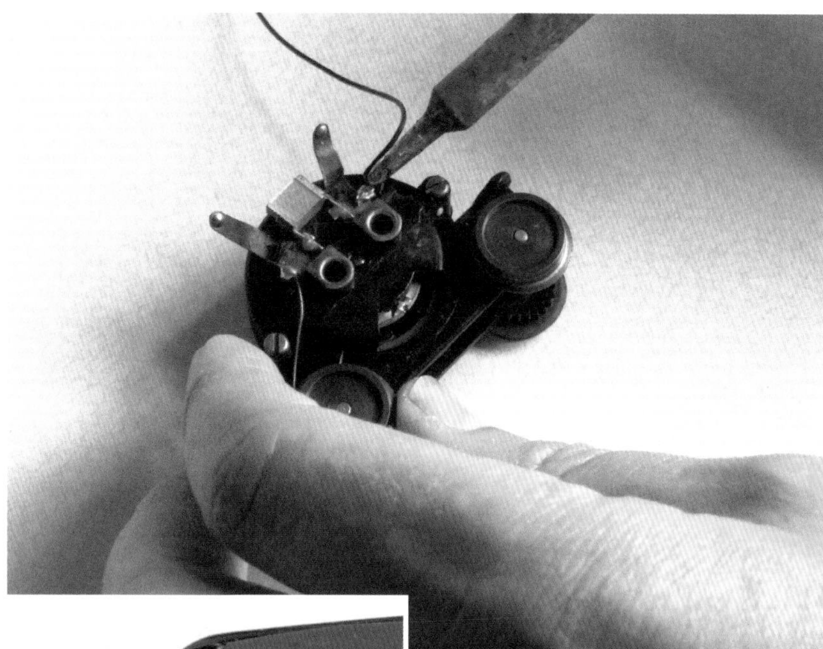

24 Once it has been disconnected, strip it back a little with a wire stripper and put a length of heatshrink tube on it.

25 Strip the red decoder wire back a little and twist it together with the wire from the unpowered bogie.

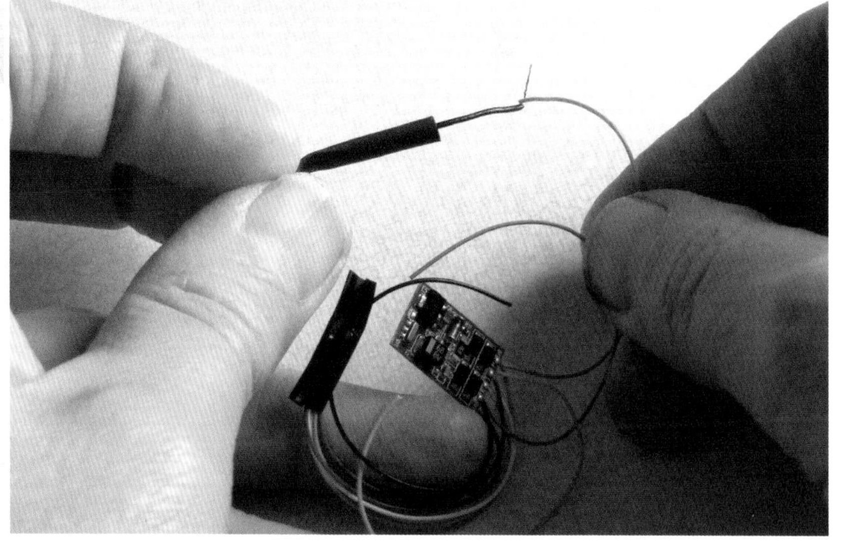

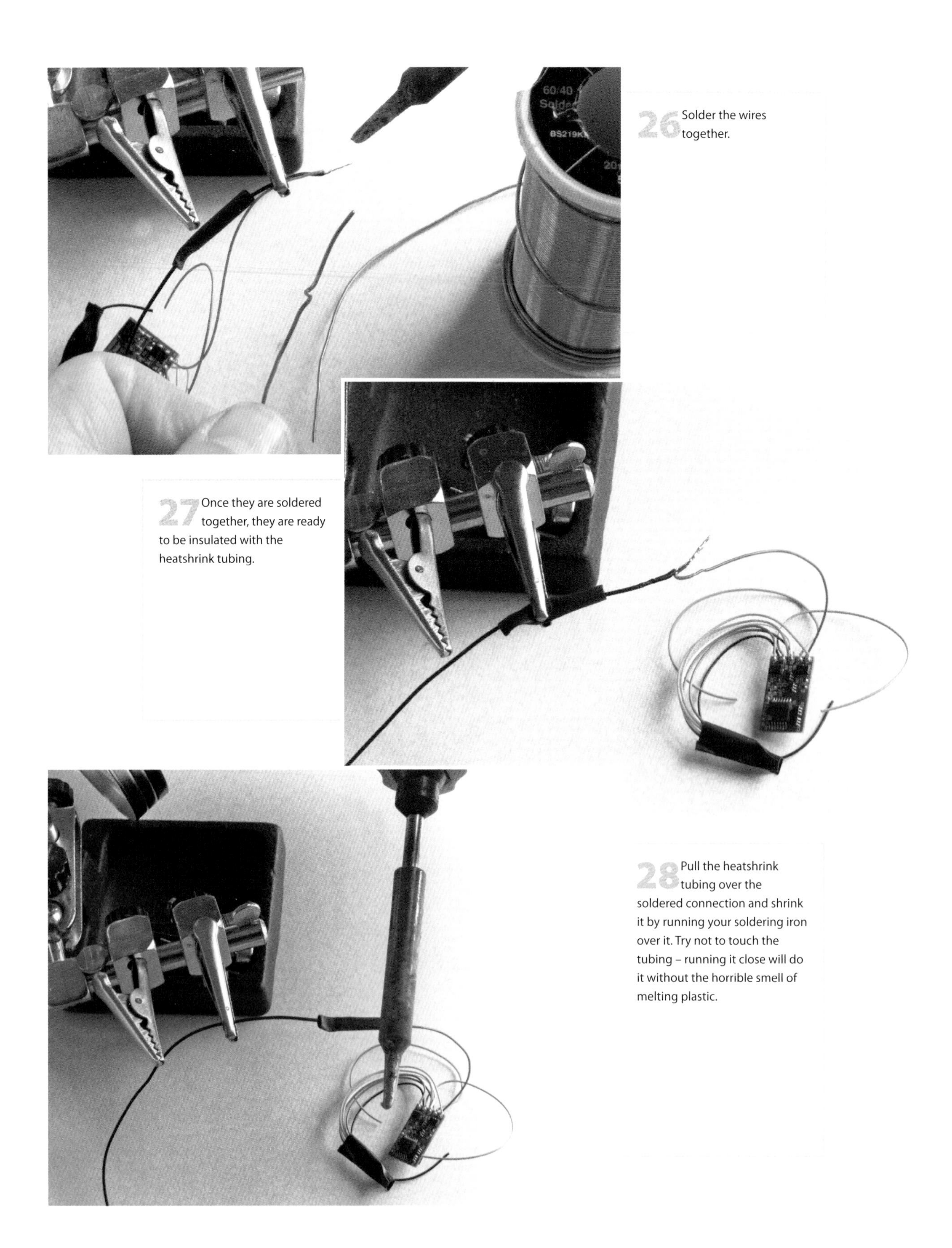

26 Solder the wires together.

27 Once they are soldered together, they are ready to be insulated with the heatshrink tubing.

28 Pull the heatshrink tubing over the soldered connection and shrink it by running your soldering iron over it. Try not to touch the tubing – running it close will do it without the horrible smell of melting plastic.

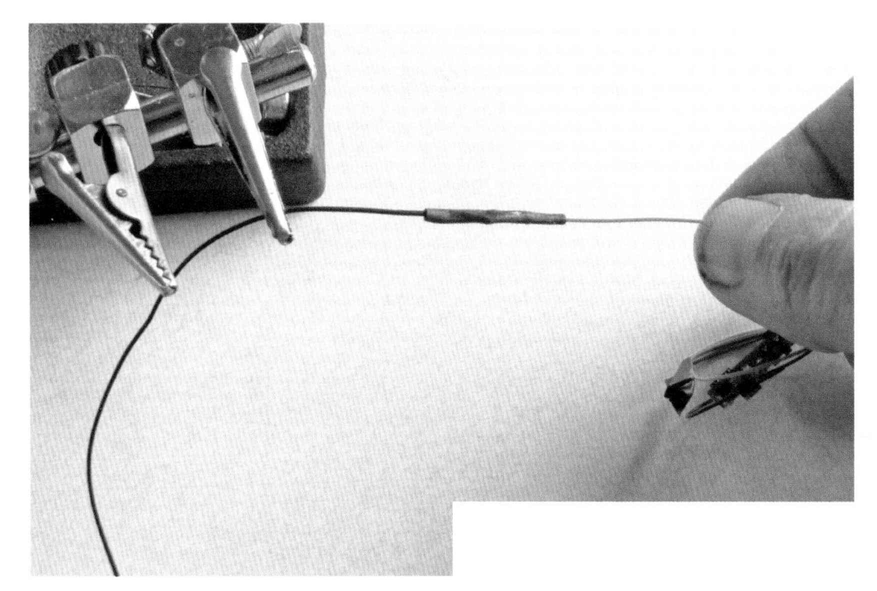

29 The shrunken tubing creates a nicely insulated joint.

30 Clean up the area where you unsoldered the wire on the motor bogie.

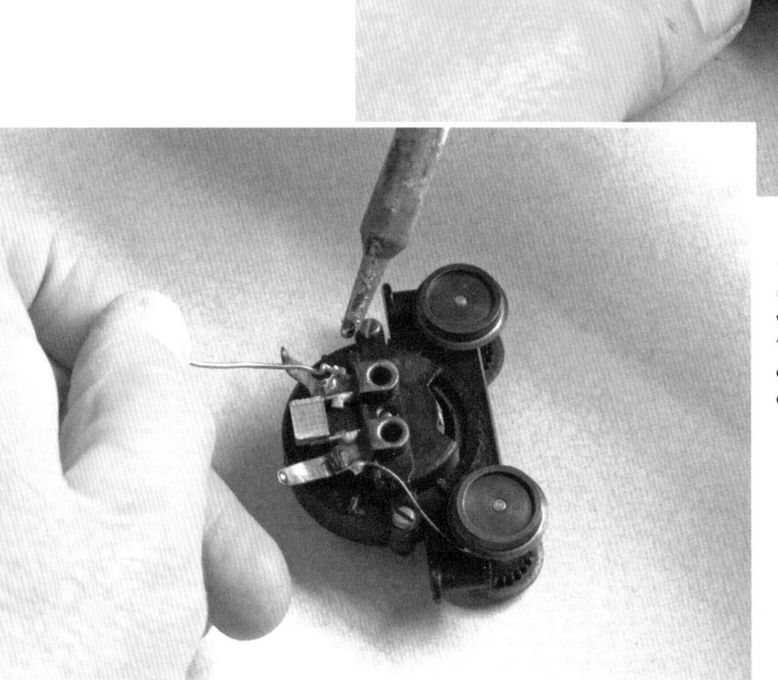

31 Melt some solder onto the area where the wire was connected. This is called 'tinning' and will make the next connection much quicker and easier.

32 Strip the orange wire from the decoder and solder it to the area that you have just tinned.

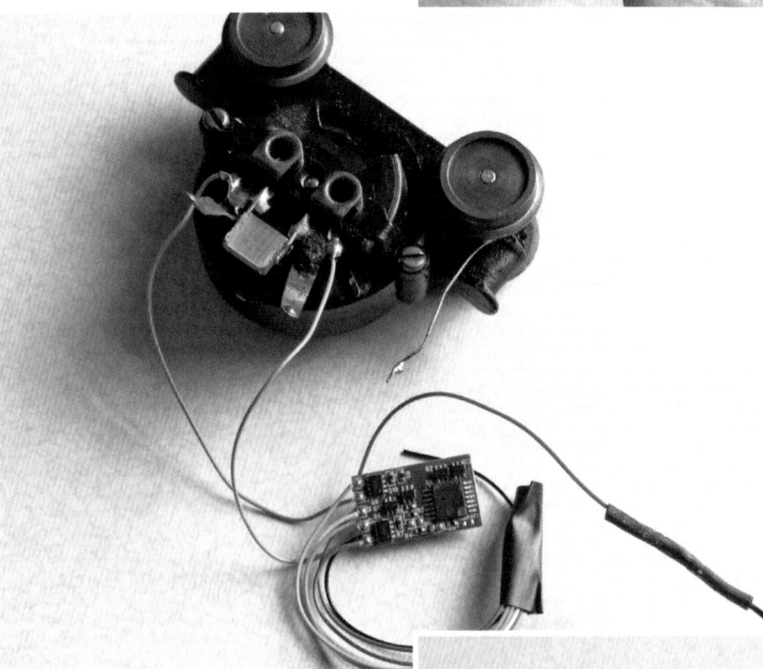

33 Unsolder the wire to the other brush holder. Tin the area, then strip and solder the decoder's grey wire into place.

34 Put a length of heatshrink tubing to the decoder's black wire, then strip it and twist it around the wire that you unsoldered from the brushholder. Solder them together.

35 Shrink the sleeving over the wire by heating it with your soldering iron. Now you can put the brushes and springs back.

36 The easiest way to put the springs back is to put them on a small screwdriver and trap them in place with the tabs of the brushholder.

37 This is what the decoder looks like once all the connections have been made.

38 A drop of glue will prevent the weight moving in future when the locomotive body is off at any point.

39 Wrapping the decoder in insulating tape will avoid any unexpected short circuits. Many decoders come with an insulating coat already in place.

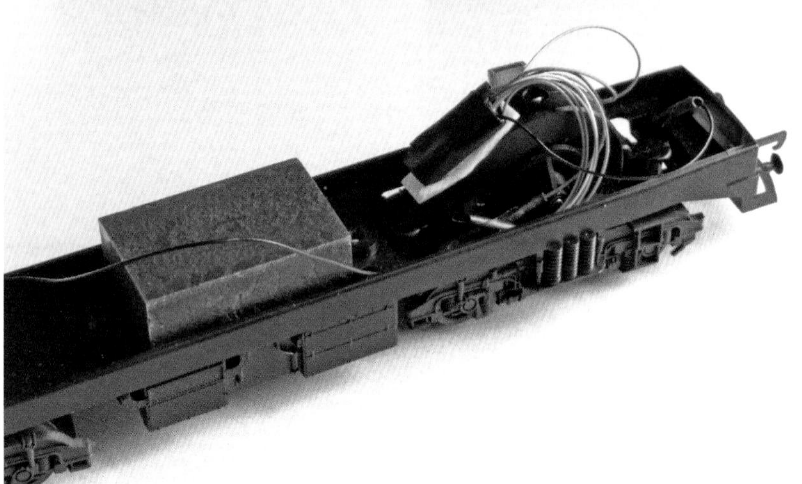

40 A sticky foam pad holds the decoder in place.

41 With the body in place, a final test is made before releasing the locomotive to the layout.

Fitting a decoder to a Hornby R855 *Flying Scotsman* locomotive

1 This is an older Hornby locomotive that many modellers will remember from their youth.

2 There are a variety of screws visible when the model is inverted in the foam cradle.

3 With experience, the choice becomes obvious – the one that is least accessible!

4 Once screw later, the chassis lifts away from the body.

5 This is an X04 motor, which was the standard in everything from the Flying Scotsman to the Great Western Pannier tank.

6 Disconnect the wire soldered to the motor.

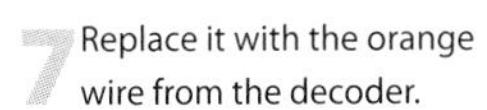

7 Replace it with the orange wire from the decoder.

8 Cut the insulating sleeve in half so that you have a piece for each retaining arm. Alternatively, you can use a length of heatshrink tubing on the second arm.

9 The grey decoder wire is soldered to the other motor brush.

10 The red decoder wire is soldered to the first wire that was disconnected.

11 Once you have made the soldered connection, slide the heatshrink tubing in place and shrink it with the soldering iron.

12 Now undo the screw that holds the motor in place.

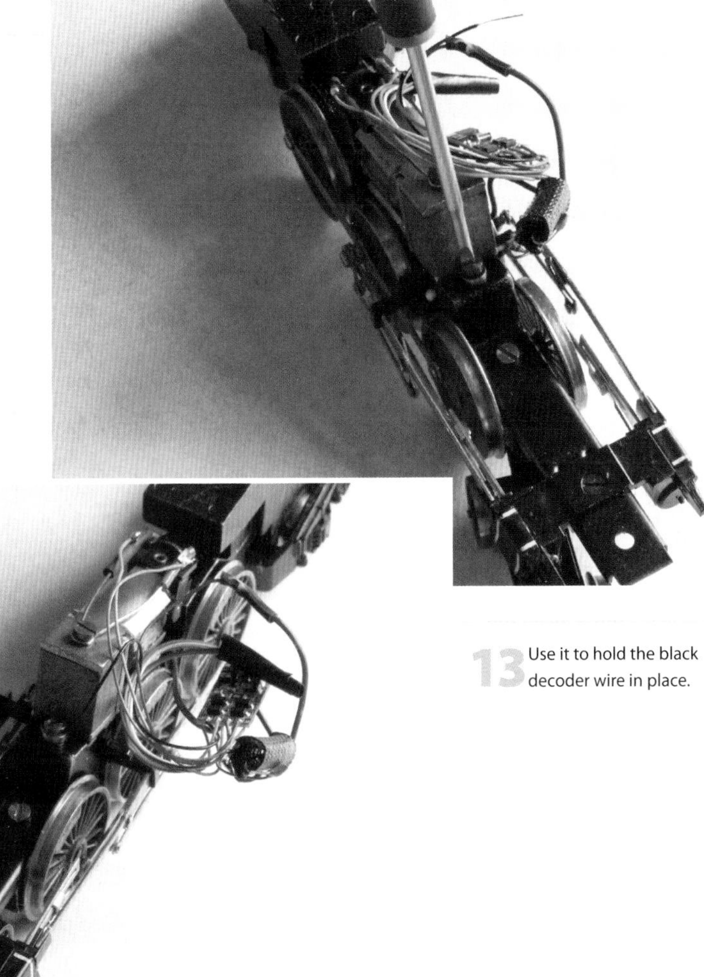

13 Use it to hold the black decoder wire in place.

14 With all the connections made, we can test the model and then reassemble it. The decoder is wrapped in insulating tape and slipped into the boiler as the model is reassembled.

CRIPPS BOTTOM No. 1 SIGNAL BOX

Chapter 4

Lights, Sound and Other Tricks

Cripps Bottom Yard is a popular exhibition layout and this picture of a BR 'Standard Four' 4-6-0 on a freight train shows why. This layout is analogue-controlled, but any layout can easily be converted to DCC to provide greater operational flexibility. PHOTO: MIKE WILD

LED lighting awaiting fitting to a class 121 railcar. The LEDs provide head and tail lights.

The railcar with the LEDs in position.

Lighting with LEDs

Light Emitting Diodes (LEDs) have many advantages over the traditional light-bulb when it comes to lighting model locomotives and coaches. They are available in a range of small sizes, they generate no heat and have a virtually unlimited life if treated properly. In addition, they draw less current than light-bulbs and so you can run a number of LEDs from a decoder function output without overloading it.

It is important to limit the current and voltage that flows through the LED to avoid damaging it. It is also necessary to connect it the right way around. The anode should be connected to the more positive side of the circuit and the cathode to the more negative side.

On a locomotive decoder, the blue wire is the common positive. All the LED anodes, for all the functions, should be connected to this wire via a resistor. The LED's cathode is connected to the appropriate function wire: white for F0 forwards, yellow for F0 reverse, green for F1 and purple for F2.

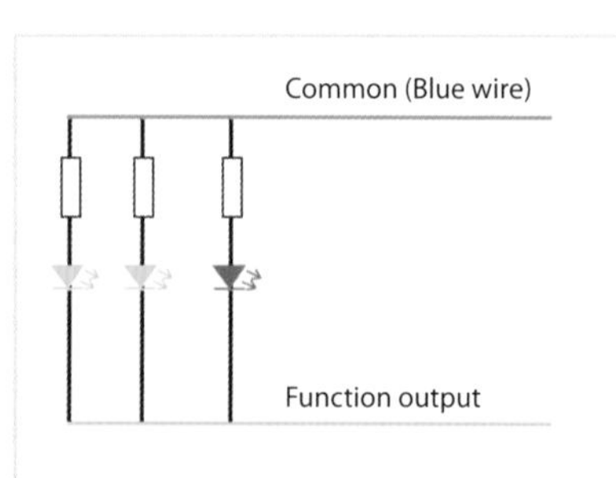

Connecting LEDs to the function outputs of a decoder.

To turn the LEDs on or off, all you need to do is select the appropriate function on your controller. It doesn't matter if the locomotive is moving or not – the lights will stay on (or off) and not dim or brighten.

You can run more than one LED from each function output. For example, you might wish to run two headlights and one tail light.

The Resistor

On a locomotive decoder the blue wire is the common positive. All the LED anodes, for all the functions, should be connected to this wire via a resistor. Typically this should be a minimum of 680Ω 0.25W, but normally a 1KΩ (1,000Ω) will work nicely. If you want the lights to be dimmer, use a higher value resistor such as a 2.2KΩ

A selection of LEDs alongside an OO gauge coach for comparison. On the left is a standard 3mm LED; at the top centre is an axial 2.5mm LED similar to the one used for the tail lamp on the coach; below that is a side-viewing LED which is ideal for portraying modern tail lamps in 4mm scale. To the right is a surface-mount LED and a 4mm-scale LED headlamp from DCC Concepts.

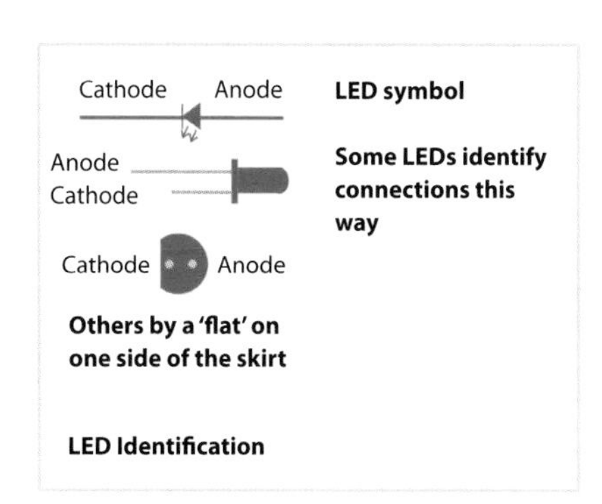

LED Identification

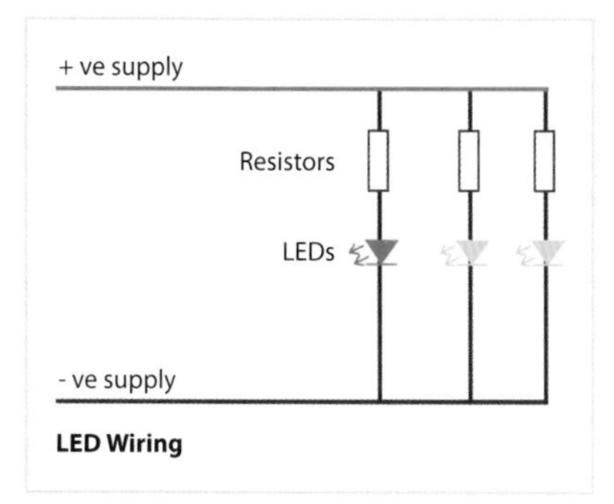

LED Wiring

Making 4mm scale LED head and tail lamps

You can make a good representation of the traditional UK head and tail lamp quite quickly, using axial LEDs. These have leads that come out from the sides, rather than the base, and a square body with a domed light on the top.

The first step is to stick one of the leads into some polystyrene or foam to hold the LED upright. Give the LED a spray of grey car primer paint and, when that is dry, a top coat of white car primer. The grey will help to cut down on any light that might show through the white top coat.

Use a craft knife or wet and dry paper to remove the paint from the domed lens. Using round-nosed pliers, bend one of the leads round to make a handle. Bend both leads through a right angle so that they can be run into a hole behind the lamp. Trim the leads to length, scrape the paint off one side of one lead, solder a wire to it, cover with heat-shrink tube and then repeat with the other lead.

The easiest way to paint the LEDs is to stick the leads into some polystyrene or foam and spray with car primer.

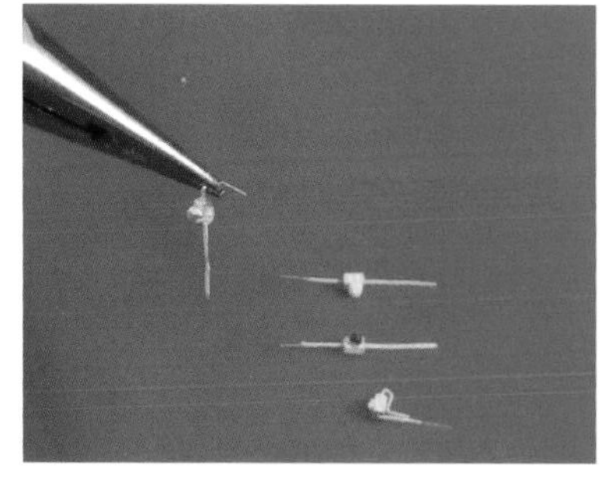

Scrape the paint away from the lens with a craft knife or file, then use needle-nose pliers to bend one lead into a handle shape.

(2,200Ω). Each LED needs to run through its own resistor. You should use 0.25W (¼W) or 0.5W (½W) rated resistors; do not be tempted to use 0.125W (⅛ W) ones as they will get hot and may damage themselves or the locomotive.

If you use a higher value resistor then the LED will draw less current. The LED's brightness will not decrease noticeably over a range of values. The higher value the resistor you use, the less current is drawn from the decoder. This can be very important if you are trying to run a lot of function outputs at the same time.

The LED

LEDs come in a wide variety of shapes, sizes and colours. In the early years of their development they were large, red and expensive, but now they come in a number of useful sizes and colours. For OO gauge, one of the most useful is the 3mm LED (also known as T1). This is a 3mm diameter unit with a domed head which is ideal for fitting in locomotives and signals. Single-colour LEDs come in red, amber, yellow, green, blue and two versions of white. The standard white LED has a blue tinge and is ideal for representing modern, high-intensity locomotive headlights, security and fluorescent lighting; the other type, usually referred to as 'golden-white' or 'warm-white', has a yellow tinge and is

Surface-mount LEDs are small, but still large compared to the head or tail lights in an 'N' gauge locomotive. The easiest way to use them is to mount them on a piece of copper-clad board and transmit the light to where it is needed using fibre optics. From left to right, the photo shows a strand of fibre optic filament on a pound coin for scale, a strip of PCB – in this case some 4mm scale sleeper – and a strip of SMD LEDs in their packaging.

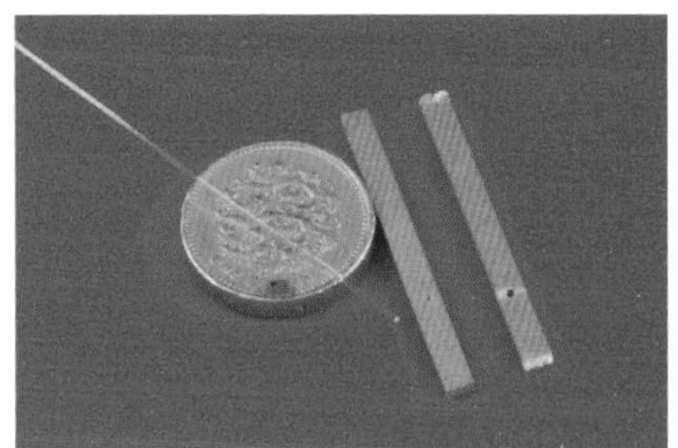

Drill a hole for the fibre optic filament into the PCB and cut away the copper coating with a razor saw or file to make a gap around it. The LED is now out of its packet and is the red speck on the pound coin.

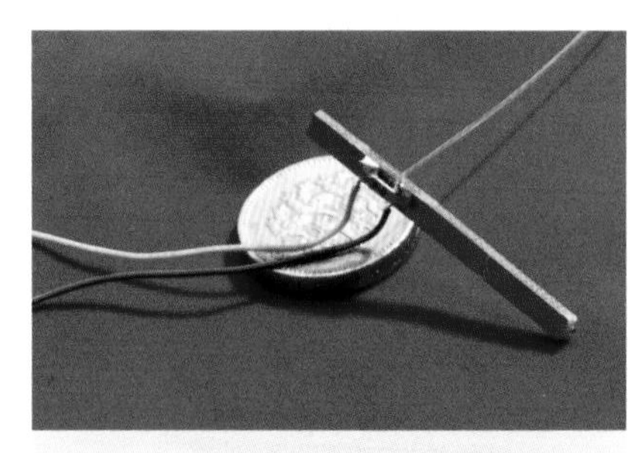

Solder the LED upside down so that the lens is over the hole and solder the wires from the decoder in place. Use superglue to fix the fibre optic filament in the hole. You can trim the copper-clad strip to a suitable length to fit and run the fibre optic to where you want the light. This gives you close to a scale-size bulb.

suitable for older headlights and traditional light-bulbs. You can also purchase bi-colour LEDs which can be used to show two or more colours. A bi-colour red/green LED can show red, green or yellow, while a red/white LED has obvious uses for train head and tail lighting.

So what is an LED? It is most definitely *not* a lamp; it is a diode. The light that it produces is a useful by-product of its function. This means that, while you can connect a bulb into a circuit either way around, an LED must be connected the right way around otherwise it will not light up. Unlike a bulb, an LED has very little resistance to current flow and so cannot be used as a current limiting device; indeed, it must be protected from excessive currents by using a resistor. A typical LED will operate from a 2V DC supply drawing a current of 20mA, or thereabouts, so in order to use them on a model railway we need to add a resistor to limit the current it will draw. In fact, most LEDs are quite bright, even on a lower current such as 15mA. Left to its own devices, it will draw as much current as the power supply will provide and have a bright but brief existence.

It is important to connect the LED the right way around. If it is connected the wrong way the LED will not light, and if it is also subjected to more than about 5V it will never work again. If you are in any doubt as to which lead is which, test the LED out on a couple of 1.5V batteries or the function output of a decoder – but if you do this, don't forget the resistor.

Surface Mount LEDs and Fibre Optics

Surface mount LEDs are miniature components designed to be placed and soldered by machine rather than by hand. Their small size makes them ideal for commercially produced models in the smaller scales. It can be difficult to handle components this size and their shape does not lend itself to home installation in models. However, by combining surface mount LEDs with fibre optics, it is possible to get small lights down to 0.5mm in size.

Fibre optic filaments are lengths of plastic that light can be beamed along. You can bend them and the light is reflected within the fibre optic, only coming out at the other end. The filaments can be purchased in diameters ranging from 0.5mm to 3mm, from specialists such as DCC Supplies. You mount one end next to an LED and the other end where you want the 'light-bulb' to be.

First you need to cut a length of copper-clad printed circuit board for the LED and its connecting wires to be mounted on. The best source, for our needs, is actually sleeper strip for soldered trackwork which is available from C&L Finescale and other suppliers.

Drill a hole in the PCB just large enough for your fibre optic filament to fit and then cut through the thin copper coating where the hole is. This will isolate the two halves of the PCB strip from each other; check with a meter that this is so. Now solder the LED *upside down* onto the PCB over the hole – so that the light will shine down through the hole. Surface-mount LEDs are very small; you will probably need to use a tiny drop of glue to hold it in place while you solder it. Solder the connecting wires to the PCB and test the LED; you should be able to see it shining brightly through the hole. Cut one end of the fibre optic at right-angles with a sharp knife and push into the hole, so that it

Modern diesel locomotives have lots of lights. By clever use of functions, all can be made to work correctly.

butts up to the LED, and fix in place with a drop of superglue. The fibre optic filament can now be cut to length and inserted into the hole where it is to be mounted. If you wish, you can heat the end by holding a soldering iron near it, to make it form a bulb shape.

Lighting with Bulbs

You can, if you wish, use the traditional light-bulb with DCC decoders. You need a resistor in series with the bulb, even 12 and 16V rated ones, to protect the decoder from the current surge when the bulb is first turned on. For a 1.5V bulb you should try an 820Ω 0.5W (½W) resistor to start with. To make the bulb brighter, drop down to a minimum of 150Ω; to make it dimmer, increase the resistor as much as necessary. If you use a resistor lower than 470Ω then you should change to a 1W resistor to stop it getting hot. Like LEDs, each bulb should have its own resistor.

Fiddling with Functions

Once you start looking at locomotive lights, you realise that the simple 'white at the front/red at the back' system used on commercial models is not really representative of how the real railway works. For a start, if a locomotive is hauling a train it won't have a red tail light – that will be on the back of the train; Similarly, if it is pushing the train then it won't have a white headlight. If a multiple unit is parked up between duties, it may well show red lights at both ends. Modern diesel locomotives show different headlight arrangements for day and night – and so the list goes on. DCC provides the technology to mimic this, but the user needs to change the decoder functions in order to do it.

Before we delve into the finer points of functions at the decoder end, it is worth mentioning that some changes can be

Always test your decoder installations on a length of track before you replace the body on the locomotive.

made at the command station. F2 is a case in point. On many sound-equipped locomotives, this is the whistle or horn; as a result, some command stations treat the F2 key as non-latching. This means that the function is only on whilst the key is pressed, rather than the usual 'push once to turn the function on and then again to turn it off'. Where a latching (push 'on', push 'off') function is used for something like a horn or some other noise, you will have to push the function button twice to get one sound; push 'on' and the noise sounds; push again to turn the function off again. Many command stations allow you to select whether F2 is latching or momentary (only on whilst the button is pressed). Some systems are more advanced, like Bachmann's Dynamis, allowing you to set which functions are latching or momentary for each locomotive. Information as to settings for your command station will be in the documentation.

To return to locomotive decoders, here is one simple example to start with: I have a narrow gauge steam locomotive that has headlights fitted at each end. In reality, the fireman would put the light on the front of the train and leave it there not only whilst the train was running but also shunting. He would only move it to the other end if the locomotive ran around its train, ready to travel in the opposite direction. So, rather than directional lighting, I need to be able to turn on either lamp regardless of which way the locomotive is currently running.

The locomotive is fitted with a Digitrax DZ125, which has two function outputs set up for 'F0 forwards' and 'F0 reverse'. By changing the CVs, the functions can be set to respond to F0 and F1 and stay on (or off) regardless of direction. Function 'F0 forwards' is fine, but 'F0 reverse' needs to be changed so that it operates the forward headlight (white wire). To achieve this, the value 1 is written to CV 34. To make F1 operate the rear headlight (yellow wire), the value 2 is written to CV35. So the front light can now be turned on and off by pressing F0 and the rear light by pressing F1.

What is even cleverer is that you can turn more than one output on for each function and can also turn an output on with more than one function. If I wish, I can program F2 to turn both the front and rear headlight on.

So how does this work?

CVs 33 through to 46 each control the outputs assigned to one particular function. CV 33 is 'F0 forward', CV 34 is 'F0 reverse', CV 35 is F1 and so on, through to CV 46 for F12. The output that each function controls is defined by the value written to each CV. Output '0 forward', the white wire, has a value of 1; 'output 0 reverse', the yellow wire, has a value of 2; output 2, green, is 4; output 3, purple, is 8 and output 4, brown, is 16. There are 14 possible outputs that can be assigned, but I haven't come across a decoder with 14 outputs yet!

By ascribing a value to the CV that controls a specific function you can define which outputs switch on. So, for example, if you write 5 to CV 38 this will turn on outputs 1 (green) and 0 (white), with values of 4 and 1 respectively, when you press F4.

Function Mapping

The table below shows the default values for each function, CV and output.

FUNCTION	CV	DEFAULT OUTPUT	DEFAULT VALUE
F0 forwards	33	0 forward (white)	1
F0 reverse	34	0 reverse (yellow)	2
F1	35	1 (green)	4
F2	36	2 (purple)	8
F3	37	3 (brown)	16
F4	38	4	4
F5	39	5	8
F6	40	6	16
F7	41	7	32
F8	42	8	64
F9	43	9	16
F10	44	10	32
F11	45	11	64
F12	46	12	128

The first block of CVs, from 33 to 37 can control outputs 0 through to 6. In practice, this is where you will make your changes.

Function	F0 Forward	F0 Reverse	F1	F2	F3
CV	33	34	35	36	37

Add up the values of the outputs that you wish to control and write them to the appropriate CV. A value of 0 indicates that no output is controlled.

Output	0 Forward (white)	0 Reverse (yellow)	1 (green)	2 (purple)	3 (brown)	4	5	6
Value	1	2	4	8	16	32	64	128

For example, to operate outputs 2 (purple) and 0 reverse (yellow) using F3, you will add 8 and 2 to give 10 and write 10 to CV 37. The second block of CVs covers F4 to F8:

Function	F4	F5	F6	F7	F8
CV	38	39	40	41	42

Output	2 (purple)	3 (brown)	4	5	6	7	8	9
Value	1	2	4	8	16	32	64	128

The final block of CVs covers F9 to F12:

Function	F9	F10	F11	F12
CV	43	44	45	46

Output	5	6	7	8	9	10	11	12
Value	1	2	4	8	16	32	64	128

Taking a more complex example, a multiple unit has head and tail lights. These lights may need to be turned off if it is coupled to another unit. When parked up, it should show red lights at both ends. We need four function outputs, one each for End A headlight, End B headlight, End A taillight and End B taillight

End A Headlight	Output 0 Fwd – White
End A Tail light	Output 0 Rev – Yellow
End B Headlight	Output 1 – Green
End B Tail light	Output 2 – Purple

We will use F0 for normal directional lighting, F1 to turn the A end headlight on, F2 to turn the B end headlight on, F3 for the A end taillight and F4 for the B end taillight. This will give us normal lighting when the unit is running on its own, along with the ability to control the lights individually when it is running coupled to another unit or parked up.

F0 Fwd	A Headlight (white), B Taillight (purple)
F0 Rev	A Taillight (yellow), B Headlight (green)
F1	A Headlight (white)
F2	B Headlight (green)
F3	A Taillight (yellow)
F4	B Taillight (purple)

So we need to write the following values to the decoder:

CV 33 – F0 Forward	Output 0 Fwd (white) = 1 Output 2 (purple) = 8	8+1 = 9
CV 34 – F0 Reverse	Output 0 Rev (yellow) = 2 Output 1 (green) = 4	2+4 = 6
CV 35 – F1	Output 0 Fwd (white) = 1	1
CV 36 – F2	Output 1 (green) = 4	4
CV 37 – F3	Output 0 Rev (yellow) = 2	2
CV 38 – F4	Output 2 (purple) = 1	1

Note that F4 is in the second block of CVs and cannot be used to control Outputs 0 or 1.

As the nights draw in, your passengers will appreciate carriage lighting.

As the maximum value you can write to a CV is 255, you are limited as to which outputs can be controlled by which function – each function can control a maximum of 8 outputs and each output can be controlled by a maximum of 8 functions – but that is more flexibility than you are likely to need.

The NMRA standards shown above are only a recommendation, as a number of manufacturers have implemented them differently. While the principle remains the same, the actual values and what they control vary. As an example, the equivalent entries for a Lenz Gold decoder – which uses the same CVs but different values – are CV 33 = (8+64) = 72, CV 34 (16+32) = 48, CV 35 = 8, CV 36 = 16, CV 37 = 32 and CV38 = 8.

Many decoders come with special lighting effects for flickering, flashing or dimming lights. These are controlled by other CVs and are unique to each manufacturer.

Believe it or not, changing the way that the decoder outputs respond to the function keys is often the easy bit, compared to getting the correct lights connected to the correct output. DCC-ready locomotives come with circuit boards that carry the socket, TV suppression components, diodes for directional lighting on analogue operation and resistors for the LEDs. The LEDs themselves are often on a separate board. You will either need to modify the circuit board by cutting the copper tracks and re-routing the functions with wires or, usually the easier option, remove the whole board and wire a decoder in directly to the pickups, motor and lights.

Installing Coach Lights

Adding coach lighting with DCC is a relatively simple project. The hardest part of this job can be finding out how to get the coach apart in the first place without wrecking it in the process. In this case, my chosen victim was a Bachmann OO gauge Mark 1 suburban.

The only visible screws attached the two bogies, so I unscrewed those and put them to one side. On some models, this reveals further screws that hold the body to the chassis – but not in this case. Careful examination revealed that the roof and body were moulded in one piece, so I experimented by running a fingernail along the join between the maroon body and the black solebar. This revealed that the two were clipped together. Some gentle lifting with a screwdriver allowed me to slip some card in the gap that opened up and I could then work my way along the side, lifting and sliding the card into place. Once the chassis had been separated from the body, I could pull out the seating unit.

Rather than wire and fix an individual LED for each compartment, I used a self-adhesive strip of LEDs. These strips can be cut into segments of 3 LEDs and the segments joined by short linking wires. This enables you to space the LEDs out so that you can get one in each compartment. For an open or saloon-type coach, you can use the strip as it comes.

Each of the 3 LED segments measures 5cms long; so for a normal coach you will need 4 segments, though for my brake coach I only needed 2. The LED strip is available in a number of colours, but for coach lighting the most suitable are warm white (for incandescent bulbs), bright white (for fluorescent bulbs) and yellow (for gaslight). Mine came from DCC Supplies, but they can be obtained from electronics suppliers and other DCC and lighting specialists.

To be able to turn the carriage lights on and off, we need a DCC decoder in the coach. This is an ideal use for old decoders that have been replaced by better ones, or obtained cheaply second-hand. For the interior lights, I used the F1 output (green wire) and added a 1K Ohm resistor in series to reduce the brightness. I soldered the green decoder wire to the resistor, then added a wire from the resistor to the bottom contact on the strip (using the printing to determine which way was up) and the blue decoder wire directly to the top contact. Using a pair of jump leads, I now connected the decoder's red and black wires to my DCC controller, selected the decoder's address and checked that the LEDs switched on and off when I pressed F1.

Now that I had working lights, I stuck them to the ceiling of the coach by removing the backing paper from each segment and then pressing in place. Check that the LEDs are spaced so that there is one in each compartment and they do not obstruct the compartment dividers. You can lift the strips and move them if necessary. You won't get the LEDs centred in each compartment but that doesn't matter. I tidied up the unconnected wires with a bit of tape and fixed the decoder in the guard's compartment. I then put the interior back in and tested the effect by turning the lights on and off.

All I needed to do now was arrange some means of getting power from the track to the decoder. For this I added some phosphor-bronze strips to one of the bogies. First I drilled a hole (about 5mms in diameter) through the bogie and chassis behind the bogie pivot. This gave plenty of space for the wires as the bogie swivelled. I passed the red and black decoder wire through the hole in the chassis and snapped it back in place. Then I passed the wires through the hole in the bogie and screwed that into place.

I cut two strips of phosphor-bronze about 3.5cm long and shaped them as shown in the photograph, using thin-nosed pliers. The little bumps on each end bore against the back of the wheels. I pulled the decoder wires out as far as I could and soldered one wire to each of the pickups.

Now I cut two small pieces of thick plastic sheeting or similar scrap material – even a flexible track sleeper will do – and glued them to the pickups with epoxy resin. This was a good time to paint the pickups black, except for the bumps that were touching the wheels – these needed

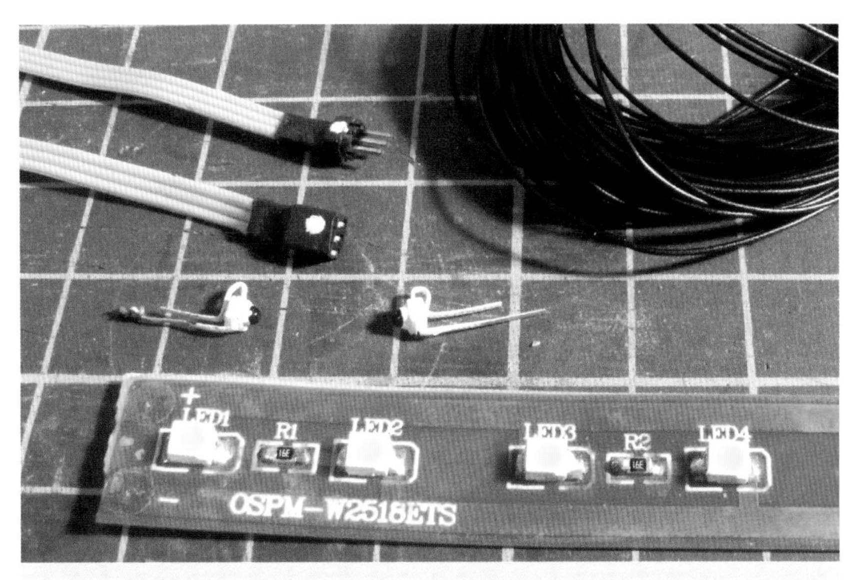

The raw materials for this project: a small plug and socket, thin wire, LED tail lamps and a strip of white LEDs.

Opening up the coach can be a difficult process. The coach is sitting in a foam cradle as the chassis and body are separated.

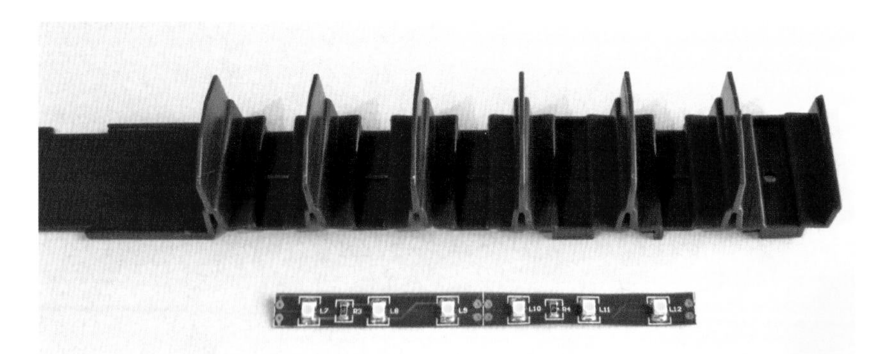

The self-adhesive LED strip alongside the seating unit. The strip needs to be split in two so that there is one LED in each compartment.

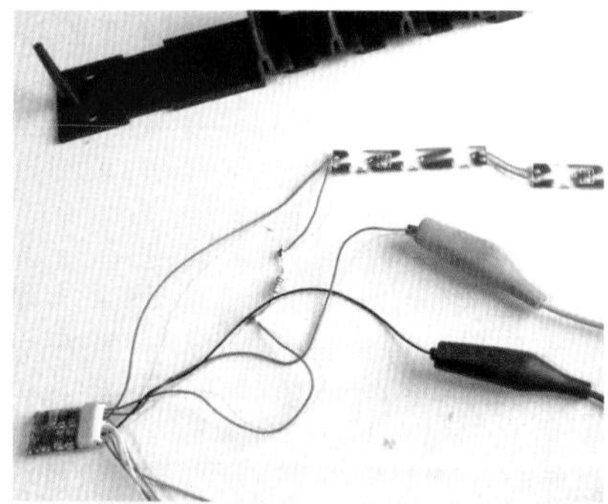

Once you have connected the LED strip to your decoder, you can test that it works correctly.

With the LED strips fixed in place and the interior replaced, you can now get a good idea of the overall effect.

to be kept clean in order to conduct electricity. Once that had set, I epoxied the pickups to the bottom of the bogie and adjusted them so that they lightly rubbed against the back of the wheels. I held them in place while the epoxy set. All that remained was to push the excess wire back through the hole and place the coach on the track. My little people were now able to travel in comfort on the long winter evenings.

One improvement that is easy to make is to add electrical pickups to the other bogie. This will reduce any tendency for the lights to flicker, especially as the train crosses pointwork. Simply fit the pickups in exactly the same way as you did on the first bogie, connect the two red wires together, the two black wires together and that's it – job done

Even on small layouts, it is unusual to have a single coach train. So what do we do to make up longer rakes of stock?

One way is to fit a decoder in each coach. This approach is straightforward but it does have a number of drawbacks. Firstly, there's the cost – even using older, second-hand decoders, the cost will mount up quickly; secondly, there's rolling resistance – each set of pickups makes the train harder to pull. If the coaches in the rake share pickups and decoders, everything becomes much more manageable.

To share a decoder between two or more coaches requires some form of electrical connection between them. You could permanently wire them together, but that would make it difficult to take them off the layout. It is far better to have some form of plug and socket to connect them together which can be disconnected for transit or maintenance. Suitable connectors in 2-, 3- and 4-way form are available from Express Models. If you are just fitting interior lights then a 2-way connector is sufficient; however, if you want to install tail lamps then you will need 3-way connectors.

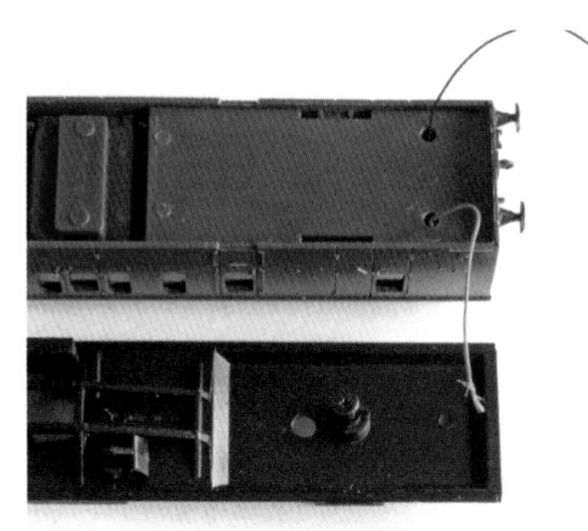

A 5mm-diameter hole in the chassis and bogie allows the wires from the decoder to pass through to the pickups that will be mounted on the bogie.

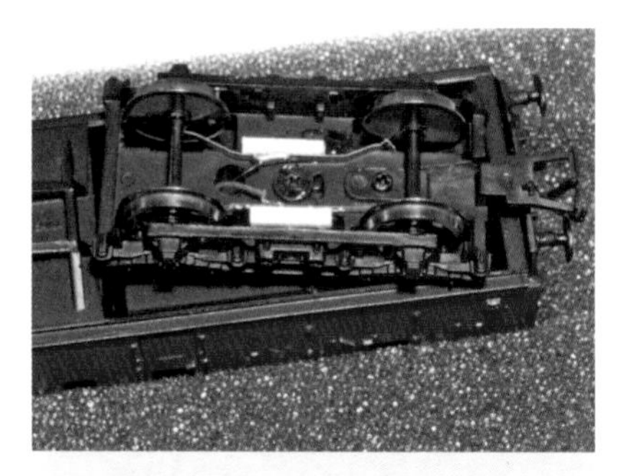

The modified bogie showing the two pickups. Apart from the parts that actually touch the wheels, the rest should be painted black to hide them from view – they have been left unpainted here so that you can see them clearly.

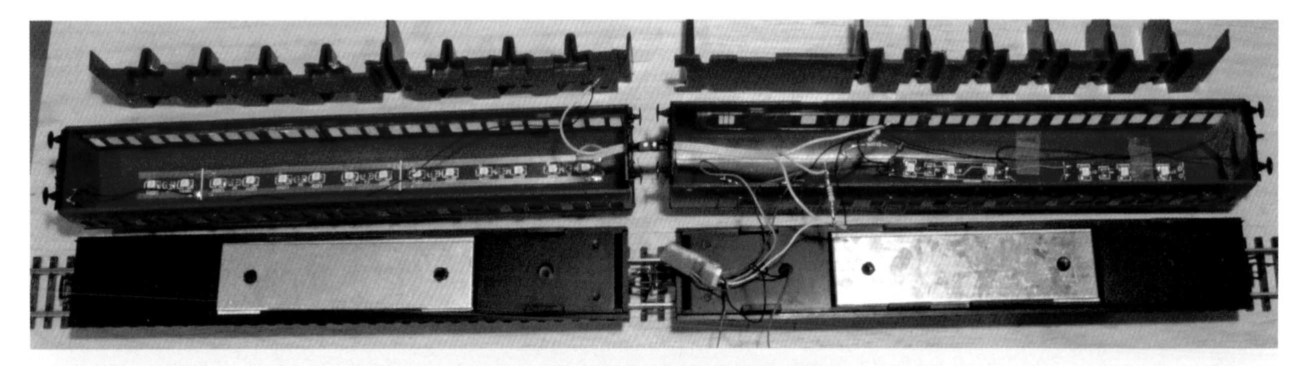

The finished installation in a pair of coaches. The LED strips are different types purchased from different suppliers.

Each coach will need a hole in the end for the wires to pass through. If you are modelling stock with corridor connections then the hole can be concealed inside the gangway; if not, then low down above the coupling is the least conspicuous place. The easiest way to make the opening is to drill three small holes with a handheld drill and then open them up into a slot with your craft knife. You may have to cut some of the chassis or interior away to make room for the wire on the inside – this will vary from model to model.

The lights in each coach will need their own resistor and should be connected up as shown in the main circuit diagram, which has been drawn for a 3-coach set. If you require a longer rake then you should split it into groups of two or three coaches, each with their own decoder and pickups. Don't forget that the decoder will have a maximum current that can be supplied on a function output and all those LEDs will start to mount up. All the decoders in the rake should be set to the same address, so that all the lights turn on or off at the same time.

On one of the connectors – in my case the plug end – you will need about an inch of free cable so that you can pull the plug out to give yourself room to get your fingers in between the coaches. Once the connectors are joined, the cable can be pushed back through its hole as you couple the coaches.

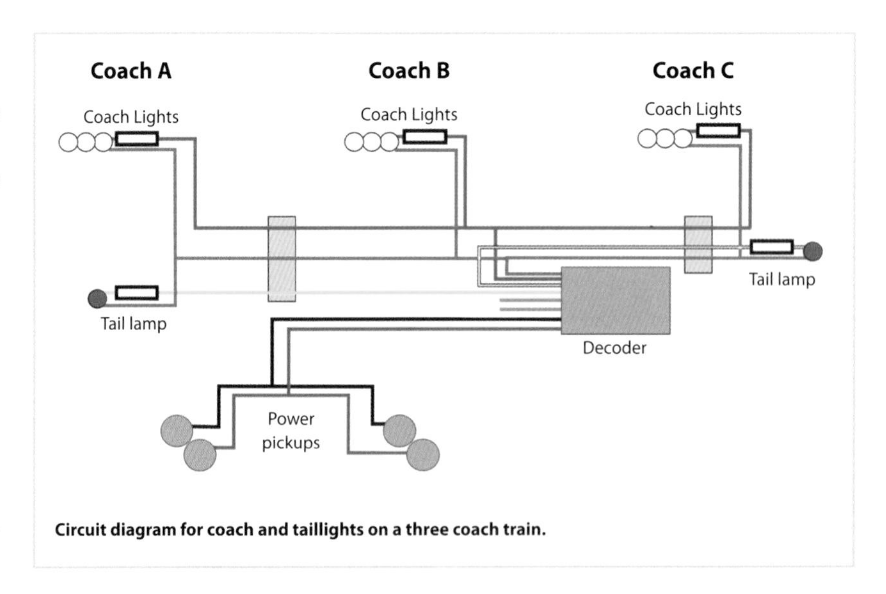

Circuit diagram for coach and taillights on a three coach train.

You will need to make a small hole in the end of each coach for the wires. If you are modelling corridor stock, then the hole can be hidden inside the corridor connection.

LED tail lamps are fitted through a small hole in the end of the coach.

Coupling up – pull the free cable out through its hole.

Push the plug into the socket.

Push the cable back through its hole as you couple the coaches.

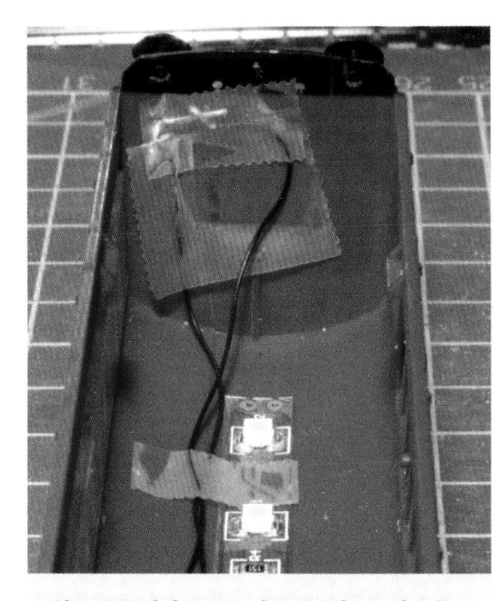

I have used clear tape here to show what is underneath – I normally use brown self-adhesive parcel tape which is thin, flexible and very tenacious.

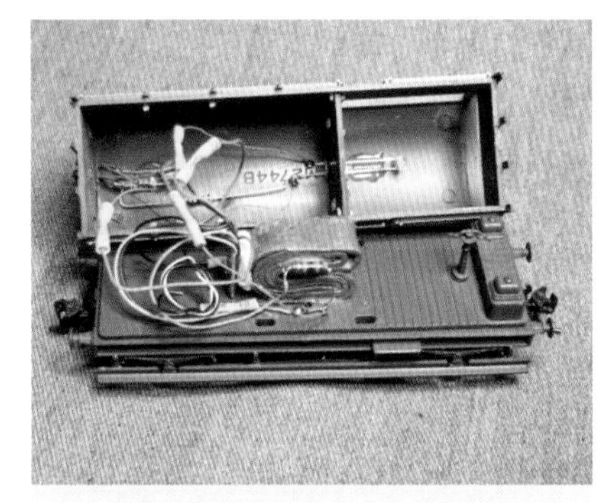

A lighting installation always tends to look like a bowl of spaghetti; as with this brake van, however, it won't be visible when the body is in place. The decoder is a TCS FL4 (function-only) and there are LEDs for the tail lamps, interior and veranda lights. PHOTO: MAX WRIGHT

The lights can all be operated individually. F1 operates the tail lamp, F2 the interior light and F3 the veranda light. The decoder allows for four functions in all. The address has been set to 6869 to make it easy to work out. PHOTO: MAX WRIGHT

Tail lamps can either be made from axial LEDs or purchased ready to use. You will need one at each end of the rake connected to the F0 directional outputs of the decoder, the white and yellow wires. As with the locomotive lights, you can adjust the functions so that you can control the lights individually if required. You need to drill a hole in the coach end for the tail lamp; most coaches have moulded lamp irons to show you where to drill. You have a choice here: you can either drill a big hole and solder wires to the LED before you mount it in position, or you can drill a small hole, mount it into position and then solder wires to the leads on the inside of the coach. The second is for those who are confident of their ability not to touch the coach with the hot iron. Either way, you should ensure that the leads passing through the hole are completely insulated with a thick coat of paint or heat-shrink tubing to avoid them shorting out.

I run the wires up the ends of the coaches and along the ceiling, held in place with adhesive tape. Thin decoder -type wire is easy to bend and conceal, ideal for the task.

If you have a short rake with 1 decoder, then the wire for the tail lamp at the far end needs to be included in the plug and socket sets, giving you a 3-wire cable. If you have a decoder in the coach at each end, then you only need two wires for the interior lights. Individual coaches need a taillight at each end but no plug or socket.

Smoke Units

Some model railway locomotives come equipped with smoke units and these must be given special attention when converting to DCC operation. While there are smoke units specially manufactured for use with DCC, those fitted to existing locomotives will be different in that they

With interior lights on and the tail lamp burning, the branch passenger train is ready to depart.

work at a lower voltage and usually draw more current.

Whatever you do, do not leave the smoke unit connected across the pickups. The units are not designed to work on the 14V or more that DCC systems put on the tracks. Unless specifically designed for DCC, smoke units cannot be run directly off a decoder function output. Typically, smoke units require around 150mA while most decoder outputs provide about 100mA.

Possible solutions are:

1. To connect the smoke unit across the motor terminals. This means that it will operate exactly as it used to, only smoking when the motor is operating.
2. To connect two function outputs together as a single feed. For example: connect the green and purple wires to one terminal and the blue wire to the other. Then set the F1 and F2 outputs so that they both operate from the same function key. This doubles the current available and should provide enough power to work the smoke unit without damaging the decoder. It also enables you to turn the smoke on and off as required. You may also wish to fit a suitable resistor to reduce the voltage supplied to the smoke unit.
3. Fit a DCC-compatible smoke unit in its place and operate that from a single function output.

If you are fitting a new smoke unit, you should pick one that is designed for use with DCC. The Seuthe range includes four such units: numbers 11, 12, 23 and 24. Each draws 70mA and works on supplies up to 22V. In the UK, Seuthe smoke units can be purchased from Express Models and M.G. Sharp Models amongst others.

Sound

Sound-equipped locomotives are one of the features that tend to convince people to use DCC, rather than conventional control. Thanks to Bachmann and Hornby, you can even buy locomotives ready to run with sound decoders installed, which gives even those who have never fitted a decoder the opportunity to experience this development.

Sound decoders are at the expensive end of the market and tend to come with the upmarket features you expect in a top-end decoder. To those who are used to budget decoders, this can be a big change; even those who normally use a high-end decoder will find that driving a noisy locomotive requires a different technique to a silent one.

To get the best from a sound decoder, you need to have a DCC controller that gives you easy access to functions 1 to 8 – or higher, depending on the facilities that the particular decoder and collection of sounds offers. Locomotive sound does tend to highlight any sub-standard or noisy mechanisms – however good the rendition of the prototype, it will be spoiled by grinding gears and screaming electric motors.

Another problem that people have with sound is that there is so much of it. One locomotive pottering around the layout is nice; half a dozen chuntering away in a station is wearing, and a dozen all doing different things around the layout can be very irritating. There is a tendency for people to set the volume of their sound-equipped locomotives too high. Remember that, even when you are standing close to your layout, it is equivalent to viewing the real thing from a distance. By turning the decoder's volume down to represent what you would hear from a distance, not only does the locomotive become easier on the ear but – on a medium or large layout – as it travels away from you the sound dies away too.

The volume setting on LokSound decoders, which are the most commonly used in the UK, is controlled by CV63. It has a range from 0 to 63 and, as a default, comes set at full volume. A value of 20, which seems remarkably low, is still loud enough when you are close to it and has the benefit of being quieter when you are further away. There is also a separate volume setting for the horn available on CV 121 and other sounds – like the clang of coupling, air brakes and so on – can be controlled using CV 123. These individual settings are separate to the main volume setting – so if the overall sound is fine but the horn is too noisy, reduce CV 121; if all the sounds are too noisy, reduce CV 63.

Sound Quality

The small speakers that we are forced to use in our model locomotives are not anywhere near good enough to capture the bass frequencies of real locomotive sound. There is a body of opinion that the only way to get a realistic sound is to use a separate sound system with large speakers. While that may well be true, there are also things that can be done to improve the quality of sound from our models.

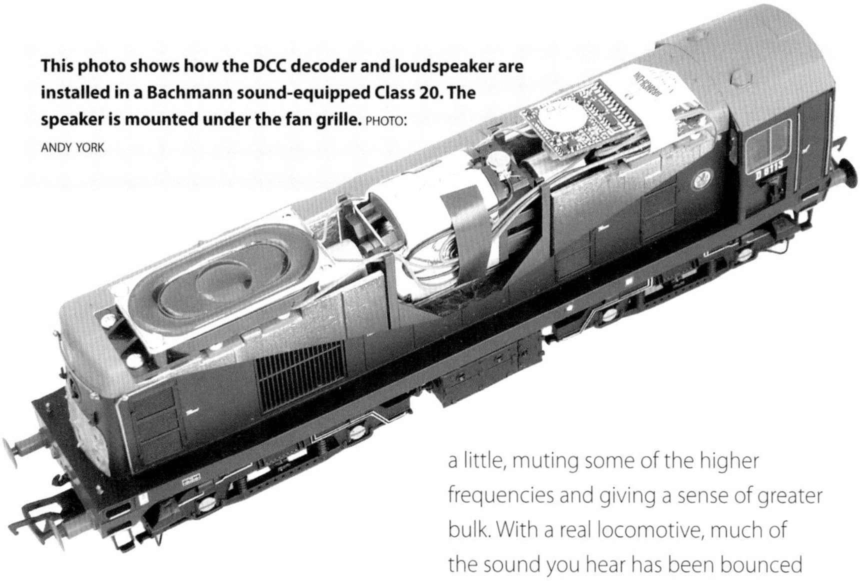

This photo shows how the DCC decoder and loudspeaker are installed in a Bachmann sound-equipped Class 20. The speaker is mounted under the fan grille. PHOTO: ANDY YORK

The first thing to do is to turn the volume down. The louder the sound, the more obvious it is that the bass is missing. This is a simple fix and does not even require you to open the locomotive up.

The loudspeaker needs to be housed in a sealed enclosure. This is a boxlike structure that encloses the rear of the speaker. It prevents the air waves in the air that are moved by the rear of the speaker cancelling out the sound produced by the air moved by the front of the speaker. If your speaker doesn't come with an enclosure, you can make your own. While many acoustic engineers devote their working lives to creating perfect loudspeaker enclosures, all we need to do is make a simple plastic card box.

The loudspeaker should be mounted so that the sound has a chance to resonate. Rather than travelling straight from the loudspeaker to your ear, the sound waves should be bounced around a little, muting some of the higher frequencies and giving a sense of greater bulk. With a real locomotive, much of the sound you hear has been bounced off the surroundings before it reaches you. To try to replicate this, fit the speaker face downwards in the fuel tank of a diesel locomotive, or similarly position it in a steam locomotive tenders The sound will be deflected off the track and bounced around by the scenery before it reaches you, adding some colour to it.

Installing Sound

Fitting a DCC decoder to a 4mm scale diesel locomotive is usually a straightforward process, especially when the model is DCC-ready: take the body off, plug in the new decoder, replace the body, job done.

So what happens when you want to fit a sound decoder instead of a standard one? Well, life gets a little more interesting. This exercise uses an early Bachmann Class 25 where a standard DCC decoder is fitted in a matter of minutes. Recent versions have been updated to supply the model with a factory-fitted sound decoder, but on earlier models much more work is required.

To add sound, I selected an ESU LokSound decoder available from various suppliers – each with their own version of the sounds produced by a class 25. In fitting a sound decoder to the Class 25, you have three options for speaker location. Many people like to place the speaker under the large circular fan on the roof; others prefer the speaker inside the body at the other end, so that the sound can resonate throughout; others still prefer the speaker to be located in the fuel tanks underneath the locomotive, facing down towards the track.

The easiest place to install the speaker is at the opposite end to the fan (the No.2 end). There is room above the chassis block for either the circular speaker supplied with the decoder or the optional 40 x 20mm rectangular speaker. Unfortunately, there is no space for the plastic enclosures supplied with the speaker and so the speaker needs to be mounted directly onto the chassis. Cover the top of the chassis block with a length of brown self-adhesive parcel tape and stick the speaker in place using an adhesive pad or double-sided carpet tape. The leads from the speaker to the decoder are not long enough for the decoder to be placed at the other end of the circuit board, so it must be mounted on top of the board. The decoder is in a plastic envelope, so it can be laid in place without any extra protection and then fixed with another length of parcel tape. Check the installation and replace the body.

If you want to place the speaker in the fuel tank, then you have to use the round model supplied with the decoder; there isn't room for the rectangular version in the bowels of the machine. Unfortunately, you have to do some major disassembly work to actually get at the tank. Firstly, you need to unscrew the circuit board and unsolder the six wires attached to it. You can now undo the retaining screws for the bogies and drop them out. With the bogies out of the way, you will see four small crosshead screws that hold the plastic underframe moulding in place; undo them and lift the chassis out. There is

Take one Bachmann Class 25 . . . The LokSound decoder comes with an NEM 8-pin plug and a circular speaker already attached. The rectangular speaker is an optional extra.

Once you have removed the body you can plug the decoder in, hold everything in place with a couple of lumps of Blu-Tack and try it out.

The DCC socket on the PCB can be a problem area, as the pins on the underside can touch the chassis block and short-circuit if the board is pressed down. Unscrewing the PCB and pressing a length of brown parcel tape onto the top of the chassis block is a wise precaution.

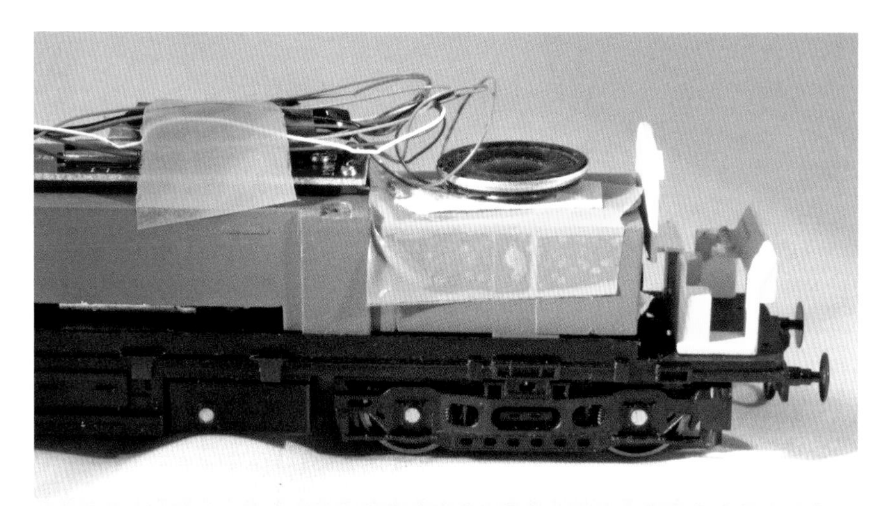

The easiest installation is at the No.2 end. There isn't room for the speaker enclosure between the chassis block and the roof, just for the speaker itself

The next step is to unscrew and drop the bogies out, which then reveals the screws that hold the underframe in place.

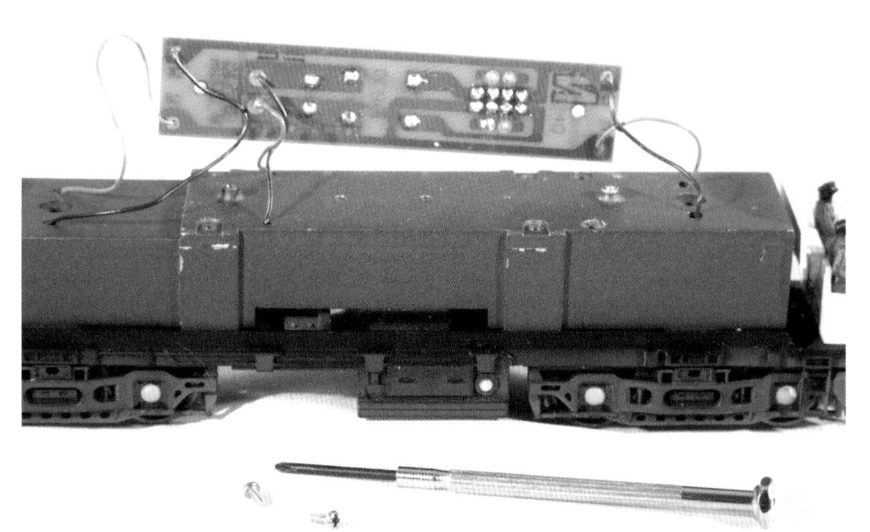

To fit the speaker underneath the fan or in the fuel tank, extensive disassembly work is required – starting with removal of the circuit board. You have to unsolder the six wires, so this photo will help you to work out how to put them back.

a weight inside the tank, unscrew this and lift it out to reveal the site for the speaker. The mounting column for the weight needs to be cut away, as do the two ribs at the front and rear of the tank. A combination of Stanley knife, craft knife and pliers will make short work of the plastic. You also need to drill some holes in the base of the tank so that the sound can get out. Do not worry about the gaps at either end of the tank – they will be hidden by the bogies and the holes in the bottom will not be visible when the locomotive is actually on the track.

The speaker can now be placed in the bottom of the tank, with a little bit of foam packing on top of it. It is held in place with a length of plastic card or girder glued across the inside of the tank. Fix the underframe back to the chassis, with the speaker wires running up the side of the chassis block. Reinstall the bogies and solder the wires back onto the circuit board. Screw the circuit board back in place (not forgetting the parcel tape under the DCC socket), plug the decoder in and fix it down to the chassis block with am adhesive pad. Check the installation and replace the body.

Finally, we come to the advanced class: putting the speaker under the fan. While this would seem to be the most obvious place, it is, in fact, the most complex of our installations. You need to dismantle the chassis as above, but leave the fuel tank weight in place. The two locating lugs at the No.2 end of the underframe need to be trimmed flat. You can now turn the underframe through a half-turn (180 degrees) and refit it to the chassis. Reinstall the bogies and solder the wires back onto the circuit board. Screw the circuit board back in place (not forgetting the parcel tape under the DCC socket).

Turning your attention to the body, unscrew the fan mounting and discard it. Superglue the fan to the bottom of the grille. Cut back the two locating pins at the fan end to match the length of those

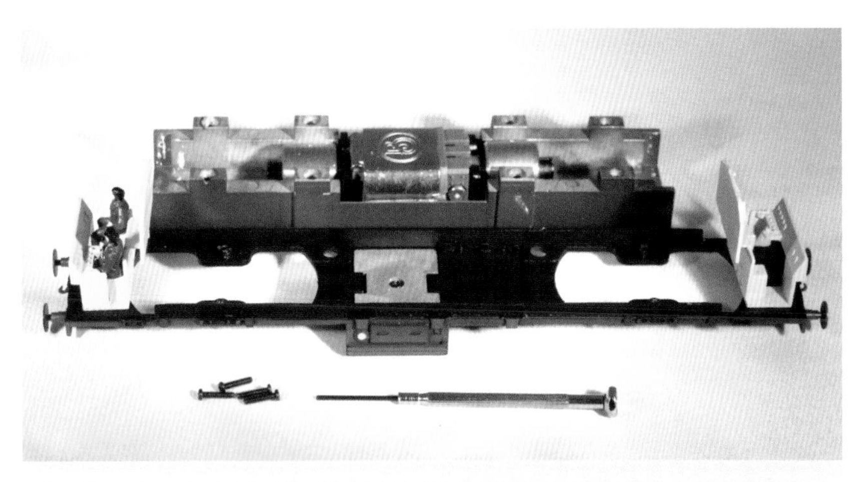

Once the underframe has been unscrewed from the chassis, you can gain access to the fuel tank. The weight occupies the space that will be used for the speaker and so needs to be unscrewed and discarded, unless you are going to mount the speaker under the fan.

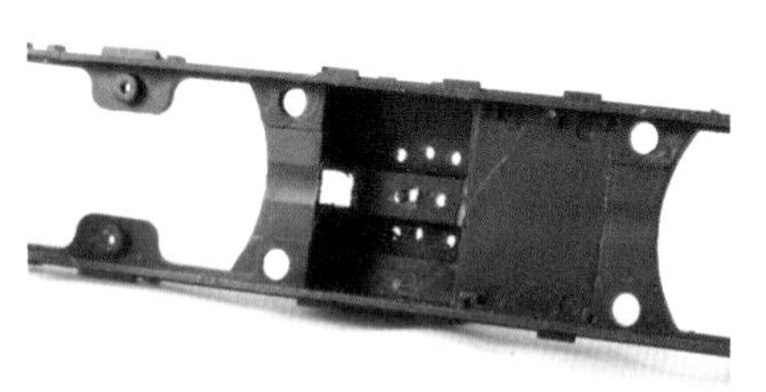

To make room for the speaker inside the fuel tank, you need to cut away the central mounting pole for the weight and the two central ribs inside the tank. Finally, you need to drill some holes in the bottom of the tank so that the sound can get out.

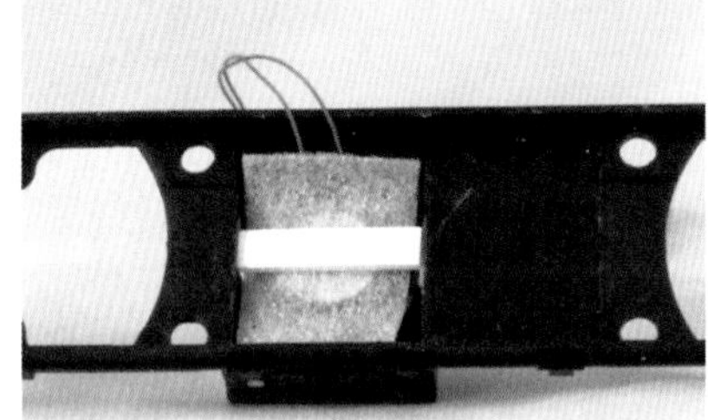

The speaker has been fitted face down in the tank. A thin layer of foam cut from the model's packaging protects it, and it is held by a strip of 80 thou (2mm)-thick plastic card lightly glued in place.

The wires from the speaker in the fuel tank run up the outside of the chassis block and the decoder is mounted at the No.2 end, using a sticky pad.

at the other end of the body. The two long lugs inside the body by the fan need to be trimmed back to match the others, otherwise the reversed chassis will not fit back in the body.

Test-fit the body on the reversed chassis and adjust the length of the locating pins if necessary. There is now room above the chassis block for either the circular speaker supplied with the decoder or the optional 40 x 20mm rectangular speaker. Once again, there is no room for the plastic enclosure supplied with the speaker, so it needs to be mounted directly onto the chassis. Cover the top of the chassis block with a length of brown self-adhesive parcel tape and then stick the speaker in place with an adhesive pad or double-sided carpet tape. The leads from the speaker to the decoder are not long enough for the decoder to be placed at the other end of the circuit board, so it must be mounted on top of the board. The decoder is in a plastic envelope so it can be laid in place without any extra protection and then fixed with another length of parcel tape. Check the installation and then replace the body.

Another Approach to Sound

The sound quality that you get from the tiny speakers that can be installed in a model is nowhere near that which can be produced by a larger speaker. An alternative approach is to install a number of large speakers around the layout and adjust the sound levels so that the sound appears to come from a specific place. By making the sound appear to be coming from where the model locomotive is, the viewer can be fooled into thinking that the model is making the sound.

Using a computer that knows where the locomotive is and what it is doing, sound can be synchronised with the model to give the impression of authentic sound. The computer program can also add in extra effects, such as ambient sound – farms, streets, factories – and so on.

At least two systems have taken this approach. The Soundtraxx Surroundtraxx unit works with Digitrax transponding decoders and the associated LocoNet detectors. The available sounds are limited to US locomotives and the system can cover a maximum of 6 areas and 6 locomotives at a time (although more than one locomotive can be in an area at once). For a larger layout, it is easy enough to add more Surroundtraxx units. The popular Railroad & Co TrainController has an add-on 4D sound module that takes information on activity and location directly from the program. Unfortunately, there are no ready-to-use sound files available, so you will have to source the sounds yourself (which isn't easy without violating someone's copyright). The JMRI project is also moving towards a similar feature, but this is currently more of an aspiration than a reality.

The idea of separating the sound from the model is appealing, not only because of the improvement in sound quality but also because you do not have to go through the sometimes tricky process of installing a sound decoder and speaker in every locomotive. This is especially so if you are working in N or OO9 gauges andhave a simple whole-layout volume control rather than having to adjust the volume on every locomotive.

If you want to fit the speaker under the fan, then the two locating lugs at the no.2 end need to be trimmed flush with the underframe before you turn it around.

The two long lugs by the fan need to be cut back so that the reversed chassis fits back into the body.

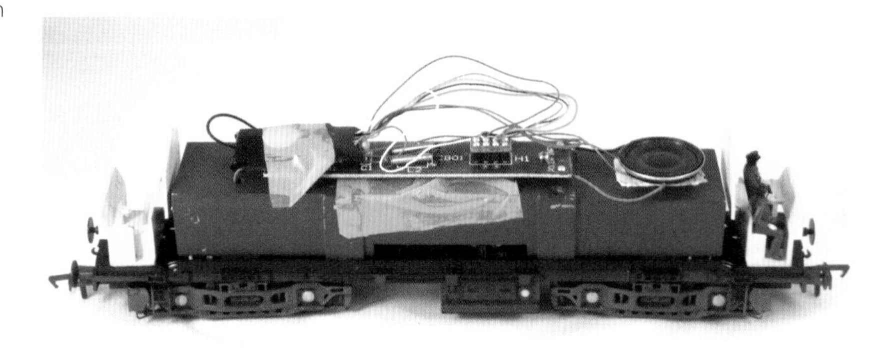

The completed installation for mounting the speaker under the fan. You can either use the circular speaker supplied with the decoder or the optional 40mm x 20mm rectangular speaker.

Uncoupling, Doors, Pantographs and Other Animation

With the ability to turn things on and off remotely, people have let their imaginations run wild with regard to operating features that can be added to their models. These range from uncoupling through to pantographs on electric trains that can be raised or lowered, spinning cooling fans, opening doors on coaches and even a driver leaning out of a locomotive's cab, whose head turns to face the direction of travel.

However ingenious the use of the function outputs, the basic mechanics come down to 4 methods: motors, electro-magnets, servos and memory wire.

- **Motors**
  A second electric motor – typically a small one such as those used to make mobile phones vibrate – can be used to power diesel locomotive cooling fans or to power the winding drum on a crane. You may well have to add a resistor or electronic circuit to reduce the voltage to suit the motor. The rotational movement can be changed to a push-pull one by use of a crank.

- **Electromagnet**
  Small 12-16V relays can be cannibalised to provide small electromagnets. These give a 'pull' motion which can be converted to 'push' by placing a small rare-earth magnet on the item being moved and aligning the magnets so that they repel each other, when the electromagnet is turned on. Bear in mind that the electromagnet's current draw must be within the decoder's limit and arrange the mechanism so that the electromagnet is normally off. This method is typically used to make couplings that can be controlled by DCC.

- **Servos**
  Specialised electric motors that are used

The Dingham coupler on the end of this 4mm-scale coach can connect to other Dingham couplers, or to the hook of a Smith's screw coupling on a locomotive. However, the coach hides a secret.
PHOTO: JIM SMITH-WRIGHT

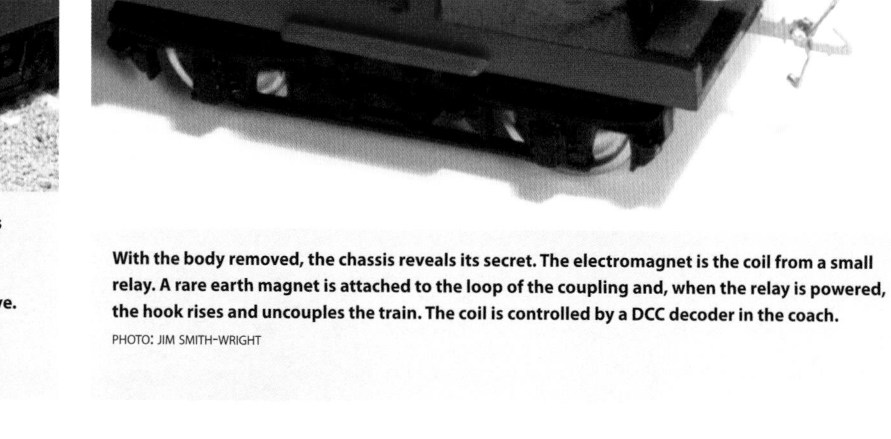

With the body removed, the chassis reveals its secret. The electromagnet is the coil from a small relay. A rare earth magnet is attached to the loop of the coupling and, when the relay is powered, the hook rises and uncouples the train. The coil is controlled by a DCC decoder in the coach.
PHOTO: JIM SMITH-WRIGHT

in radio-controlled models to give a controlled position. The position arm of the servo (or more accurately the shaft to which it is attached) is defined by the signal that it receives. So, for example, by alternating two different signals you can make the arm move from a position of 0 to 132 degrees and then back again. Some decoders, such as those produced by Zimo, can control servos. The motor shaft is set to move between two positions, dependent on the function output, and can be used for operating anything from a pantograph to a driver's head.

- **Memory Wire**
  A special wire that changes length when a current is passed through it. When the current is turned off, it returns to its original length. It is silent in operation and very powerful. The drawback is that you need a long – in 4mm-scale model terms – piece of wire to get a useful movement. It has been used to operate pantographs and doors, both hinged and sliding. As with electromagnets, the current draw is a consideration and the normal state of the device should be with the wire off.

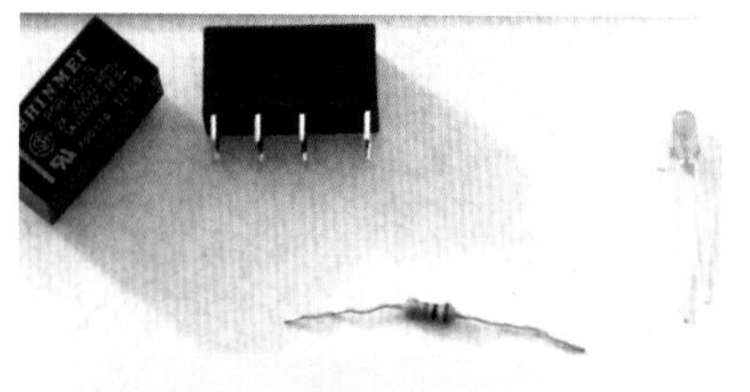

Relays small enough to fit inside locomotives are available, if you need to operate an accessory that requires more current than the decoder can provide. A standard resistor and 3mm LED are shown alongside for comparison.

If you have some electrical device that needs more current than the decoder can provide, then you can use a function output to operate a relay. This is an electrically controlled switch that connects the device to the pickups so that it can draw current directly from the track.

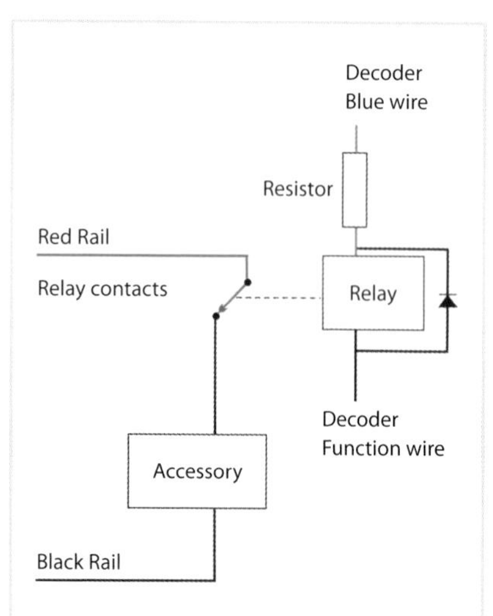

The relay coil should be connected to the decoder's function common (blue) and appropriate function wire, along with a resistor to guard against excessive current draw. A diode needs to be wired across the coil to avoid any pulses getting fed back into the decoder when the relay is operated. The accessory should be connected to the track pickups via the relay's switching contacts. You may have to include diodes or resistors, depending on the accessory's needs.

Road Vehicles

Believe it or not, you can get DCC decoders for fitting into model road vehicles. First, let me introduce you to the Faller Car System.

The Faller Car System is one of the best kept secrets in the hobby. Even the importers of this German made system seem to be reluctant to advertise it. The concept is very simple: each road vehicle is fitted with a motor powered by a rechargeable battery and a steering arm to guide the vehicle around roads. The arm carries a small magnet that follows the path of a steel wire underneath the road surface, so both the guidance and propulsion systems are effectively invisible to the viewer. Add to this the ability to start and stop vehicles, as well as to switch routes at junctions, and the resulting display verges on magical. A range of vehicles is available in HO and N scales, along with various accessories.

This photo shows just how small the DCCar decoder is. It is double-sided; on this side is the circuitry to increase the supply voltage from 2.4V to 5V. (The decoder circuitry is on the other side.) It is sitting on the roof of a 4mm (1:76)- scale Cortina and the ruler is showing millimetres.

Claus Ichmann, in Germany, has developed the DCCar system which allows the Faller Car System and similar vehicles to be operated by DCC controllers, or dedicated function modules using an infrared communications link. In addition, it also provides an anti-collision system based on infra-red.

Adding moving vehicles to a model railway brings life and movement to scenes outside the railway fence. This OOC die-cast model has been fitted to a modified Faller CarSystem chassis and is passing underneath a railway bridge, as a DMU rumbles overhead. The magnetic steering arm can be seen below the number plate.

Even if you don't use the DCC control feature, you have the ability to trigger functions from infrared LEDs by the roadside so that vehicles slow, stop, speed up and indicate at certain places. This is a facility that would be of great benefit to automation in standard DCC decoders.

To operate DCCar decoders, you need to connect one or more infrared LEDs to the track outputs of your DCC controller. (You can still use the controller to drive trains as well.) The DCCar decoders have miniature infrared detectors which are mounted on the front of the vehicles, picking up the signals transmitted by the controller and acting on them just like a normal DCC decoder. Each vehicle will have its own address and can be driven just like a locomotive – the only difference being that, due to the way the Faller CarSystem works, you cannot reverse. The decoders can control head and taillights, trafficators and flashing lights.

D8200

Chapter 5

Accessory Decoders

The manufacturers of ready-to-run OO gauge models now provide DCC sockets for their new releases. This means that models like this Heljan Class 15 – seen pulling away from *Bawdsey* with a mixed goods train – should be easy to convert. Sometimes, however, the DCC socket is not easy to access, making installation harder than it should be. PHOTO: MIKE WILD

Provided it is fitted with a decoder, you can operate just about anything from a DCC controller – from locomotives and points to cranes and lights.

DCC can not only control your locomotives but also your points, signals and other accessories. Accessory decoders come in a variety of types for different purposes. As they have to control everything from streetlights to solenoid point motors, this is hardly surprising. Most accessory decoders can control 4 different items and many can operate a mix of devices.

The main stumbling block is cost. Many layouts do not have motorised points anyway. If yours does, then finding an extra £5 to £10 per point to cover the cost of a decoder is a pretty strong disincentive. So why bother?

1. You don't need a control panel – having got rid of all those section switches, you can now get rid of the switches for points and other accessories and dispense with the control panel altogether. This not only saves on space but also the cost of switches and all the wiring from the panel to the point motors.
2. You can operate everything from your DCC handset. This is really useful when you are following your train around the layout – no need to dive back to the control panel to change a point.
3. If you prefer to have a control panel, then you can use a computer screen as a 'glass panel'. If you change the layout, only a little work on the computer program is needed rather than wrestling with wires, switches and solder. The computer can also interlock points and signals to stop conflicting routes being set up.
4. A computer can operate for you. Many DCC systems have computer interfaces and a PC can be used to automate sections such as the fiddle yard, fill in for missing operators or run the mainline traffic whilst you shunt the yard.

One common misconception is that you cannot use the same numbers for points or routes as you can for locomotives. This is not true. The two types of decoders each have their own range of addresses, so you can have both a locomotive number 1 and a point number 1. The cab should make it clear which one you are trying to operate at any given time.

Running your accessory decoders can cause problems on large layouts. The high current draw needed to operate twin solenoid point motors can lead to a momentary loss of power if a large number of trains, or accessories, are in operation. Also, if a locomotive causes a short circuit by running into a point that is set against it, this will shut down the control station and you will be unable to change the point to remove the short. It is far better to feed the accessories from a separate bus, fed from either its own cut out or a separate booster.

Controlling the accessories is normally handled by your command station. Most command stations will allow you to control individual accessories and many allow you to set up 'routes'. A route is a selection of accessories which are set at the same time. This allows you to set all the points and signals for a manoeuvre, for example, with a single operation. As you can imagine, the saving in time and reduction of errors on even a medium-sized layout makes this worth considering.

Depending on your choice of accessory decoder, you can choose from a number of ways to operate semaphore signals. Possible methods include solenoid point motors, slow-motion point motors, servos from radio control models and memory wire. Whichever method you choose, the signal will operate the same way as far as the command station is concerned. These signals are on John Dew's DCC-controlled Great Western layout. PHOTO: JOHN DEW

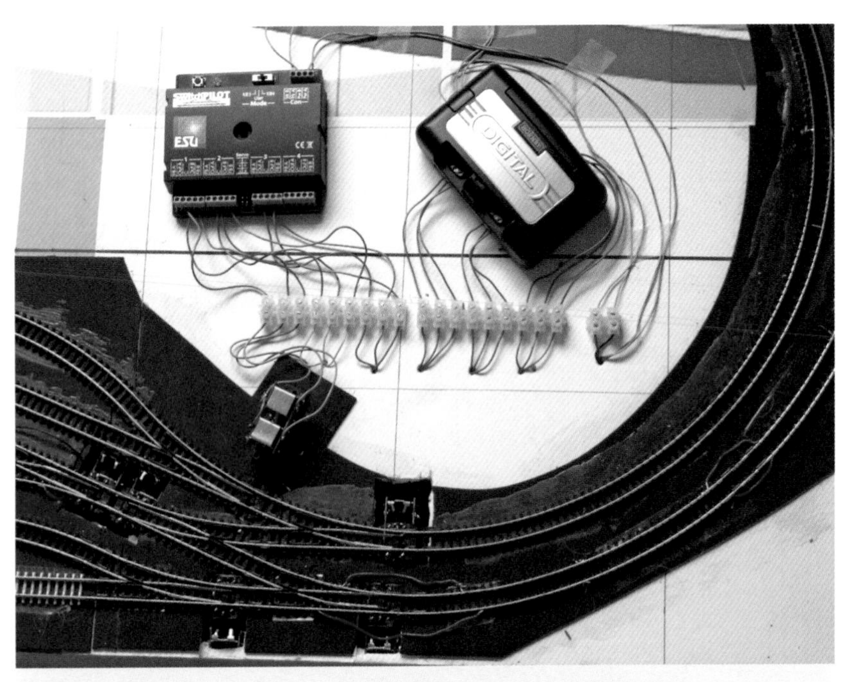

ESU and Hornby accessory decoders wired to operate the points leading to a fiddle yard. You can mix and match accessory decoders in the same way you can use different manufacturers' locomotive decoders.

A Typical Accessory Decoder

Most accessory decoders have four pairs of outputs. These can be used to control point motors, signals, electric uncouplers, lights and many other electrically powered accessories. The four pairs of outputs are usually numbered in a block so that a decoder may, as an example, use addresses 1 to 4 or 85 to 88.

Each pair of outputs can normally be programmed to give a burst of power or to be left on continuously. Both the outputs of a pair have the same setting, but different pairs of outputs can have different settings.

All decoders need to be connected to the track bus in order to pick up the DCC commands. However, some can be connected to a separate power supply. This is very useful if you use solenoid point motors which take a lot of power. Using a separate power supply means that you do not drain the power from the track bus, which could cause your locomotives to behave erratically.

The decoder outputs provide either a DC or AC output of around 12-16V. Different devices need to be connected in different ways. Different accessory decoders have different facilities and it is a good idea to think about what you would like from your decoders before you purchase. You can, of course, mix and match using different decoders for different jobs if you wish. There is an amazing variety of decoders available, from basic models like Hornby's R8216 – which is the cheapest of the readily available units, operates 4 solenoid point motors and takes both signal and power from the DCC bus – to the Digitrax DS64 – with four outputs which can be configured to operate dual-solenoid or slow-motion point motors – but only one type for all four outputs. It can take its DCC information either from the track bus, or by plugging into the Digitrax LocoNet.

The power for the accessories is 12V DC, either from an accessory bus or a plug-in transformer. The output addresses can be set either as a group of four or individually. An additional feature is that you can set addresses to be part of a route. A route can consist of up to 8 points that are all set from a single command. External switches can be used to operate outputs or routes manually.

The ability to operate accessories manually seems, at first glance, to be pointless. After all, when you can control a point from your DCC handset, why would

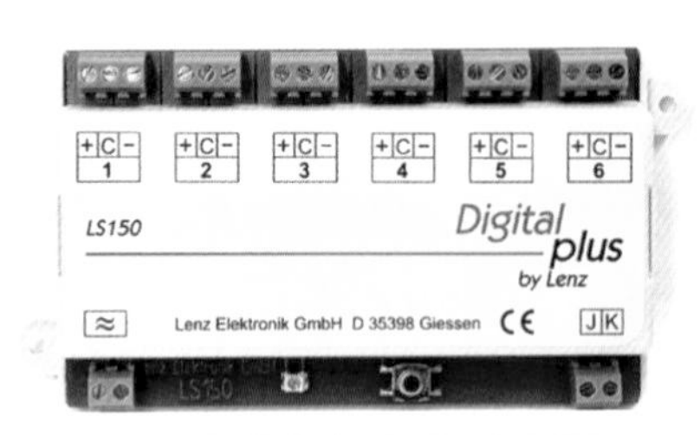

The Lenz LS150 is a fairly typical example of a DCC accessory decoder, except that it can control six accessories rather than the more usual four.

DCC accessory decoders do not only operate points, but also items like streetlamps. They can be switched on and off from your DCC controller without any extra wires or switches.

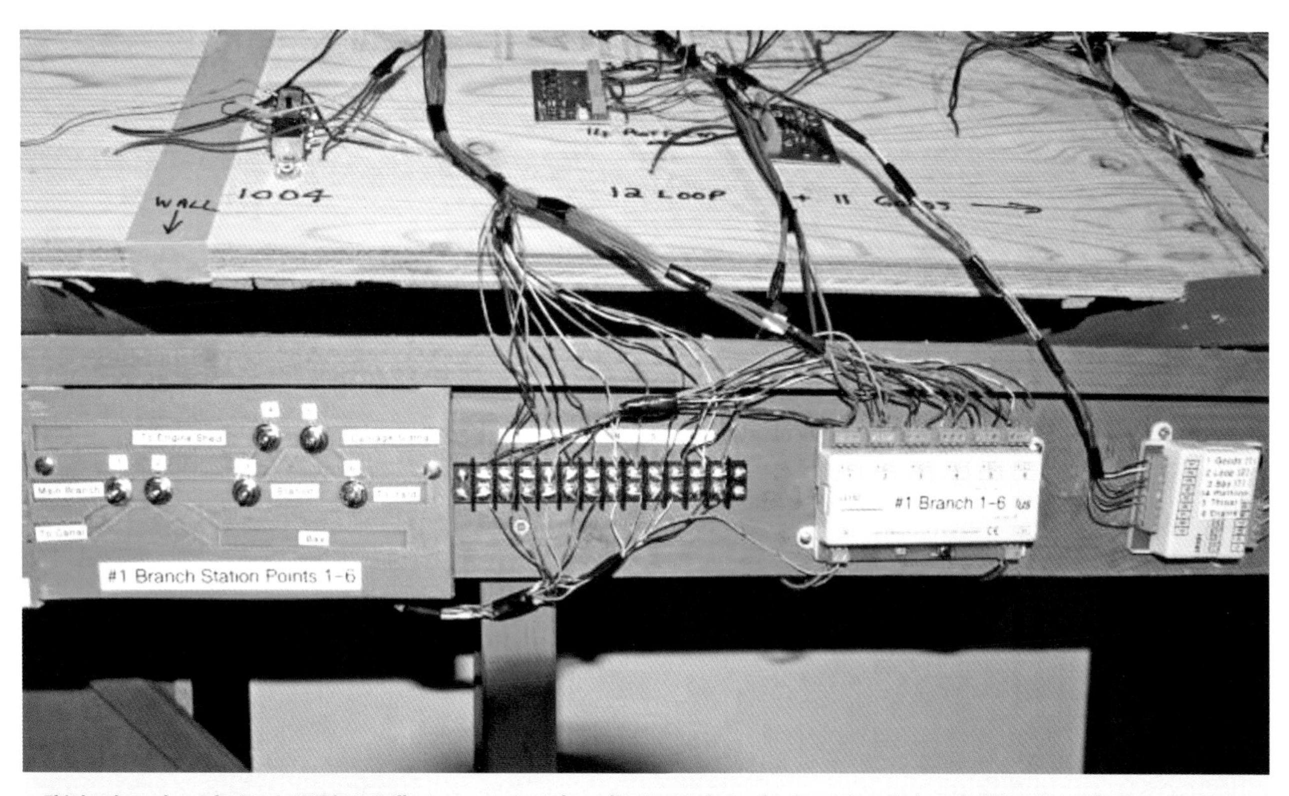

This local panel on John Dew's GWR layout allows an operator to have direct control over the six points at the branch station. Normally, the points are controlled by a computer running Railroad & Co or from the cab handset. However, sometimes it is easier, when shunting, to use these panel switches.
PHOTO: JOHN DEW

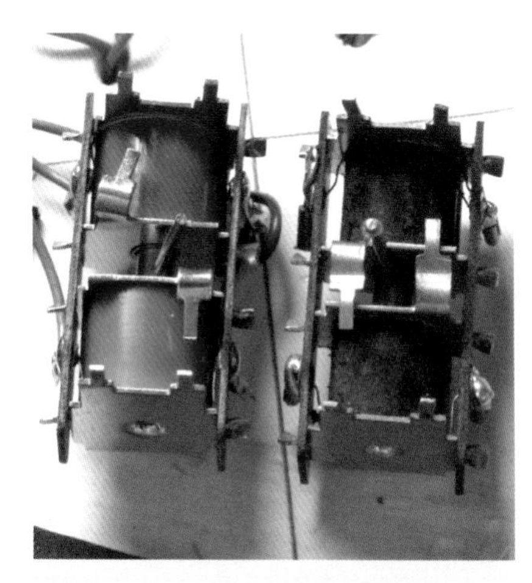

Peco produce a special version of their point motor for DCC use. It has a lower current draw than the standard unit, which can overload some accessory decoders. The DCC version (left) has green coils for easy identification.

you want to push a button on a control panel? The answer is flexibility. If you are shunting then you will be changing your locomotive's speed and direction frequently, as well as changing points. To switch from locomotive running to point operation, entering the point's address and setting it requires a lot more keystrokes than a single press of a button – so a button situated conveniently for shunting operations will make operation much easier and more enjoyable.

The DCC decoder allows you to operate the point from elsewhere in the room, when you are running a train through the area and as part of a route. There is no need to have all your points fitted with DCC decoders or point motors – you can motorise those on your running lines and leave the sidings for local or manual control.

Programming Accessory Decoders

Accessory decoders use a different set of addresses to locomotive decoders and run from 1 to 2044, although not all systems cover the full range. Accessory decoder addresses can duplicate your locomotive addresses; it is perfectly acceptable to have a locomotive with an address of '1' and an accessory with the same address – the DCC system can work out which one you are trying to operate from which keys you press, and the decoders can work it out from the message that the command station sends.

The normal way to program an accessory decoder's address is to press a button on the decoder, which puts it into program mode, and then operate the accessory address that you wish to set it to. The decoder sets to the first

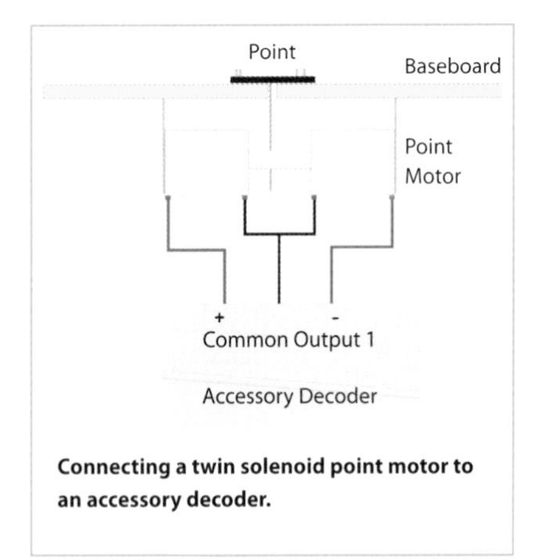

Connecting a twin solenoid point motor to an accessory decoder.

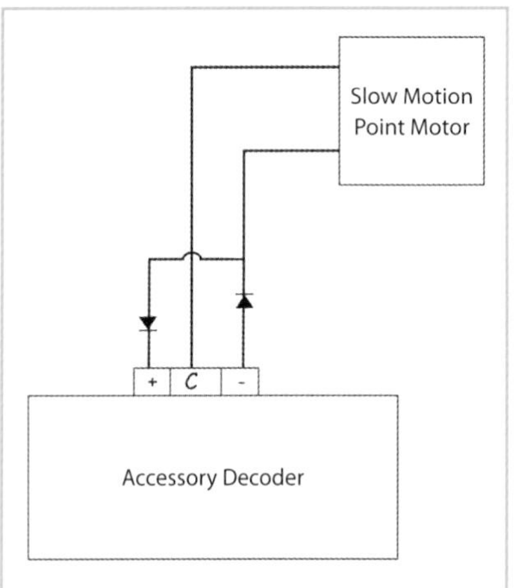

When connecting a slow-motion point motor to an accessory decoder designed to operate a twin-solenoid point motor, you need to configure the decoder so that the power is on long enough for the motor to move the point all the way across. Some decoders are designed for use with both types of motor and have the extra circuitry built in.

accessory address it receives when it is in program mode.

Many decoders come with other features that can be set by programming CVs. These may need the programming button to be pressed or may simply be programmed on the main. Depending on the complexity and functionality of the decoder, there may be many CVs that can be set to define the accessory type, how long it should operate for and so on. As each decoder is different, you will need to refer to its manual to establish what it can do and how to make it do it.

Twin Coil Solenoid Point Motors

The typical model railway point motor consists of a pair of solenoid coils which need a pulse of electricity to operate them. If they are subjected to a continuous voltage, they very quickly burn out. Most accessory decoders are set to operate this type of point motor as a default.

One output is connected to each coil and the common wire is connected to both. This is exactly the same method as would be used for conventional operation, with push buttons or similar switches. If your point motor has an auxiliary switch and your decoder has a feedback facility, the switch can be connected to the decoder so that the point's setting can be read by the command station.

Where 2 point motors need to be operated at the same time, for example on a crossover, you should not connect both to the same decoder output. Instead, you should connect each point motor to its

Slow-motion point motors like this Fulgurex unit are based on small electrical motors, and they need a different type of power supply to solenoid-based ones.

A class 47 diesel is held at a 2-aspect colour light signal. The signal was built from an Eckon kit; similar models are available from CR Signals in 'N' gauge.

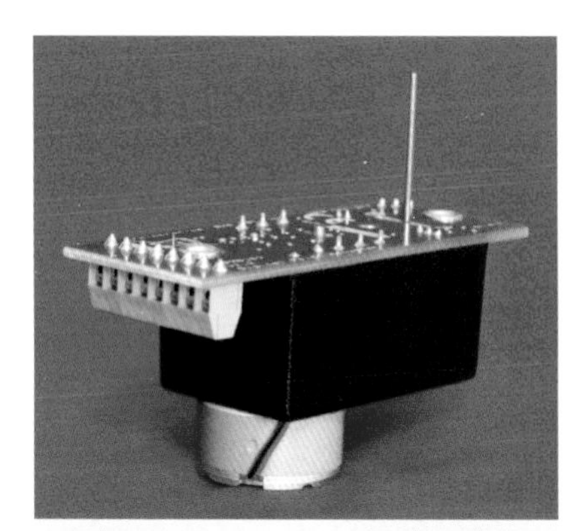

The TrainTronics TT300 is a slow-motion point motor with a built in DCC accessory decoder. This makes it ideal for locations where only one or two points are close together as you don't waste outputs on an accessory decoder.

own individual output and set them both to the same address.

A number of people have experienced difficulty using Peco point motors with accessory decoders. Older Peco point motors tend to have a very low resistance and thus draw a large current which can be beyond the capabilities of the decoder to supply. To solve this problem, Peco have introduced a low-current version of their motor, the PL-10W, which is better suited to DCC use. It is easily distinguished from the conventional version by the green coloured coils.

Slow Motion Motors

Slow motion point motors, such as the Tortoise or those produced by Fulgurex, need to be connected differently to the twin solenoid types. They require a constant DC voltage in one direction or the other to operate and hold the point blades in position.

Many decoders are able to control either thin-solenoid or slow-motion motors, but not both types on the same decoder. Some decoders do let you mix-and-match while others are only for one type. If you plan to use (or may wish to upgrade to) slow-motion motors, check

that your chosen decoder is compatible.

The Traintronics TT300 works on a different system; while it is a slow-motion motor like the Tortoise, it has a built-in DCC decoder and takes its power directly from the DCC bus. The advantage of having a built-in decoder is that no matter how many or how few point motors you have in an area, you will always have just the right number of decoder outputs for them.

The built-in decoders also have a route-setting system: the decoder will respond to a number of different addresses for both normal and thrown outputs. For example, point number 27 could be set so that not only would it respond to address 27 but also move to its normal position for addresses 107, 110, 124, 136 and its thrown position for addresses 106, 108, 109, 113, 114, 116 and 130. By setting each point along a route

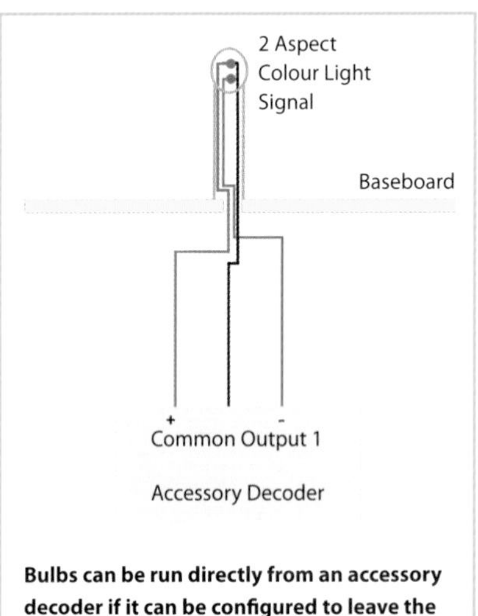

Bulbs can be run directly from an accessory decoder if it can be configured to leave the outputs on constantly, rather than just giving the pulse needed for a solenoid point motor. This enables you to control signals, such as this two-aspect model with red and green bulbs connected to a single decoder output.

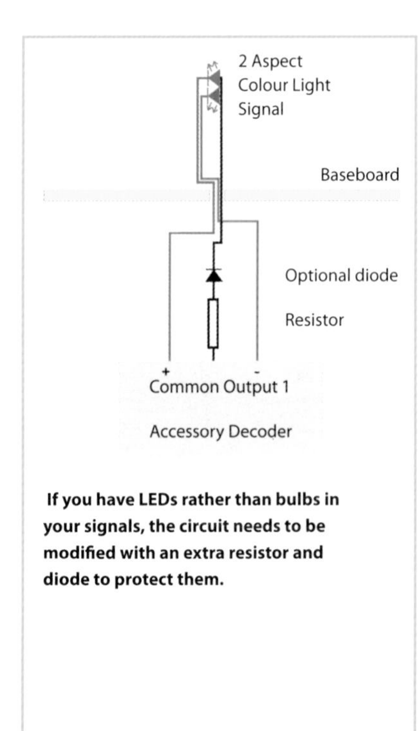

If you have LEDs rather than bulbs in your signals, the circuit needs to be modified with an extra resistor and diode to protect them.

DCC can be used to control all sorts of accessories, from point motors to container cranes. This operating crane is a Heljan product seen on Nick Gurney's OO gauge Holland Park Container Terminal layout.

to respond to the route's address you can select a route, rather than individual points; even if your DCC command station doesn't have route setting.

Colour Light Signals

Two-aspect colour light signals with 12V bulbs can be connected directly to the outputs of the accessory decoder. Signals that use LEDs need a current-limiting resistor in order to work properly. Note also that the LEDs need to have the anodes connected together and to the common terminal on the decoder. Current flows from the common terminal through the LED to the + or – terminal. If you use LEDs on an AC ouput decoder (such as the Lenz LS150), you will also need to add a normal diode between the signal and the resistor (with the anode at the resistor end and the cathode at the signal end) to protect the LEDs from the AC voltage.

For a supply voltage of 16V AC, the resistor should typically be 1K5Ω, rated at 0.25W or greater. If your supply voltage is lower the LEDs may appear dim, and in that case the resistor can be reduced to 1KΩ. If the LEDs are too bright for your needs, then they can be dimmed by using a higher value resistor – normally 1K8Ω or 2K2Ω.

Multiple-aspect colour light signals cannot be directly operated using an accessory decoder, but this accords with prototype practice as on real railways the signals cycle through the different aspects automatically. The signalman can set a signal to red to stop a train and then clear the signal, but the actual aspect that it displays (green, double yellow or yellow) is dependent on the position of other trains on the line.

If you have a multiple-aspect colour-light system installed, then the accessory decoder can act as the signalman's set/clear switch to replace the equivalent control on your signalling panel. To do this, it will probably be necessary to connect a relay to the accessory decoder and use the relay contacts to replace the mechanical switch.

Other Accessories

You can, of course, use an accessory decoder to control just about anything that you would normally operate with a switch. Roco and Heljan produce DCC-operated cranes and it is easy to connect up lights, level crossings and other animated scenes.

If you have a working level crossing, it can be fitted with a DCC accessory decoder and operated from your DCC controller.

Route Setting

Once you have a DCC controller to drive your trains, it is tempting to use it to control points as well. The advantage is that you can dispense with control panels altogether and operate everything from the one controller. The disadvantage is that, for many controllers, the number of key presses needed to operate a point is excessive if you require more than a couple of points.

One solution to this problem is to use the route-setting facility offered by some controllers and also by some accessory decoders. This enables you to set a number of points just by using one address.

Of course, some operations – such as running around a train on Platform 5 or moving multiple units to and from the sidings – will almost certainly be

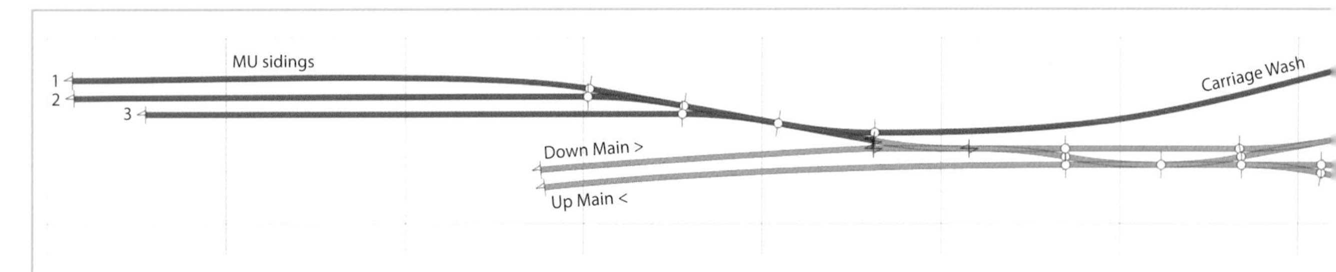

You can combine DCC route setting and manual control of shunting moves. The red points are controlled manually, the blue ones solely by the DCC system and the grey ones by both the DCC system, for arrivals and departures, and manually for shunting moves.

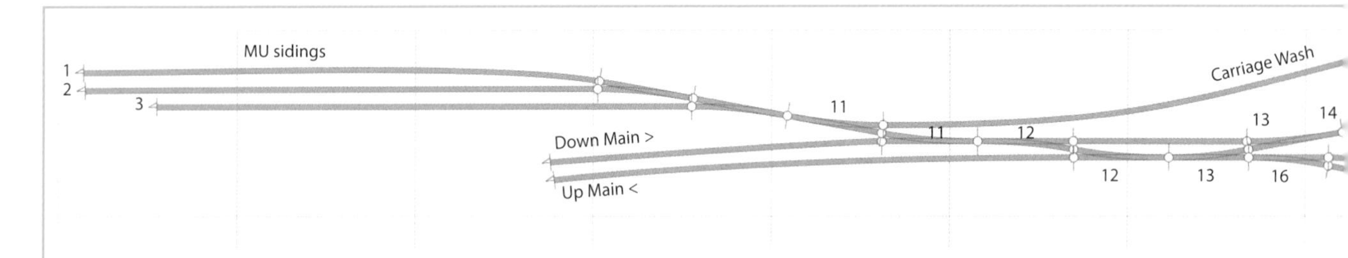

This track plan for a modern image station shows the benefit of route setting when operating using a DCC handset. Arriving and departing trains only need a single series of keystrokes to set all the points for their movement, instead of around 5 series to change each point individually.

Taking the track plan in the example you could set up routes for main line arrivals and departures like this:

Down Main to Platform 1
Down Main to Platform 2
Down Main to Platform 3
Down Main to Platform 4
Down Main to Platform 5
Platform 2 to Fiddle Yard 1
Fiddle Yard 1 to Platform 3
Platform 1 to/from MU Siding 1
Platform 1 to/from MU Siding 3
Platform 2 to/from MU Siding 2
Platform 3 to/from MU Siding 1
Platform 3 to/from MU Siding 3

Platform 1 to Up Main
Platform 2 to Up Main
Platform 3 to Up Main
Platform 4 to Up Main
Platform 5 to Up Main
Platform 2 to Fiddle Yard 2
Fiddle Yard 2 to Platform 3
Platform 1 to/from MU Siding 2
Platform 2 to/from MU Siding 1
Platform 2 to/from MU Siding 3
Platform 3 to/from MU Siding 2
Platform 4 to/from MU Siding 1

Platform 4 to/from MU Siding 2
Platform 4 to/from MU Siding 3
Platform 5 to/from MU Siding 1
Platform 5 to/from MU Siding 2
Platform 5 to/from MU Siding 3
MU Siding 1 to/from Carriage Wash
MU Siding 2 to/from Carriage Wash
MU Siding 3 to/from Carriage Wash
Platform 5 Run Round (via Platform 4 to Up Main)

The above is 33 routes as opposed to 17 points. The benefit comes with the number of key presses to route a train through the station. Let's take a train on the Down Main heading for Platform 2 as an example. The points that need to be set are numbers 11 (Normal), 12 (Normal), 13 (Reverse), 14 (Normal) and 15 (Reverse).

performed whilst standing close to the station. These could be controlled locally by manual override switches on the layout fascia, close to the points that they control. This would reduce the number of accessory decoders that you need; for example, the points in the multiple unit sidings would not need to be linked into the DCC system. Some points would be controlled both manually and by the DCC system, while others – such as the hidden crossover in the fiddle yard – would only be controlled by the DCC system.

Unfortunately, there is nothing in DCC to stop you setting conflicting routes. If you want to have points and signals interlocked, you either need to use a specially-constructed conventional point and signal control system or else operate them via a computer interface and a suitable program.

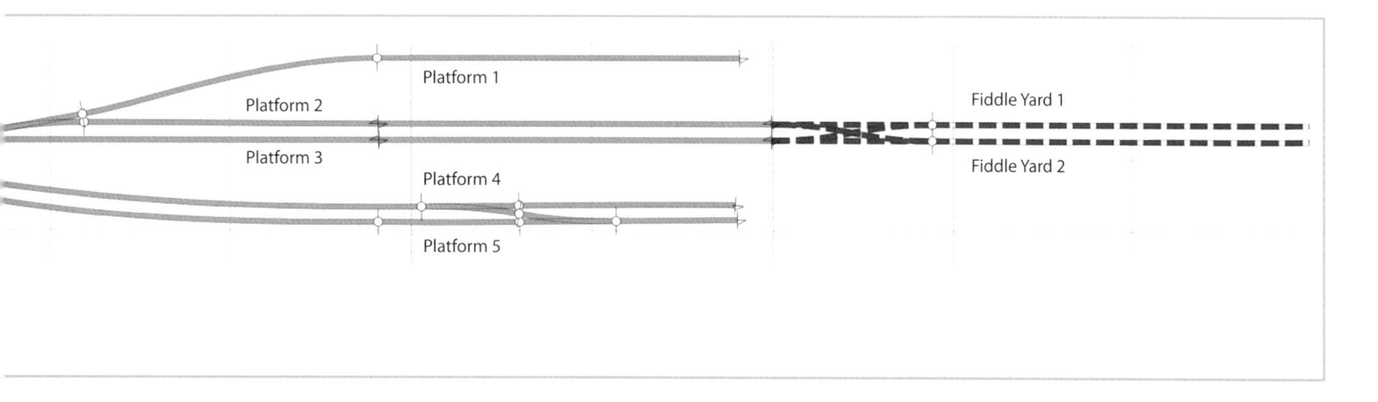

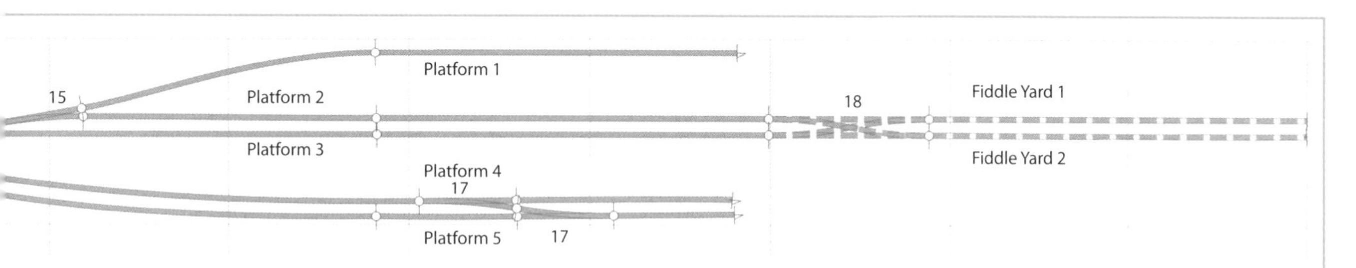

On a Digitrax Zephyr, which is one of the easier controllers when it comes to operating points, the commands to set the individual points would be:

<SWITCH> - Select accessory decoder mode
11 <c> - Set point 11 to closed (normal)
12 <c>
13 <t> - Set point 13 to thrown (reverse)
14 <c>
15 <t>
<EXIT> - Return to normal operation mode.
A total of 17 key presses.

By comparison, to set the route numbered 51 you would need to enter:
<SWITCH> - Select accessory decoder mode
51 <t> - Set route 51
<EXIT> - Return to normal operation mode.
A total of 5 key presses.
Remember that you will need to set the route for every train that arrives at and leaves the station and you can see why route setting is such a benefit.

LEVEL
1 IN 73

Chapter 6

Wiring for DCC

DCC has the capability to significantly reduce the wiring required on a medium or large sized layout, giving you more time to spend on scenery. A Maunsell 'N' 2-6-0 approaches Treneglos with a van train. PHOTO: MIKE WILD

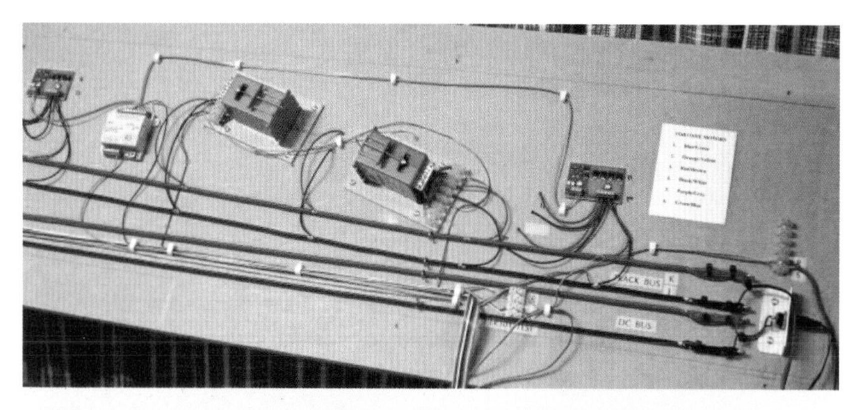

While you do need more than two wires under all but the simplest DCC layout, the amount of wiring is much reduced compared to the equivalent analogue (DC) layout. The bus wires feed the accessory decoders and are then connected to the point motors and other devices. The tracks are fed directly from the DCC bus. This is the underside of a layout built by Max Wright.

PHOTO: MAX WRIGHT

Bus Wiring

In wiring terms, a 'bus' is a wire (or group of wires) that carries traffic around the system. In the case of DCC layouts there may be a number of them – all doing different things:

- **DCC or Track Bus.** This is the DCC power feed to the track, either system-wide or as part of a power district. Each local track feed is connected to this pair of wires. The bus wires should be much larger than the track-feed wires, as they can be called upon to carry a higher current.

- **Accessory Bus.** If you have separated the DCC track power from the DCC accessory decoders, this will be the DCC supply to your accessory decoders. The bus wires should be the same size as the track bus, as they too can be called upon to carry high currents.

- **Cab Bus.** This links the sockets that you plug your handheld cabs into. It may also connect to other devices, such as a computer interface. These wires will be smaller than the track-bus wires as they do not need to carry large currents. Depending on your DCC system, there will be between 4 and 6 wires in the cab bus, usually in a multi-way cable.

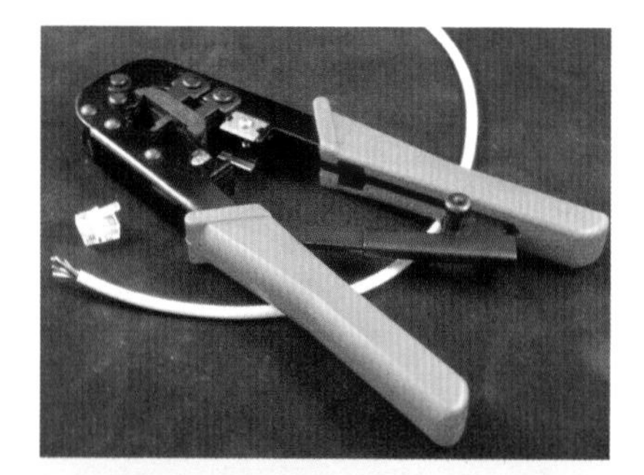

To make your own Loconet or XpressNet cables you need plugs, cable and special crimping pliers. All of these are available from electronic parts retailers or eBay.

- **Feedback Bus.** This links the devices that are sending information back to the command station. Typically, these will be block occupancy detectors and switches that show which way the points are set. Again, the wires will be smaller than the track bus wires and the number of them varies depending on your system.

- **Power Bus.** If you have accessory decoders or other items that require their own power supply, then they will get them from this bus. The number and size of the wires will depend on your specific requirements.

Depending on your system and needs, you may not require a full set of buses around your layout. Digitrax's LocoNet combines the cab and feedback bus into one system. If you don't need feedback or a separate power supply, you won't need a feedback or power bus.

The Cab Bus

DCC systems come with their own preferred connector, usually some variation of a telephone plug. These are typically – though technically incorrectly – called RJ11 and RJ12, while Lenz handsets use an audio connector, a 180° 5-pin DIN. The DCC manufacturers are happy to sell you socket panels to install around your layout, but the canny modeller can usually save money by buying panel mounting sockets from electronic retailers.

Digitrax's LocoNet uses RJ12 telephone/computer connectors with 6 contacts and all 6 are used. These plugs and sockets are identical to the more common RJ11, except that RJ11 only has 4 wires connected. You should always check that all 6 connections are available or, in the case of a cable connection, when buying leads and sockets from other sources.

Lenz's XpressNet uses two different connectors. Handheld cabs tend to come with a 180° 5-pin DIN plug – sockets for these are available cheaply from electronic and audio retailers. Other XpressNet devices, such as computer interfaces, tend to come with an RJ11 plug – this is a telephone/computer plug with 4 of the 6 wires connected. RJ11 leads are much easier to come by and you can always use an RJ12 cable with 6 wires, if that is all that is available. Other manufacturers use the same plugs and sockets but cannot be interconnected; doing this may well ruin one or both DCC systems.

You don't have to use the manufacturer's standard plugs and sockets for inter-baseboard connections; any suitable plug and socket will do, even combining the bus with other wires if necessary.

It is possible to make Loconet and XpressNet cables yourself, but you need a special crimping tool to do it. Therefore, if you only need a few cables it is easier and cheaper to buy them readymade. To make your own you need the plugs, cable and the crimping tool.

The plugs are known variously as RJ11, RJ12 and Stewart, and come in different versions for use with flat or round cables. The Rapid Electronics part numbers are 24-0476 for the flat cable version and 24-0478 for the round cable one. The other ingredient is the cable, 4 core for XpressNet and 6 core for Loconet.

The crimp pliers will usually have a set of cutters built in that will cut the cable and strip the outer sheath off at the correct length. Put the coloured wires in the correct order for your system and push the cable into the plug, making sure that the individual wires slide into the channels at the plug end. Do not strip the insulation from the individual wires, as the crimp connections will break through it.

At this point, make sure that all the wires run all the way down to the end of the connector. Check once more that the wires are in the correct order, place the plug in the pliers and crimp. Once you have fixed the plugs to both ends of the cable it is a good idea to test it, either with a cable tester or swapping it for one currently in use on your layout. If you don't test your cables then you will have a major job identifying the faulty one that is shutting down the entire layout.

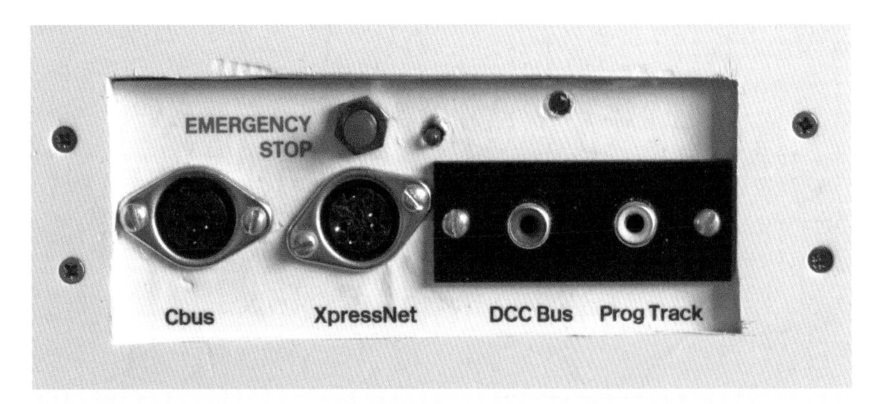

This socket panel shows the versatility that creating your own panels affords. From left to right: a socket for the feedback bus (the MERG CBus system), an XpressNet socket with a green LED (to indicate the XpressNet is working) and an Emergency Stop button for use when there's no handset plugged in, DCC bus 'power in' from the command station with a red LED (to indicate the track power is on) and the DCC supply for the programming track from the command station.

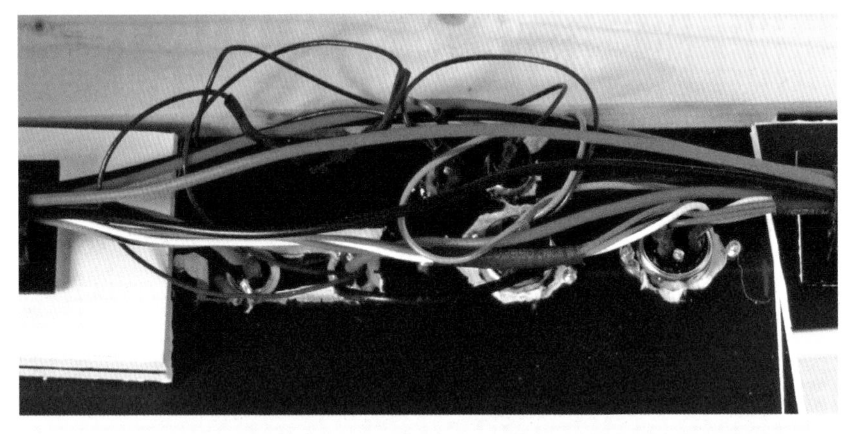

The rear view of the same panel. The bus wires in each direction are joined at their sockets. The indicator LEDs and pushbutton are connected by short lengths of wire to the appropriate terminals. The resistors for the LEDs have been soldered directly to their leads and covered with shrink-wrap tubing.

Whilst you are installing your own connectors, it is easy to add indicator LEDs and, with Lenz systems, an emergency stop button. This is of great use on those occasions when there just isn't time to get a cab plugged in before disaster strikes. A track-power LED and a cab-bus power LED are useful troubleshooting tools.

To wire a Lenz emergency stop requires you to run an extra wire from the command station around the layout. The extra wire should be connected to the 'E' terminal on the command station and, at each location where you want an emergency-stop button, you need to fit a normally-open pushbutton that connects this wire to the XpressNet 'M' (ground) wire. Digitrax users don't have this facility as they need a device that can generate the necessary LocoNet message to instigate an emergency stop.

To wire an XpressNet cab bus-power indicator you need to connect an LED and

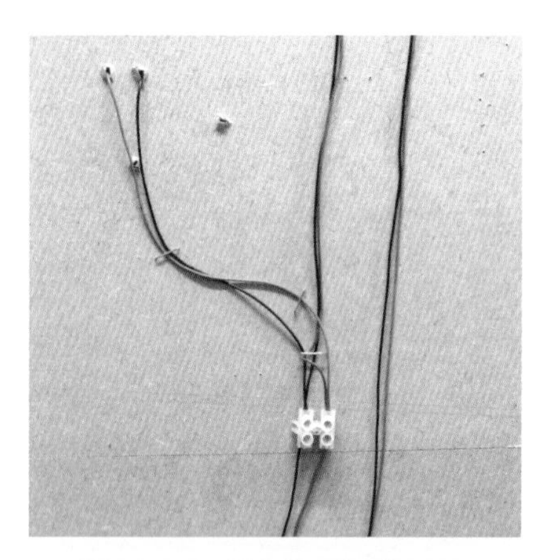

DCC wiring at its simplest. Here we have two pairs of bus wires with one set connecting to the track. If you have more than one bus, always keep their wires separate to avoid mistakes.

Self-adhesive copper tape can be used for the bus wires in place of conventional wires. Track and accessory feeds can be soldered directly to the copper tape.

resistor between the 'L' (+12v) and 'M' (ground) wires. The resistor needs to be 3KΩ or larger and the LED's cathode connects to 'M'. Use as high a value resistor as possible to reduce the current drain on the bus.

To wire a LocoNet live indicator, you need to connect an LED and resistor between pins 1 RailSync B (white wire) and 2 Ground (black wire), or pins 6 RailSync A (blue wire) and 5 Ground (yellow wire). The RailSync lines are at 7V DC ,so you can use a 1KΩ or larger resistor. The LED's cathode connects to ground.

To wire a track-power live indicator you need to connect an LED, a resistor and a diode between the red and black track-bus wires. The anode of the LED should be connected to the cathode of the diode. The resistor should be 3KΩ or larger and the diode can be any standard rectifier diode, such as a 1N4001, 1N5401, etc.

The Track Bus

There is a marketing myth that you just need two wires for DCC. While this does have some truth in it, it is likely that you will need more than that – but a lot less than a conventional analogue DC layout. If you already have your layout wired up, then it is possible to reuse that wiring. However, you may find it beneficial to rewire it, which can be done in stages over time.

The two most important wires on a DCC layout are usually called the track bus. These are the 'two wires' of popular myth. Their job is to distribute the power and DCC signal to the track and anything else that happens to be connected to them.

These should be made of thick cable to minimise any loss of power and should, as far as possible, run parallel to each other. Usually they are coloured red and black for easy identification. The track bus is connected to the track by short thinner wires. Ideally, each piece of rail should be connected to one of the bus wires; at the minimum, the latter should be connected to the track at intervals of 3 to 6 feet. The table opposite gives the minimum recommended sizes for bus wires. If you have long wires, in excess of 4 metres, then you will need to use thicker cable to avoid the track voltage dropping as you get further away from the booster.

As an alternative to wire, you can use self-adhesive copper tape to carry the DCC power around your layout. The tape is sold for wiring dolls' houses and can be fixed to either the top or, more usually, the underside of the baseboard. As you only need two bus wires, copper tape is a viable option – it would not be suitable for analogue DC, where there may be dozens of wires serving the same purpose. Track

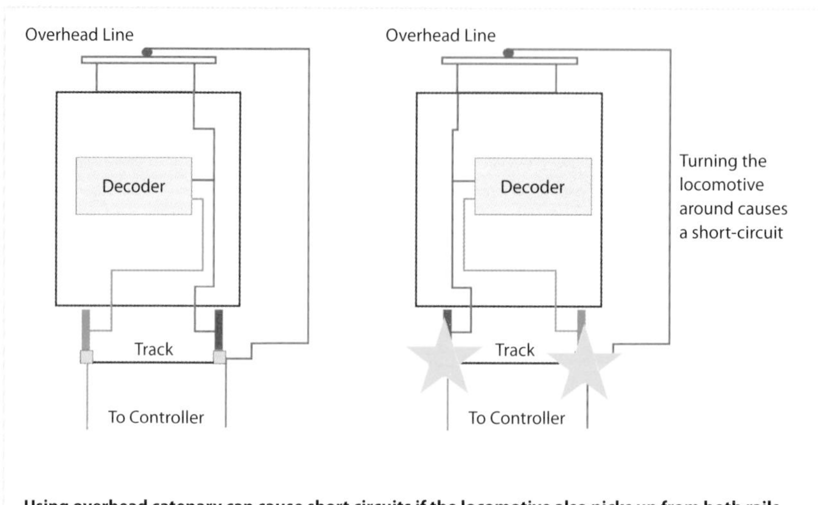

Using overhead catenary can cause short circuits if the locomotive also picks up from both rails. If it only picks up from one rail (the blue rail in the left-hand illustration) then turning it round will leave it unpowered.

BOOSTER CAPACITY	BUS CABLE SIZE
3A bus	Single core wire – 20AWG
	Stranded wire – 16/0.2mm
	Conductor area (stranded or single core) – 0.5mm2
6A bus	Single core wire – 18AWG
	Stranded wire – 24/0.2mm
	Conductor area (stranded or single core) – 0.75mm2
10A bus	Stranded wire – 32/0.2mm
	Conductor area – (stranded or single core) – 1.0mm2

Some commercial power clips come with built-in suppressors which can disrupt the DCC signal. If you use power clips rather than soldered connections, always make sure that they are DCC-compatible.

feeder wires and links to accessory decoders can be soldered to the tape to make the short run to their destination.

It is recommended that DCC is not used for pickup from overhead wires, unless both rails are electrically linked. If the overhead is connected to one of the running rails, then turning a locomotive around – either manually or by running around a reverse loop – will cause a short circuit. If you were to use a different booster for the overhead wire to that being used for the track underneath it, placing a locomotive the wrong way around would double the track voltage supplied to the decoder, destroying the latter very quickly. In addition, electrical pickup from an overhead wire tends to be far more erratic than from the rails, leading to unreadable DCC signals and the decoder losing power.

When a short circuit occurs on the layout – for example, when a locomotive derails – then the full current from the booster will flow along the bus and through the short. As this will typically be between 2 and 5 Amps, the booster is fitted with a high-speed circuit breaker that detects the sudden current surge and shuts the power off, thus preventing any damage to the booster, wiring or locomotives. However, if the bus wires are too thin, they can cause the track voltage to drop to such an extent that the booster cannot detect the short circuit and activate the circuit breaker. If that happens and the short is not removed, or the power shut off manually, the short can generate sufficient heat to damage track and rolling stock, or even start a fire. You can test if your wiring is good enough to allow the booster to detect a short, simply by placing something metal (such as a screwdriver or coin) across the tracks at various places. The booster should shut down and indicate a short circuit every time. If it does not, then you will need to increase the size of the bus wires or add extra feeds in the areas where short circuits are not detected.

Inadequate wiring also causes poor performance. Nickel-silver rail has a much higher electrical resistance than copper wire and, if there are long runs without feeders from the track bus, there will be a significant drop in the voltage at the track. This will cause locomotives to run slowly or even stop, as the locomotive's decoder will shut down if there isn't enough power to operate it. This is particularly noticeable if you have locomotives with additional functions such as lights and sound.

Having got your booster to shut down every time that there is a short, you will probably find it very irritating that all trains stop whenever you have a problem. To avoid a derailment in the goods yard stopping the main line trains, you need to have either a number of boosters or electronic cut-outs, each supplying a separate area of the layout. Each booster or cut-out will have its own bus. Do not connect the track buses together as this will defeat the object of the boosters and could well damage them. There is no need for the track sections attached to a booster to be contiguous. For example, you might have three boosters – one for the up mainline, one for the down mainline and a third for the locomotive depot on the downside of the station – and the goods yard on the upside. A benefit of adding extra boosters is that you have more power available for operating locomotives and accessories such as coaches with interior lighting.

If you are installing multiple boosters, ensure that you are consistent in connecting the red and black bus wires in each section. The easiest way to check that you have done this correctly is to use a meter set to its AC Volt scale and connect it to the 'red' rail in two different sections. If the meter reads 0V, then both rails really are 'red'. If it reads the full DCC voltage (around 14V) then one rail is 'red' and the other 'black'. Swap the connections over in one of the sections and try again.

If you operate point motors and other accessories using DCC, you may wish to have a separate booster and track bus for them to avoid their current draw affecting the trains. Another possibility is to use point motor decoders that have their own capacitor discharge unit (CDU), which will provide the large kick that solenoid point motors need to operate without leaving the rest of the layout short of power.

Regardless of the number of boosters or cut-outs that you have installed, you will find it really useful to add a number of switches along each track bus to turn off sections of track for troubleshooting purposes. This makes it far easier to locate a short circuit. The track connected to each section of the bus will need to be isolated from the other track sections on both rails for the switches to work.

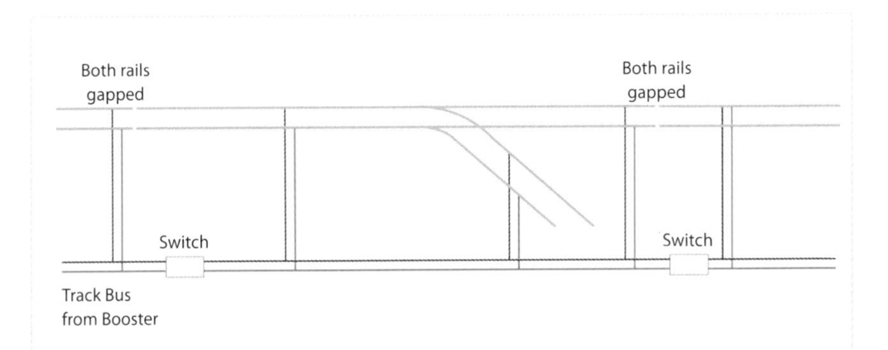

When trying to locate a short circuit you can turn the switches off one by one, working back towards the booster until it clears. This tells you that the short is in the section controlled by the last switch that you turned off. Using the diagram above as an example, suppose that there is a locomotive causing a short at the point. Turning off the right-hand switch would not clear it; turning off the left-hand switch would. From this, you would quickly home in on the fact that the short was in the centre section of the track.

Points and Crossings

Despite the myths and misinformation, there is no fundamental difference from analogue DC in wiring up points for DCC. The only thing to remember is that, with DCC, all rails that have power fed into them are always live, whereas with analogue the power can be switched off.

The illustrations below all show live frog points. As with analogue DC, these ensure electrical contact for the locomotive and make for smoother running. Peco Streamline 'electrofrog' points can be laid in exactly the same way as dead, or insulated, frog points with no extra wiring. Most other brands require the frog and associated rails to be electrically switched when the point is changed. This can be done by a switch linked to the point motor or lever.

The secret of pointwork is to always feed electrical power from the toe of the points. Never feed the frog. One feed can run through a number of points as long as they all face in the same direction – or, to put it another way, when coming from the feed you should always pass the point blades before you get to the frog.

You will note that the turnouts retain their power-switching function under

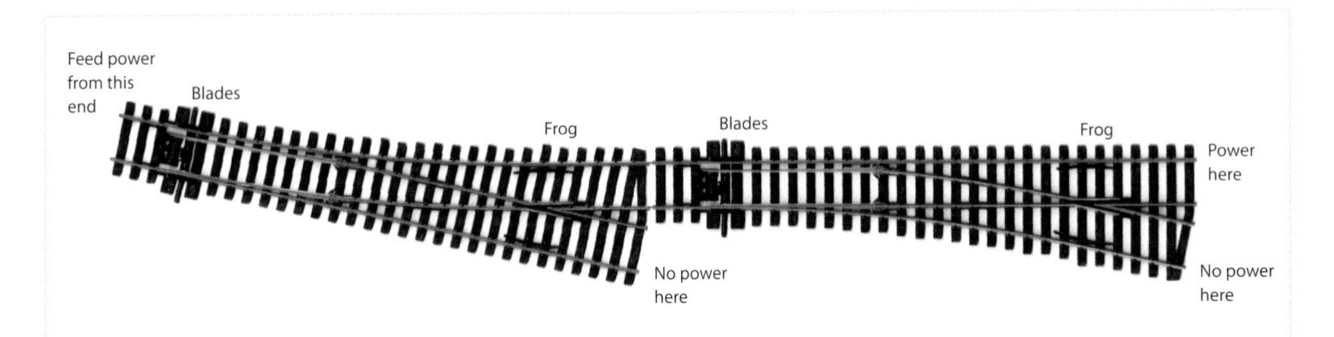

The secret with any pointwork is to always feed electrical power from the toe of the points. One feed can run through a number of points as long as they all face in the same direction.

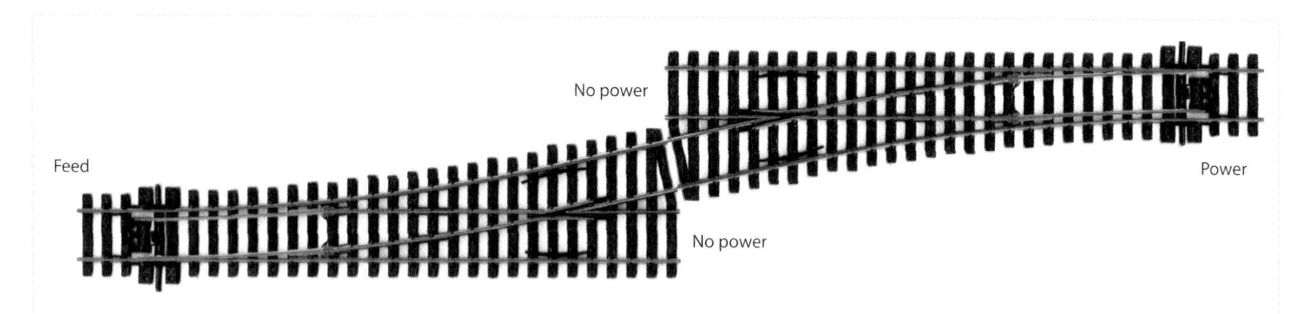

One situation to avoid is when you reach the frog before the blades. While the power flows normally if the route through the points is set, things start to get complicated when you change the points.

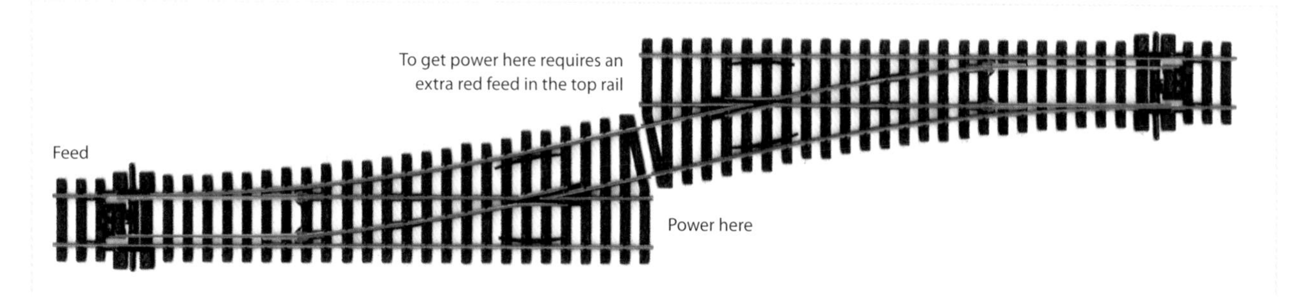

If the points are both set against each other, then trains will still run on the lower line. To get a train to run on the upper line, you will need to provide an extra power feed in the top rail. Do note, however, that it is the opposite polarity to the previous illustration.

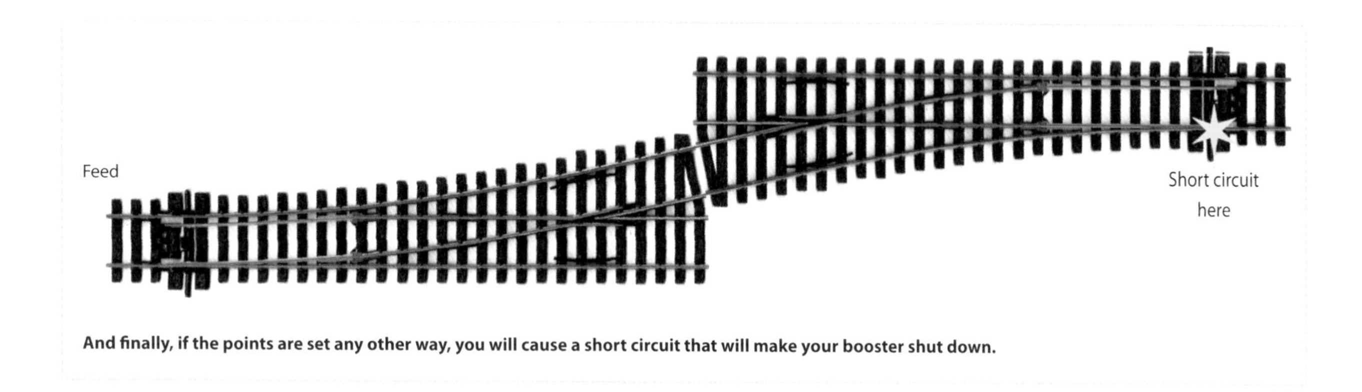

And finally, if the points are set any other way, you will cause a short circuit that will make your booster shut down.

DCC and that the sidings with the points set against them are electrically dead. This is an advantage if you are running unconverted locomotives on the layout, as they can be isolated by setting the points against them. On the downside, it means that any DCC-equipped locomotive on the isolated siding will not respond to the controller.

To make a siding live at all times, you need to put insulating rail joiners on both rails after the frog and then run feeder wires to the siding. The siding will now be live at all times, but you will be able to run a locomotive into a point that is set against it and cause a short circuit which will shut down the booster. This is the single most common cause of short circuits on DCC layouts.

Don't forget that there can be a long length of track between any of the points and that they can fan out in both directions from the feed.

Where you have points that join 'frog to frog' the solution is to put insulating rail joiners between the two points and feed each one from its toe. Do not forget that there can be many feet of track between

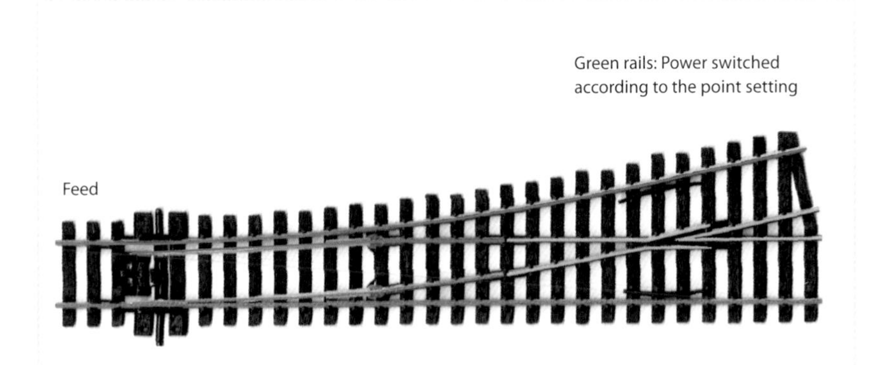

What is often referred to as 'DCC Friendly' is just good practice for live frog points and is also the way that many people wire them for analogue (DC) layouts. By electrically connecting the point blades to the adjacent rail, most problems caused by out-of-gauge wheels can be eliminated.

the points and it can sometimes be hard to spot this configuration.

The other problems that can occur with points is when out-of-gauge wheels bridge the gap between the frog rails and running rails to cause a short, or where locomotives with long, rigid wheelbases are running around sharp curves. If you must do this, then the point needs to be modified so that the blades are connected to the adjacent running rail and the frog is electrically switched by the point motor or lever. The instructions supplied with Peco points explain how to do this.

Power Routing Points

Dead frog points usually send power only to the route that is selected, leaving the route with the point set against it electrically dead. This is an ideal situation for analogue (DC) layouts, as it means that by default sidings can be isolated and locomotives left on them will not move.

With DCC there is no need to isolate sidings, as the locomotive's movement is controlled by the DCC decoder inside it. Obviously, if the siding is not powered then, regardless of whether the locomotive is DC or DCC, it will not move. However, if you have lights or sound installed in the locomotive then, if the siding is isolated, these will not work either. As a result, the normal practice is to ensure all lengths of rail are powered at all times by running extra feeds to sidings, passing loops and anywhere else that would normally be isolated by dead frog points.

Live frog points that lead to a dead-end siding are also sometimes wired to isolate the siding, by the omission of the insulating rail joiner on its leg of the frog. Again, if you require locomotive lights and sound to be operational when the point is set against the siding, you will need to install the appropriate insulated rail joiner and feed from the DCC track bus.

In some places, however, power routing can be an advantage with DCC – typically in the fiddle yard. By ensuring that fiddle yard tracks are only powered when they are selected, you can avoid the possibility of selecting the wrong train on your cab and driving it into a point set against it. If you have sound-fitted locomotives or carriage lighting, power routing will reduce the current drain on your layout from locomotives and coaches that are on hidden tracks.

One quick tip for any siding or length of track that can be isolated by changing the points against it: wire a diode, LED and resistor across the tracks; the LED will illuminate when the track has power and provide a visual check that it has been selected. Again, this can be especially useful in a fiddle yard, where a number of points have to be set correctly in order to select a track.

Hidden Siding Stop Sections

Taking the idea of isolating locomotives further, you can provide an automatic stop section on hidden sidings to ensure that trains stop automatically in the right place without manual intervention. The locomotive will then be held until released. By using normally open pushbuttons, you can ensure that the wrong locomotive cannot be started by mistake and that the stop section cannot accidentally be left on.

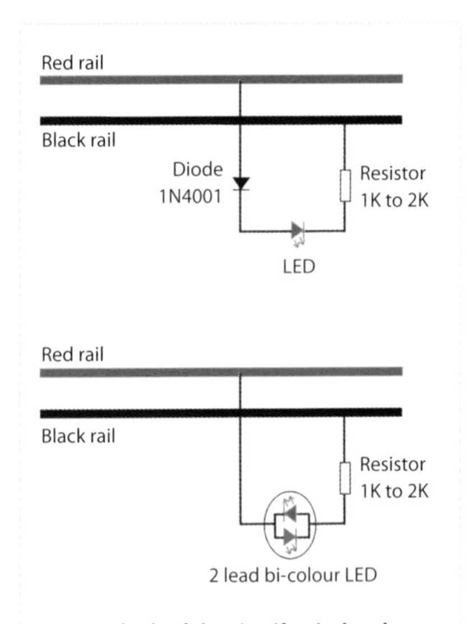

Two methods of showing if an isolated section of track has power: A standard LED needs a diode to protect it from reverse polarity and a resistor to limit the current that it draws. Alternatively, a two lead bi-colour LED can pass current in either direction, so you can dispense with the diode. A red/green bi-colour LED will show yellow on an AC supply such as DCC.

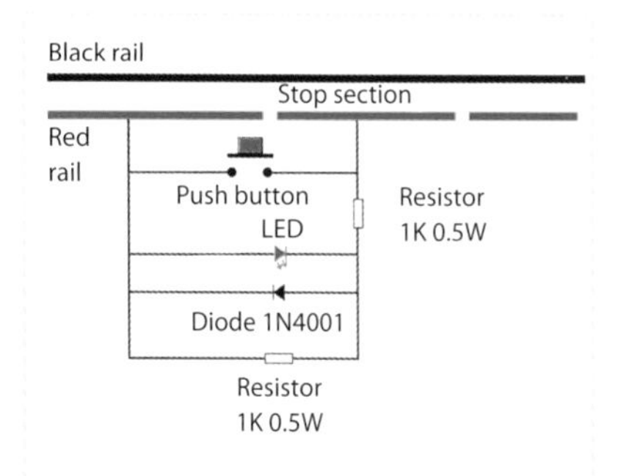

Isolated3: You can make an automatic stop section on a hidden siding like this. The LED will light up when a locomotive is stopped, but the resistors will stop it drawing enough power to move. When the button is pressed, normal DCC is restored to the section and the locomotive can be driven out.

If you have a reverse loop on your layout, then at some point a rail connected to the 'red' track bus will meet a rail connected to the 'black' and a short circuit will be created.

Reverse Loops and Wyes

Despite its many advanced capabilities, DCC is still a two-rail system and, as such, suffers from the same problems with reverse loops and wyes as analogue DC model railways. The problem is that, at some point, the right-hand rail meets a left-hand rail and vice versa, resulting in an immediate short circuit.

For conventional analogue systems, the most common solution is to use a switch to change the polarity of either the loop or the rest of the layout. This is either operated manually or linked to a point. Assuming that the loop is fed through the switch, the system is operated like this:

1. Set the switch for the inbound direction
2. Run train onto loop and stop
3. Change the point and switch
4. Run the train out of the loop (with the controller set to the opposite direction).

Fortunately, you can use DCC in just the same way – with the exception that the train will still go forwards without having to change the direction on the controller.

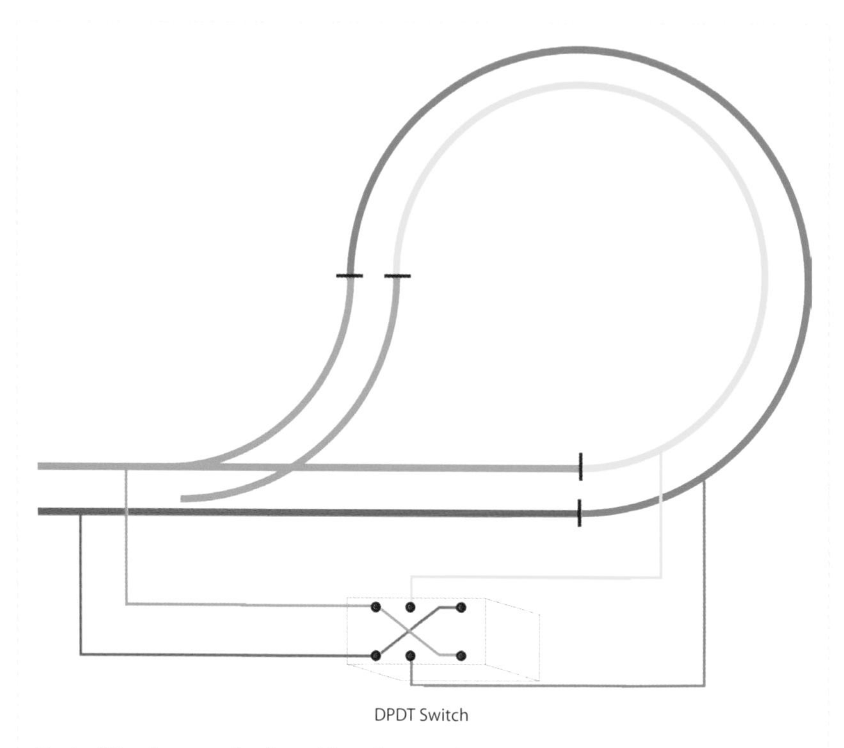

The traditional way to solve the problem of a reverse loop on analogue (DC) layouts is to use a separate reversing switch for the loop. This method works equally well for DCC.

Some manufacturers produce reverse loop modules which allow you to run a train around the loop without stopping or having to change a switch. These work by detecting the short circuit caused when the train enters or leaves the loop and quickly switching over the power feeds to the two rails. The decoder does not register the interruption in the power and continues

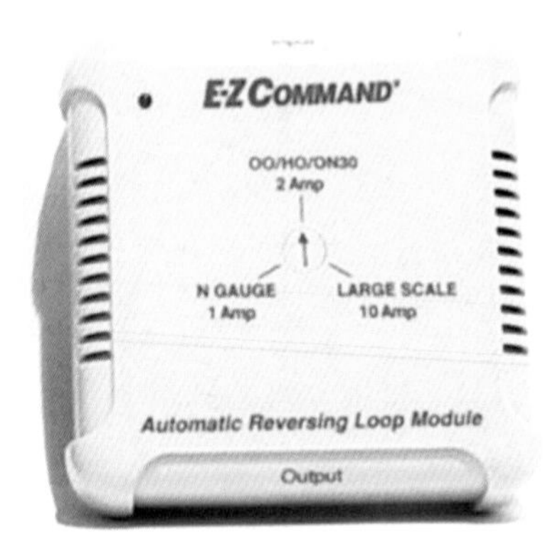

The Bachmann 36-525 reverse loop controller has a switch to select the current draw which will trigger its operation.

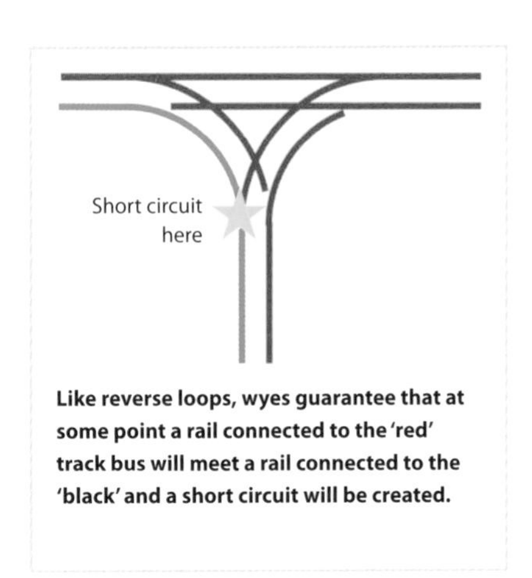

Like reverse loops, wyes guarantee that at some point a rail connected to the 'red' track bus will meet a rail connected to the 'black' and a short circuit will be created.

running as before. These units cost upwards of £30. While you can connect more than one reverse loop to them, they can only cope with a single train at a time, so in most situations you would need one for each reverse loop.

If you have divided your layout into power districts using circuit breakers like the NCE EB1, as discussed in Chapter 2, then the reverse loop unit needs to be connected between the track and the circuit breaker rather than the circuit breaker and booster. This ensures that the reverse loop unit is the first to see the short and will take action before the circuit breaker responds.

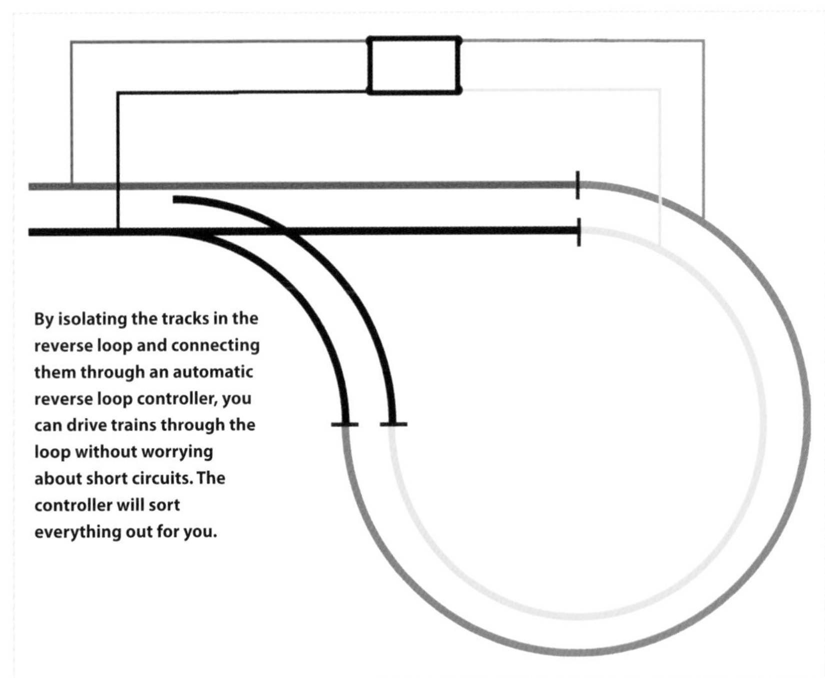

By isolating the tracks in the reverse loop and connecting them through an automatic reverse loop controller, you can drive trains through the loop without worrying about short circuits. The controller will sort everything out for you.

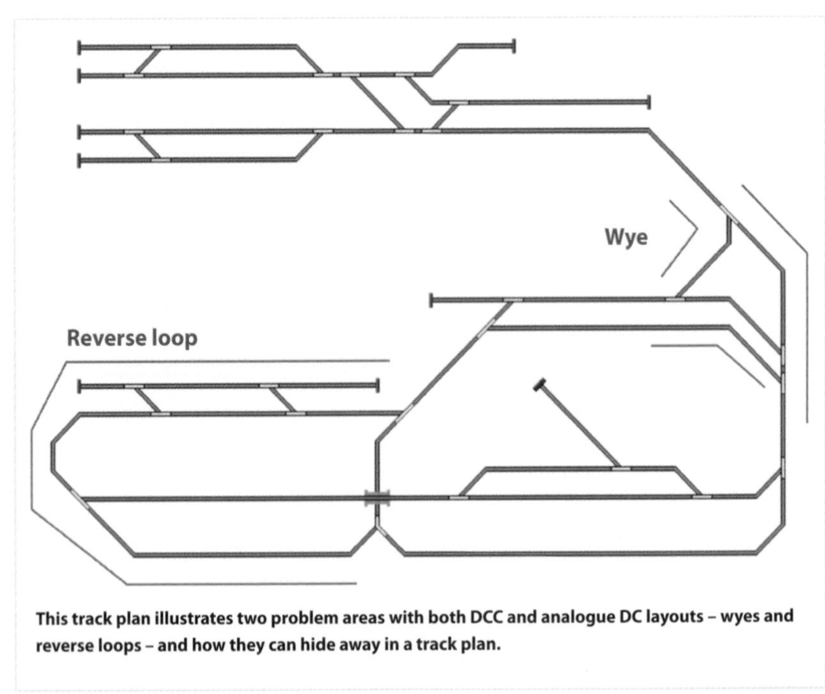

This track plan illustrates two problem areas with both DCC and analogue DC layouts – wyes and reverse loops – and how they can hide away in a track plan.

Wyes have exactly the same problem and solution. Both reverse loops and wyes can hide in track plans that seem to be perfectly innocuous. It is always worth drawing out the track plan with both rails marked in colour so that you can spot any problem areas.

As with the isolated tracks discussed above, you can use LEDs to indicate which end of a manually operated reverse loop

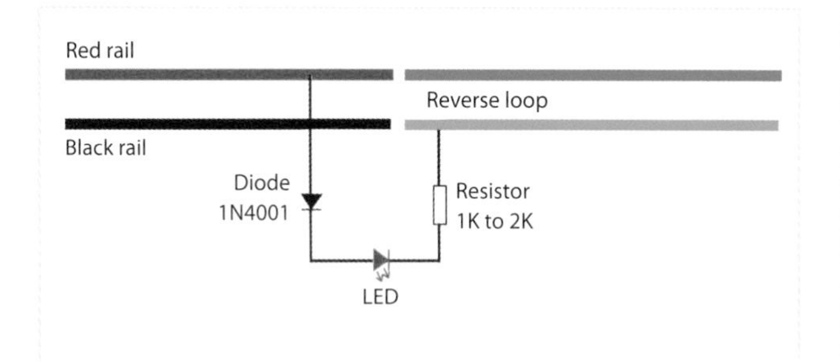

If your reverse loop is not controlled by an automatic reverser, then you will need to know which end is currently set so that a locomotive can enter without causing a short circuit. An LED wired like this – similar to the circuit for isolated sidings shown above – will be lit when it is safe to cross the isolated gap.

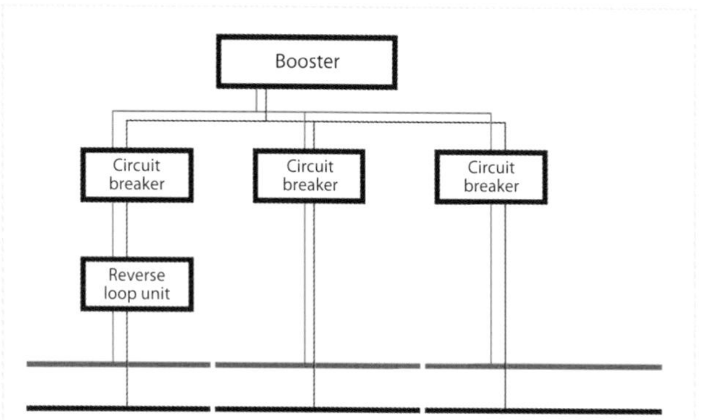

If you are using circuit breakers as well as reverse-loop units, then you need to connect the unit between the track and the circuit breaker.

or wye is correctly set for a train to enter. In this case, the LED should be wired across the rails and across the gap as shown in the diagram. When the red and black rails are the same way around on both tracks, the LED will light.

Programming Tracks

It is useful to have a programming track on your layout, but you will probably want it connected to the rest of the trackage so that you don't have to lift locomotives off the rails to change their CV settings. Even if your DCC system allows you to program on the main, you will find that in order to read the settings you will still need to use the programming track. If you have a simple system (such as the Bachmann E-Z controller) that does not have a separate programming track output, it is still useful to create a programming track to save you having to take the other locomotives off the layout every time you want to set one of their addresses.

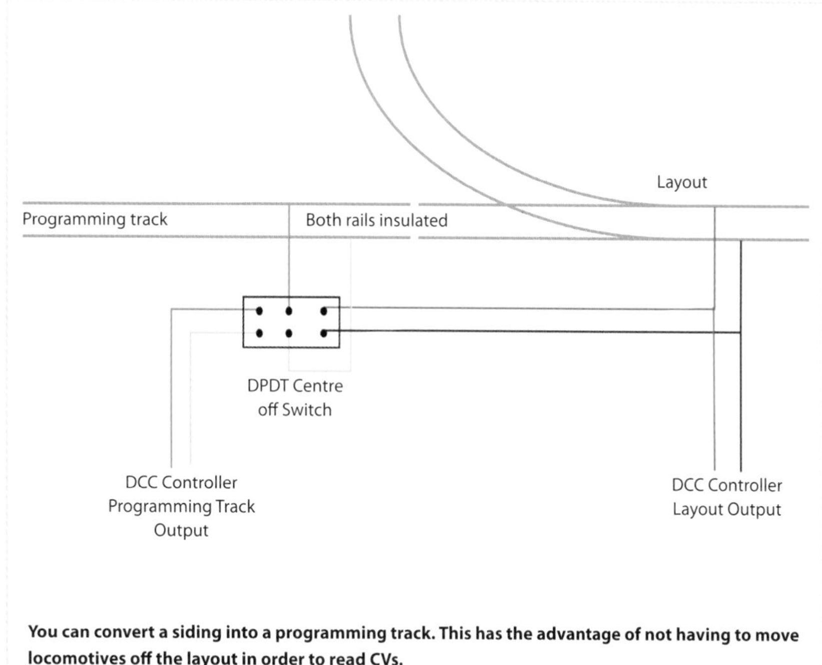

You can convert a siding into a programming track. This has the advantage of not having to move locomotives off the layout in order to read CVs.

The diagram above shows how to convert a siding on your layout into a programming track, using the programming track outputs from your DCC system. It is important that the DPDT switch is a centre-off type, so that there is no possibility of the programming and normal outputs of the controller being connected to the track at the same time. Both rails need to be electrically isolated from the main layout using insulated rail joiners.

In normal use, the switch would be set to connect the siding to the layout and it would behave just like any other siding. To program a locomotive, you need to drive it onto the siding. Make sure that the whole locomotive is in the siding and no wheels are on the layout side of the insulated gap. Change the switch to connect the siding to the programming output of the controller. You can now program the decoder. Once you have finished, change the switch to connect the siding back to the layout and drive the locomotive off the siding.

E W &
60041
60041
25

Chapter 7

Computer Control and the Internet

The Wirral Finescale Railway Modellers have embraced DCC to the full, even developing their own computer systems to generate train movements. Here, we see a Class 60 passing through with a long rake of empty steel wagons. PHOTO: MIKE WILD

Miniatur Wundeland in Hamburg has taken DCC to the limit. It is the largest digitally-controlled model railway in the world, as well as being a major tourist attraction. This is part of the main control console – and you thought that your wiring was a nightmare! PHOTO: CHRISTIAN FINKER

DCC and computers is an idea that you either find appealing or appalling. The usual negative reactions are along the lines of, 'I don't want a computer to run my layout,' 'I can't program the microwave, let alone a computer' and 'It's far too complicated and expensive.' In fact, a computer can offer both simplification and cost savings in some cases and add to your enjoyment in others.

So what can a computer bring to a DCC system? Many people assume that full layout automation is the point of adding a computer; while this is possible, there are a number of ways to use this powerful combination:

1. Decoder programming
2. Control panels
3. Partial and full automation

Decoder Programming

DecoderPro is part of the JMRI suite and is an easy way to program locomotive decoders. (Its use is covered in Chapter 3, 'Locomotive Decoders'.) If your DCC system has a computer interface, I strongly urge you to give DecoderPro a try.

Control Panels

Unless you have chosen to operate everything from your cab, then some form of control panel is a necessary evil. While it is possible to create small local panels that control a few things in an area, most UK layouts are designed with some form of large panel. This may enable the lone operator to control everything or a signalman to control points and signals whilst other operators drive the trains.

It is not easy to arrange for buttons and switches on a centralised panel to control

DCC accessories. While some accessory decoders allow local control via pushbuttons, running the necessary cables to a central panel defeats the object of having an accessory bus in the first place.

CML Electronics produce electronic modules that can be used with Digitrax Loconet to control accessories and show feedback. This combines the ease of a physical control panel with the convenience of being able to operate accessories from a cab – the best of both worlds. The only problem with such a scheme is that, as with any physical control panel, changes to the layout can mean a lot of work in rebuilding the control panel.

Many control panels in industry have been replaced by 'glass panels'. These are computer screens that display the necessary information and allow the user to set controls, just like a physical panel. Glass panels are used to operate everything from nuclear power stations to airliners and have the advantage of being more informative and easier to change than the conventional panels they have replaced.

You can use a computer as a glass panel for your model railway. Using the computer interface on your DCC system, it can send and receive commands just like a cab. It can control locomotives and accessories, as well as receiving feedback information from the layout. Using a computer screen allows the controls to be more informative and intuitive. As an example, the F0 button on your cab can read 'Lights' and only appear if the locomotive you are controlling actually has them fitted. The computer can also perform route setting even if your DCC system does not support it, and can stop you setting up conflicting routes. You do not have to buy an expensive new computer; older machines that have been replaced are perfectly adequate for the job and are often available very cheaply.

There are a number of programs available that can be used as glass panels. I would strongly advise downloading samples and trying a number of them. They all differ in style, features and complexity, so it may take a while to find the one that is right for you.

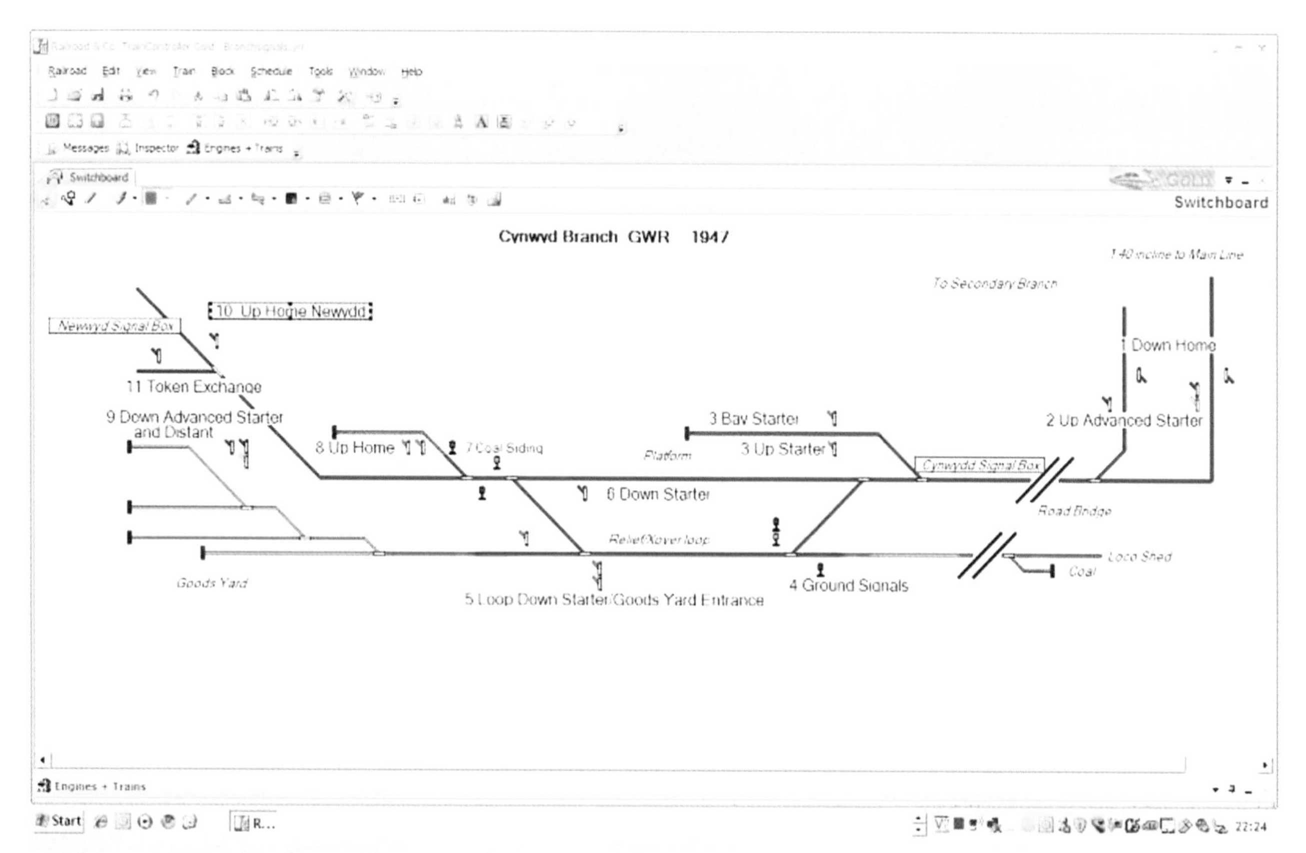

Railraod & Co can be used as a control panel. You operate points and signals by clicking on them with the mouse, and set up rules so that signals do not clear until the appropriate route is set. Therefore you cannot set up conflicting routes. This screen shows part of John Dew's GWR layout.

IMAGE: JOHN DEW

If you want to automate some or all of your layout, then everything needs to work reliably. John de Frayssinet's OO9 masterpiece 'County Gate' is a fully automated DCC layout using Digitrax controllers and Railroad & Co software. It runs as well as it looks.

Here are a few to get you started:

- **JMRI PanelPro/Railroad & Co/Rocrail**
  Available for most DCC systems that support a computer interface. PanelPro allows you to draw control panels of differing styles and link the items on the panel to your layout. Operating the panel causes a message to be sent to the layout to operate the corresponding device. Similarly, feedback information from the layout can be displayed on the panel.

You can create rules and routines that specify how things operate. This enables you to provide route setting, interlocking and signalling to suit your specific requirements.

http://jmri.sourceforge.net
http://www.railroadandco.com
http://www.rocrail.net

- **SSI Model Railway Control System**
  Available for Lenz XpressNet, Hornby Elite, Littfinski LDT s88 feedback system, MERG RPC control system and the MERG CBUS control system. SSI offers a highly realistic level of layout control as it looks and operates like the real IECC (Integrated Electronic Control Centre) systems, commonly used across the world. It gives full control of turnouts and signalling, full interlocking support (which is highly configurable) and Entry/Exit (NX) functionality.

SSI supports an advanced timetable system which can operate according to a real-time clock or a 'fast' clock. Events can be configured to set routes, activate layout devices, play sounds (such as station announcements) and set signal-box bell-sequence codes.

www.gppsoftware.com

Partial and Full Automation

Once you have DCC-controlled locomotives, points, signals and block detectors, the next step is to connect them to a computer running software that can operate them. Why would you want to do that? Well, for many people, railway modelling is a solitary activity for much of the time. Even if you are fortunate enough to have friends who join you to operate your layout, they aren't always there every time that you feel like running a few trains. Some people like to be engine drivers; others signalmen. The computer can take on the roles that you don't want and fill in for missing operators. If you are shunting the yard, the computer can run passing mainline trains in the background.

Before you embark on any form of automation you need virtually 100% reliability of operation on your layout. Points must throw first time, every time. Locomotives must respond to the cab and not stall, stutter or refuse to start. Stock that is supposed to be coupled must stay coupled until required to uncouple. Run through your proposed automated sequence and put a pound in a box every time something goes wrong. At the end of the session, put the money towards improving your track, locomotives and rolling stock – then try again!

There are a number of programs available for running part or all of a DCC controlled-layout from a computer, but all of them have a number of requirements in common:

1. Your DCC system must support a computer interface. Some have an interface built into the command station, some have separate modules that connect to the cab bus, while others do not have any interface at all. Your chosen system must be able to work with the program that you intend to use. Some

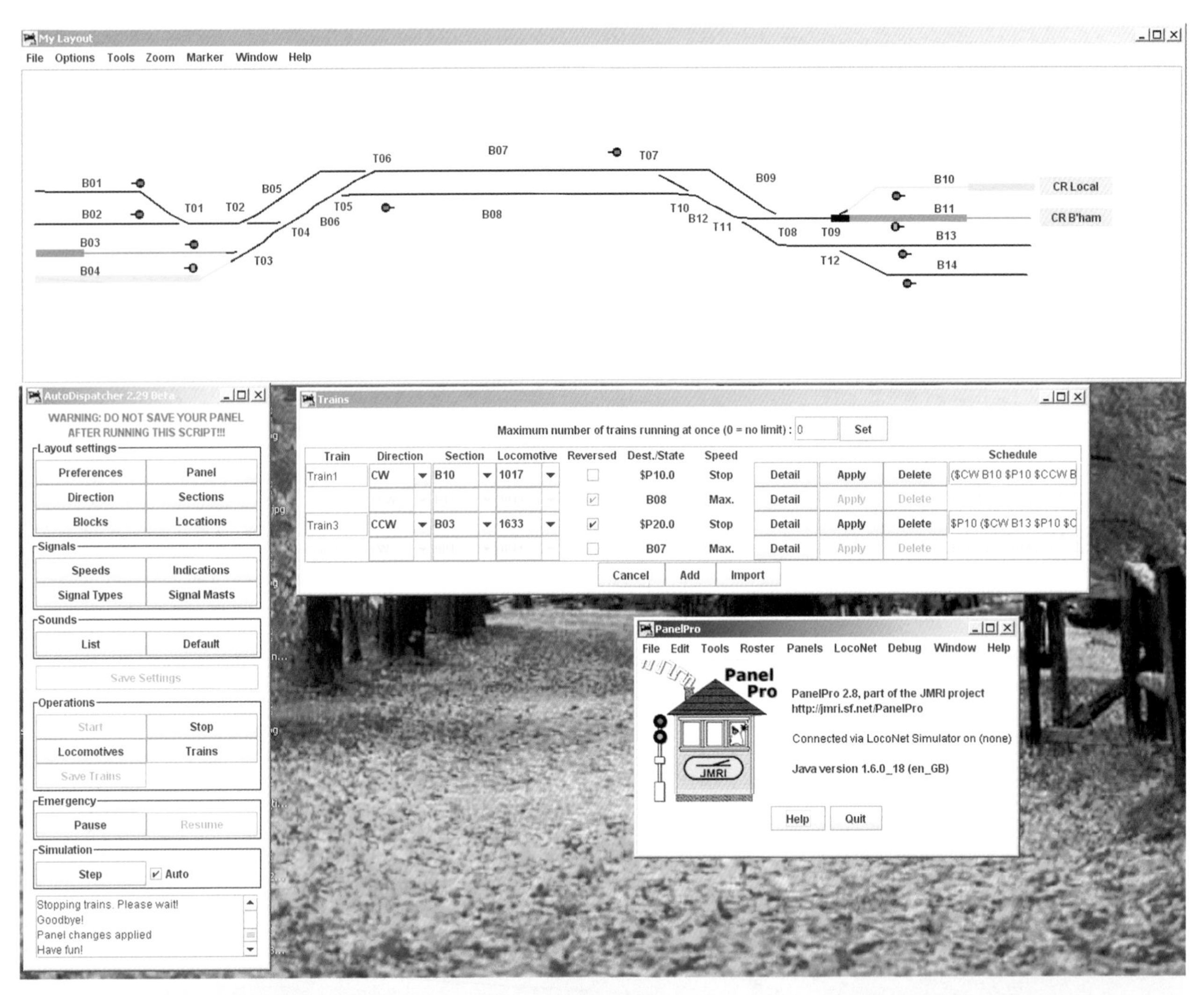

This Minories to fiddle yard layout is run automatically via JMRI. The blocks (sections) are shown with 'B' numbers – the fiddle yard is B01-04 and the platforms are B10-14. Points (turnouts) have T numbers and the trains are shown in blue and purple. The signals show the current aspect only, although the underlying logic controls 3 aspect signals. Apart from the standard JMRI suite, you also need to use the separately available Train Despatcher script.

programs are designed specially to work with particular DCC systems.

2. If you want the computer to be able to control points and signals for you, then these will need to be operated by DCC accessory decoders. You may decide – on grounds of convenience, cost or operating pattern – that some points, such as those in the locomotive depot and goods yard, will always be manually operated, with the computer having control of the main line. In prototype terms, the manual points would be operated by a local lever frame or hand lever with the main line operated by the signal box.

3. To get the computer to operate trains, it will need to know where the locomotives are. This will mean fitting block occupancy detectors to establish which tracks on the layout have a train on them. DCC block occupancy detectors normally work by detecting the current drawn by a locomotive decoder, even when the locomotive is standing still. Alternatively, you can use more traditional methods such as magnets underneath the trains operating reed switches under the track, or trains breaking infrared beams.

Armed with this information the computer can send commands to the DCC command station to drive trains, change points and signals and even operate lights and sounds. There are a number of programs that offer automation in full or part. It is much easier to write a program that can act as an automatic signalman than as an automatic driver. Of the programs listed in the 'Control Panels' section above, the SSI system can only act as a signalman and not as a driver. RocRail and Railroad & Co both have provision for automatically driving trains as well as operating points and signals. JMRI does not have any automation built into the basic program as downloaded, but libraries of automation routines are available that cater for automatic operation of both trains and points.

Automating a model railway is not an easy task and will involve a considerable investment of time and money. You also need to be patient, methodical and willing to spend money on things that don't add to the visual appeal of your layout, like block detectors.

The ultimate in hands free control. Spoken commands are relayed by the Bluetooth headset in my ear to a computer running GTCommand. This interprets them and sends instructions through a computer interface to the DCC command station, which in turn controls the trains.

Feedback can get expensive very quickly for automation – you often need more detectors than blocks, so that the computer knows when to start decelerating and when to stop. Railroad & Co can work the train's position out within a block, provided the locomotive has been profiled within the program, thus saving on the cost of extra detectors and offsetting the cost of the program.

JMRI is free, but needs a big investment in time and effort if you go down the automation route. Fortunately, most of the computer programs have free downloads that you can play with – try a few to see what they can and cannot do, and what they require in order to do it.

Getting to grips with any of these programs is a difficult task. They are complex and you are configuring them to operate a complex system. However, with Railroad & Co the process is more accessible. JMRI represents a much bigger mountain to climb, and you need to be happy tinkering under the bonnet of Java code to do it.

I have created and run simulated Minories-to-fiddle-yard layouts in both RR&Co and JMRI. I can honestly say (as a computer programmer in a past life) that the only reason I persevered with JMRI was out of sheer stubbornness. I got them both to work as simulations (eventually), but if they were connected to a real-world layout it would be a lot harder to get things to stop in just the right place via JMRI. For use as a control panel, JMRI PanelPro is great; for use as a locomotive programmer, JMRI DecoderPro is unequalled; for automating some or part of your layout, it is very hard work.

Voice Control

Controlling your locomotive by voice is possibly the ultimate in hands-free operation. GamesOnTrack (*www.gamesontrack.com*) produce a voice recognition program that lets you do just that. It picks up what you say via a headset, converts this to an instruction to your DCC system and sends that via a computer interface to your command station. The command station sees this input as a perfectly normal cab and actions the instruction as normal.

The system is currently limited in the vocabulary that if offers and you cannot add words to it yourself. But, as it matures, the words that it recognises should increase and become more useful. Each locomotive is given a name from the vocabulary – like 'Odin' – or a combination – such as '66-1-3-5', to give one locomotive's number. You can then control trains by spoken instructions about which locomotive, what it has to do and how much. For example, 'Odin Forward 14' would set the locomotive moving forward at speed step 14 and '66-1-3-5 Lights On' would turn the lights on for locomotive 66135.

The software also controls accessories and allows you to set up routes, even if your command station does not. You can also set up sequences of commands, for example to set a route, sound the locomotive's horn and then move off, all from a single command.

The software uses a lot of computing power to process the verbal commands and so needs to run on its own computer with its own interface. You cannot run it on the same computer as something like Railroad & Co. You are also restricted by the length of the cable for your headset. The solution to this is to fit a Bluetooth wireless headset to your computer, which gives you complete freedom of movement. Unfortunately, getting many computers to recognise a Bluetooth headset can be tricky. So if you are not confident about how to achieve this, it would be a good idea to buy the necessary hardware from someone who will install it for you.

Making Your Own

Making your own decoders and cabs may seem a strange idea, but it can have benefits. While you would be hard-pushed to improve on the size of a modern decoder, in some cases things can be made cheaper than their commercial equivalents and better suited to your needs. Designing something from scratch is not easy, but there is plenty of information on the Internet that can be used as a basis. You can also buy kits from individuals and societies who have done all the hard work for you; all you have to do is assemble the parts.

Building electronic modules such as occupancy detectors, accessory decoders or computer interfaces can save you money, especially on a large layout. However, it does require you to invest time in assembling and testing them. Some electronic modules also provide facilities that are just not available commercially.

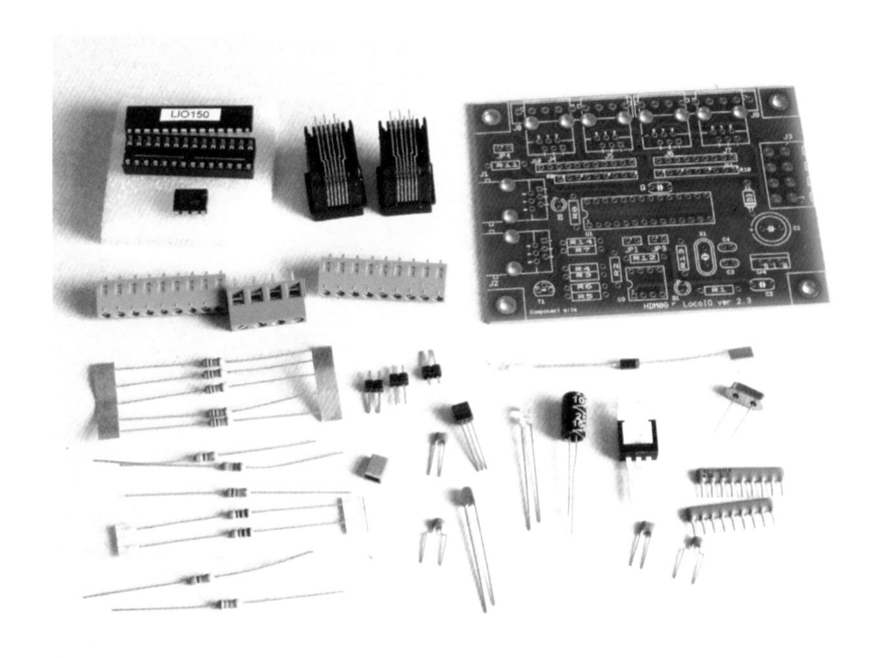

These are the parts for one of Hans De Loof's 16-channel input/output modules. Full instructions can be found on his website and, if you can solder a DCC decoder into a locomotive, you should have no problems in assembling this kit.

MERG Accessory Decoder

MERG (Model Electronic Railway Group) provide a range of kits for their members – including 2 for DCC accessory decoders, 1 for dual-solenoid point motors and another for slow-motion motors. While you do have to solder the components in place yourself, the process is quite straightforward and the instructions are clear and easy to follow. If you have a need for more than two decoders, then it is well worth considering joining MERG and building your own. The output addresses are set as a group of 4 and the decoder should be the only one connected to the DCC controller for programming.

Whilst the decoder is fairly basic, it is perfectly adequate for many uses – either in its twin-solenoid or steady-state forms – and has the great advantage of economy at around £10 for a 4-output unit.

HDL Loconet Modules

Hans de Loof is a Belgian hobbyist who has designed a number of modules for use with Digitrax's Loconet. These include a computer interface, a servo controller and an input/

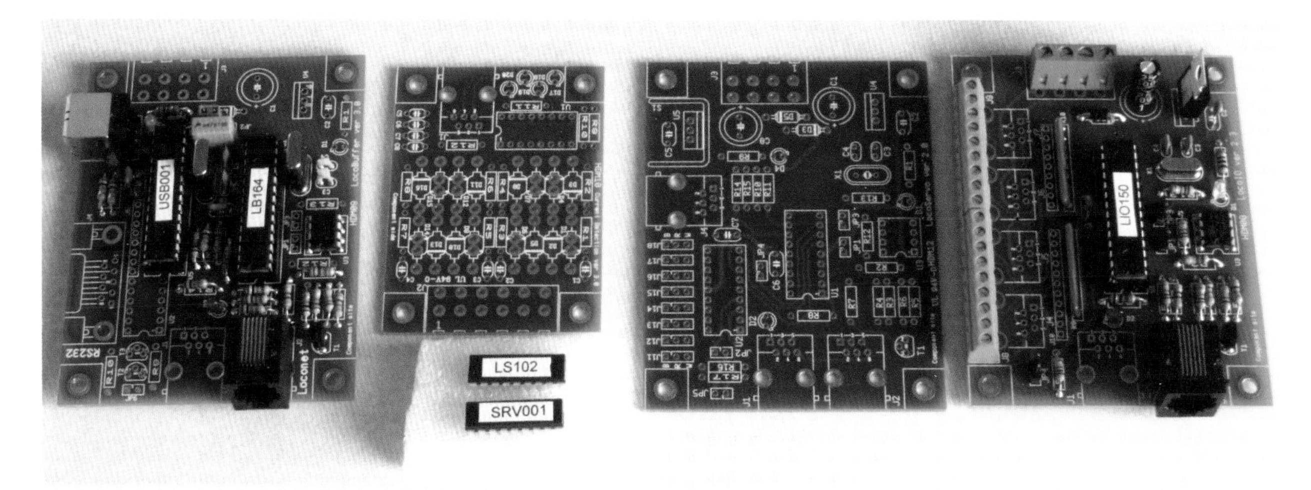

Two assembled HDL modules flank two printed circuit boards that are yet to be started. The module on the left is a USB computer interface while that on the right is a 16-channel input/output board.

output board. They can be purchased as kits, or you can buy the boards and source the components yourself.

Using these modules adds a great deal of flexibility to a layout controlled by a Digitrax command station. You can even use the computer interface unit to run a 'stand alone' Loconet without a Digitrax unit, or connect all your accessories to HDL modules and run them independently of your DCC system.

The input/output (I/O) board has 16 lines which can each be configured as an input or output of various types. They can be used for block detection, point or signal control, indicator lights and input buttons; you can create local control panels with LEDs showing which tracks are occupied and switches to control the points.

The modules are well designed and easy to build with all the necessary information being available on-line in English. Hans's website is at *users.telenet.be/deloof/*. The modules and PCBs can be obtained from Het Spoor and can be ordered on-line from *shop.hetspoor.com* (under Electronics – HDM).

Other Sources

There is a vast amount of information on self-build DCC on the Internet. Many of the designers offer printed circuit boards (PCB) which make it easier to construct the units. A search engine, such as Google, will throw up many entries if you search for things like 'Loconet modules', 'DCC circuits' and so on. A good place to start your search is on the MERG links page at *www.merg.org.uk/links.htm*, which includes links to a variety of DCC-related sites.

The Internet

The Internet is an invaluable resource for the modeller. There are many thousands of websites devoted to railways – both real and model – along with dozens of forums and groups for discussion. Naturally, many of these cover DCC.

There are also websites which cover DCC topics both for beginners and the more advanced. A good starting place is Alan Gartner's *Wiring for DCC* (*www.wiringfordcc.com*), which contains a lot of good advice. The MERG website not only includes details of their own self-build DCC kits but also a good selection of links to other relevant sites.

The major DCC manufacturers all have websites which describe their ranges and how to use the various items that they manufacture. Usually, the manuals are available for download, which is very useful if you have mislaid your copy or wish to find out what a particular item can do.

There are Yahoo groups which cover all the major DCC systems, as well as specialist interests such as DCC sound, JMRI and Railroad & Co. Start your search at *groups.yahoo.com*. Some examples are: DCCUK (*groups.yahoo.com/group/DCCUK*), for DCC users in the UK; JMRIUSERS (*groups.yahoo.com/group/jmriusers*), for people using JMRI; and DIGITRAX (*/groups.yahoo.com/group/Digitrax*), for users of Digitrax DCC systems.

Finally, there are the model railway forums, such as RMweb (*www.rmweb.co.uk*) and Model Rail Forum (*www.modelrailforum.com*), where you can discuss model railway matters online. These are great resources, as you can normally get a quick answer to a problem that has you completely stumped.

SOUTHERN
1016
HORSLEY

Chapter 8

When It All Goes Wrong

You don't need to build a new layout for DCC. A layout like Horsley takes a lot of time and skill, but you can convert it without any impact on its visual appeal. DCC decoders are usually completely hidden and much of the wiring can remain unchanged. At its simplest, you can install decoders inside the locomotives, turn all the section switches on and replace the analogue controller with a DCC version. PHOTO: MIKE WILD

It only takes a few minutes browsing the various railway modelling forums to see that people have no end of problems with DCC. If all these people are having trouble, then surely there must be something fundamentally wrong with this new-fangled technology?

But in fact DCC is hardly new-fangled. The first NMRA DCC standards were published over 15 years ago, based on work started in the late 1980s, which in turn was based on commercial designs going back well before that. And people have had similar problems with mobile phones, computers, video recorders and just about any other piece of consumer technology.

So, what do you do when it just doesn't work?

Well, if things had gone to plan then you should have designed out the problems as you built – or converted – the layout and locomotives. So ask yourself the following questions:

- Did you test the locomotives on DC before conversion to DCC?
- Did you check the back-to-back measurement on all metal wheels so that they would not short-out on points and crossings?
- Did you test the track wiring with a coin to ensure that the overload tripped when shorted out?
- Were you consistent with which rail was connected to the black and red wires?
- Did you doublecheck the wiring on your cab bus?

If you haven't done all of the above, make a note to deal with them. Those five checks will eliminate a lot of seemingly inexplicable faults that occur every so often and then just disappear again. If you still have a problem, then it will be one of two types: it has never worked or it has stopped working.

Sometimes things just don't work. Fortunately, many DCC problems are easy to solve with a bit of thought.

It Has Never Worked

It could be faulty, but unless you have purchased it second-hand from an unscrupulous seller it's unlikely. DCC equipment is mass produced and most of the time it will work straight out of the box. So first of all, check that the problem isn't you:

- Have you connected it up correctly? Check the manual. Double-check the connections – reconnect them if you are in doubt.
- Are you using the right control, address, switch, etc? Check the manual.
- Have you disrupted something when installing the new part? I had a DCC decoder that I was convinced was a dud. I had tested the locomotive on DC, taken the body off, installed the decoder and the whole thing was dead. So I took it out, replaced the blanking plug, put the body back and put it in the box to return it. Guess what? The locomotive no longer worked on DC either. When I'd fitted the decoder I'd put some pressure on the circuit board which had moved some contacts, and now nothing would work. The decoder itself was fine.
- Still stumped? Read the manual. Most manuals include a section on what to do when things don't work. The problem that you're having is probably described there.
- If you can, try the faulty part elsewhere. If it is a controller, plug it into another socket or directly into the command station. If it is a decoder, try it in another locomotive. If it works in the new location then – like my locomotive with the dodgy circuit board – the fault lies elsewhere.
- Ask for help. The retailer is your first port of call; most DCC specialist retailers are very good at solving problems. They like happy customers. Join an internet forum like RMweb (*www.rmweb.co.uk*); these are fantastic resources and can often provide you with a variety of solutions. Finally, if you are still stuck, contact the manufacturer.

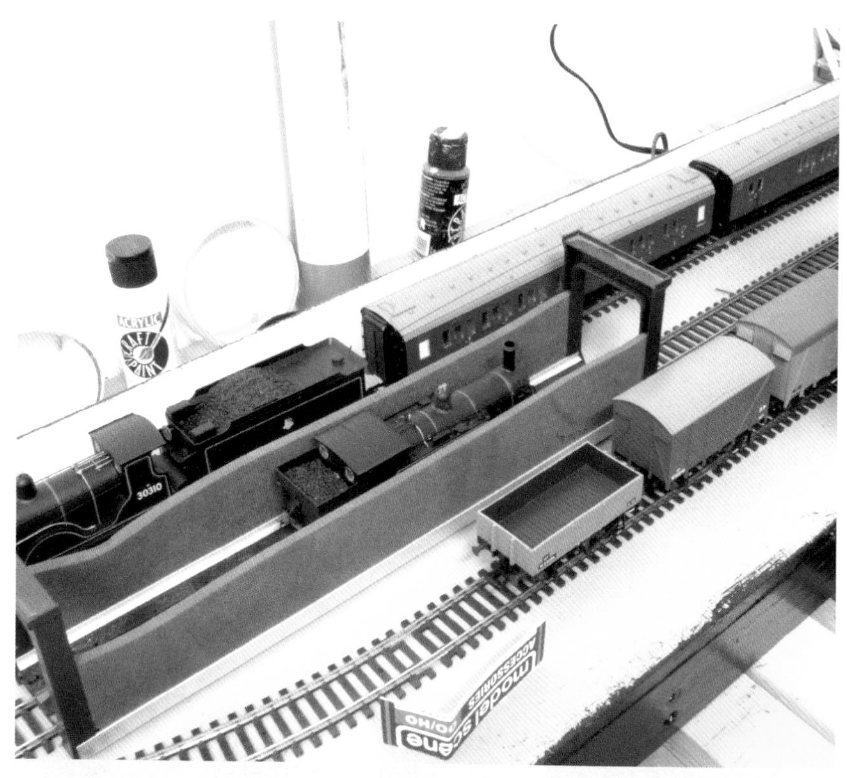

It is easy to cause a short circuit that shuts down your DCC system when putting locomotives on the rails. To move them from one end of the fiddle yard to the other on this OO-gauge branch terminus layout, I use a Peco Loco Lift. Place the Loco Lift on the end of the track, run the locomotive onto it, pick the Loco Lift up, place it at the other end of the train and you can run the locomotive off again.

It Has Stopped Working

The first rule of troubleshooting is: what happened? What changed just before the problem struck? Unfortunately, life, unlike computers, doesn't have an 'Undo' key. It is always helpful to know how things were put together and set up before they went wrong, as with the following:

- Make sure that you have some form of wiring diagram, so that you can replace the wire that's been pulled out in the correct place.
- Label and colour-code your wires so that, when faced with a number of loose ones, you know which is which.
- Make sure that you have a record of the CV settings of your locomotive before you try to remap the functions – so that F28, for example, turns the firebox glow on when travelling in reverse.
- If you have accessory decoders with special settings to operate the servos on your level crossing gates, make sure you have a note of what they are.
- Keep the manuals for your various command stations, controllers, decoders and locomotives somewhere to hand, so that you don't have to spend hours trying to find out how to set something up or open it up.

DCC makes it easy to replicate real operations. Here, a class 25 diesel is coming to the rescue of a failed DMU.

Some simple details to check

- Is it getting power? Check that the mains is on, the various leads are plugged in, there isn't a short circuit, the locomotive is on the rails and there is power going to them.
- You can't run a train on the programming track. You program on the programming track.
- Has a rail gap closed up? Rail gaps, if not fitted with an insulating rail joiner, are not permanent! They will close up due to temperature and humidity changes and cause all kinds of misery. A 16V bulb or multi-meter set to AC Volts will quickly establish if you have power where it shouldn't be.
- Has a rail gap opened up? If a length of rail doesn't have its own feed wire, then it is reliant on current from a neighbouring rail. Heat, dirt, vibration can all lead to a poor contact and loss of DCC in the section concerned. Again, a 16V bulb or multi-meter set to AC Volts will quickly establish if you don't have power where it should be.
- Are you using the right address? I have a DCC system that defaults back to address 1 after a short. More often than not, I forget this and wonder why my locomotive isn't responding.
- Check the track with a coin. If the overload trip does not cut the power

then you have a wiring problem.

- Check the back-to-back measurement of any metal-wheeled stock involved and, ideally, the gauge of the track.
- Locomotives and stock sitting on points and across isolating gaps can cause numerous problems, with the current going into all sorts of places where it shouldn't be.
- Still stumped? Try putting everything back as it was before the problem. If that fails, ask for help. The retailer is your first port of call; most DCC specialists are very good at solving problems. They like happy customers. Join an internet forum like RMweb (*www.rmweb.co.uk*); these are fantastic resources and can often provide you with a variety of solutions. Finally, if you are still stuck, contact the manufacturer.

That Old Chestnut

There are some problems that crop up regularly; here is a selection of them.

I can't program or read any decoders – my system says, 'not found/incorrectly connected/Err02,' or something similar.
Your programming track and/or locomotive wheels are probably dirty. If they are clean, then your wiring between the booster and programming track has too high a resistance – probably due to a bad connection or soldered joint. You can confirm this by running wires straight from the booster unit to the programming track and attaching direct to the rails, using crocodile clips.

I can run analogue (DC) locomotives, but DCC-installed locomotives do not work.
Your wiring between the booster and layout has too high a resistance – probably due to a bad connection or soldered joint. You can confirm this by running wires straight from the booster unit to a length of track and attaching direct to the rails, using crocodile clips.

All trains stopped suddenly.
There is a short circuit somewhere, or else someone has triggered the emergency stop. Check the command station or handset – it should tell you which it is. Have you run a locomotive up to a point that is set against it? If you can isolate sections of your layout, do so to try to locate it. Remove the locomotives one by one, to see if any of them are causing the short circuit. For an emergency stop, simply reset it.

If you use the same DCC supply to power both the track and the accessory units driving twin-solenoid point motors, check that operating the points does not cause the problem. If it does, connect the accessory decoders to a separate booster.

One or more locomotives have suddenly started to run away and won't respond to the controller.
Turn the command station off for a while and then back on again. There are two probable causes. Most likely is that a mains fluctuation (known as a 'brownout', where the voltage drops) has upset the command station's processor. Turning it off will reset the processor. The other is that one of the locomotive decoders has suffered a similar problem and is interfering with the DCC signal.

If you have a locomotive that is consistently running away, then first of all try turning the DC mode off in CV29 – Bit 2; some decoders seem to be temperamental when this is set on. If it fails then try a decoder reset; it could well be that a power supply problem has corrupted the dceoder's settings. Resetting a decoder normally involves writing a value to CV 8, the manufacturer ID. Check the decoder's instructions to find out how to do it.

The controller keeps on cutting out.
If you are running a lot of trains when it happens, then the railway is taking more power than the system can supply. Reduce the number of locomotives and accessories in use. If this cures the problem then you need to install one or more booster units. It is possible that something which has wheels that have an incorrect back-to-back measurement is shorting out as it crosses over points.

DCC is not restricted to any particular branch of railway modelling, but is suitable for all scales, gauges and formats – from ready-to-run 'G' gauge in the garden to kit-built 009 locomotives, running on hand-laid track like this.

My locomotive won't respond to the controller.
Check that you are using the correct decoder address! Have you entered the address correctly? Have you recently changed the loco's address and are entering the old one?

Check that there is power to the track. Is the locomotive in a siding that has been isolated by a power routing point?

Has it been removed from a consist? Maybe the consist information has not been cancelled in the decoder.

Check that no wires have come loose in the locomotive.

Is the command station set for a 128-speed step operation but the decoder does not support this mode?

If you have changed a CV setting since the locomotive last worked – change it back.

My locomotive just stopped and now won't respond to the controller.
Is the track dirty? Are the locomotive wheels dirty?

The decoder might have overheated. Remove the locomotive from the track and let it cool down before trying to run the locomotive again.

The decoder CVs may have been corrupted. Check them on the programming track and, if they seem strange, perform a decoder reset (see the decoder's manual).

My locomotive's headlight and other functions are controllable, but it won't run.
This sometimes happens when you clear a consist but, for some reason, the decoder misses the command. Set CV19 to 0 to clear the consist information.

The headlight won't switch on.
The command station and decoder are in different speed-step modes. Alternatively, is the headlight wired to the correct function output? Has the headlight bulb blown? Is there a headlight fitted?

All my locos are running erratically.
Clean the track thoroughly. Dirty track can impair the DCC signal. If you use the same DCC supply to power both the track and

Modern passenger services are performed by multiple units; often two or more sets are coupled together for all or part of the journey. DCC's ability to control locomotives – individually or in multiple – allows this type of operation to be replicated in model form.

accessory units driving twin-solenoid point motors, check that operating the points is not causing the problem. If it is, connect the accessory decoders to a separate booster,

One locomotive travels in the wrong direction.
The wires to the motor brushes in the locomotive have been reversed. This can be corrected, without rewiring the loco, by setting bit 0 of the basic configuration register (CV 29) to 1.

A locomotive did not respond to a function key press.
Try again. The locomotive may have been on dirty track and may not have received the command. Is that function valid for that locomotive and decoder? Check that no wires have come loose in the locomotive.

The headlight goes on and off as the locomotive changes speed.
You are operating a locomotive with an older 14-step decoder in the 28-step mode.

My locomotive won't run on an analogue (DC) layout
Check that the DC mode bit is set in the basic configuration register (CV 29, Bit 2).

Appendix A

Major Manufacturers and Suppliers

A&H Models
UK distributor of Lenz DCC equipment.
95 High Street, Brackley, NN13 7BW.
Tel: 01280 701410
www.aandh-models.co.uk

Bachmann
Manufacturer of DCC equipment and models.
Moat Way, Barwell, LE9 8EY.
www.bachmann.co.uk

Bromsgrove Models
Supplier of Hornby, Digitrax, ESU, MRC, NCE QSI, Soundtrax, TCS, Umelec and Zimo DCC equipment.
www.bromsgrovemodels.co.uk

DCC Supplies
Supplier of Digitrax, Hornby, ESU, Lenz, MRC, NCE QSI, Soundtrax, TCS and Zimo DCC equipment and ESU sound decoders with UK locomotive sounds.
Unit 17A, Top Barn Business Centre, Worcester Road, Holt Heath, WR6 6NH.
Tel: 0845 224 1601
www.dccsupplies.com

Express Models
Supplier of lighting kits.
65 Conway Drive, Shepshed, Loughborough, LE12 9PP.
Tel: 01509 829008
email: sales@expressmodels.co.uk
www.expressmodels.co.uk

GamesOnTrack
Produce the GTCommand voice control system.
Uhresøvej 35, Dk 7500 Holstebro, Denmark.
email: Admin@gamesontrack.com
www.ganesontrack.com

Gaugemaster
UK importer of MRC DCC equipment.
Gaugemaster House, Ford Road, Arundel, BN18 0BN.
Tel: 01903 884321
www.gaugemaster.com

HDM
Hans de Loof – designer of electronic modules for use with Loconet.
email : hans.deloof@compaqnet.be
users.telenet.be/deloof

Het Spoor
Supplier of HDM electronic module kits for Loconet.
T SPOOR Parkstraat 90 3053 Haasrode Tel: 016/40.70.42
email: info.spoor@telenet.be
Parkstraat 90, 3053 Hassrode, Belgium
email: info.spoor@telenet.be
shop.hetspoor.com

Hornby plc
Manufacturer of DCC equipment and models.
Westwood Industrial Estate, Margate, CT9 4JX.
Tel: 01843 233535
www.hornby.com

Howes Models
Suppliers of ESU sound decoders with UK locomotive sounds.
12 Banbury Road, Kidlington, OX5 2BT.
Tel: 01865 848000
www.howesmodels.co.uk

M.G. Sharp
Suppliers of Bachmann, Lenz, TCS, Digitrax, NCE & Roco DCC equipment.
712 Attercliffe Road, Sheffield.
Tel: 01142 440851
www.mgsharp.com

Maplin Electronics Ltd.
Supplier of wire, electronic components, solder and tools.
Stores nationwide.
Tel: 0870 4296000
www.maplin.co.uk

MERG Model Electronic Railway Group
Society for people interested in using electronics with model railways. Have their own range of self-build DCC items available as kits.
MERG Membership Secretary, 40 Compton Avenue, Poole, Dorset, BH14 8PY.
www.merg.org.uk

Modellautobahnen
Supplier of DCCar decoders and equipment for Faller CarSystem vehicles. Although the website is in German they can answer email queries in English.
www.shop.modellautobahnen.de/
Claus Ichman, the developer of DCCar, has information in German on his own website:
www.modelleisenbahn-claus.de/

Rapid Electronics Ltd.
Supplier of wire, electronic components, solder and tools.
Severalls Lane, Colchester, C04 5JS.
Tel: 01206 751166
www.rapidonline.com

SPROG DCC
Small DCC controller ideal for use with JMRI DecoderPro on a portable programming/test track.
31 The Gables, Haddenham, Aylesbury, Bucks, HP17 8AD. (No callers.)
email: sprog@sprog-dcc.co.uk
www.sprog-dcc.co.uk

South West Digital Ltd.
Supplier of ESU Lok-Sound decoders with UK locomotive sounds.
1 Savernake Road, Weston-super-Mare, BS22 9HQ.
Tel: 01934 517303
www.southwestdigital.co.uk

Sunningwell Command Control Ltd.
Supplier of Digitrax and Soundtrax DCC equipment.
PO Box 381, Abingdon, OX13 6YB.
Tel/Fax: 01865 730455
www.scc4dcc.co.uk

Squires Model & Craft Tools
Supplier of wire, electronic components, solder and tools.
100 London Road, Bognor Regis, PO21 1DD.
Tel: 01243 842424
Fax: 01243 842525.

ZTC Controls
Manufacturer of DCC equipment.
PO Box 4454, Yeovil, BA20 9EZ.
Tel: 01963 441219
www.ztccontrols.co.uk

Appendix B

CVs and What They Do

CV 1 Primary Locomotive Address

As supplied, all decoders have CV 1 set to 3. This means that the decoder will respond to locomotive number 3. To change the locomotive's address, you change the value of CV 1 to a number between 1 and 127. If the decoder and your base station support extended addressing, then the numbers 128 through to 9999 can be used – but there is a special method to do this.

CV 2 Start Voltage

This sets the voltage that will correspond to the first speed step. Decoders vary as to how the value is interpreted, so you should check the instructions but the normal range is 0 to 255. This value should be set as low as possible to just about keep the locomotive moving. In a perfect world it would be set to zero, but the friction of the locomotive's mechanism means that the optimum value will be larger than that. The correct figure is best established by experimentation and could well be different for apparently identical locomotives. A high figure, over 70, would indicate that the locomotive mechanism could do with some remedial attention.

CV 3 Acceleration Rate

This determines how quickly the locomotive will accelerate. Large freight locomotives will normally take longer to reach a given speed than an express locomotive and this enables you to replicate these differences. Many analogue controllers have similar features, usually labelled 'momentum'.

The rate of acceleration is worked out as CV3 x 0.896 / Number of speed steps seconds per speed step.

For example: if CV3 = 2 and number of speed steps =128 then the acceleration rate is 2 x 0.896 / 128 = 0.014 seconds per step. So to accelerate from 0 to half-speed (64 steps) would take 64 x 0.014 = 0.896 seconds.

Or: if CV3=100 and number of speed steps = 28 then the acceleration rate is 100 x 0.896 / 28 = 3.2 seconds per step. So to accelerate from 0 to quarter speed (7 steps) would take 7 x 3.2 = 22.4 seconds.

If CV3 is set to zero then the change in speed is immediate.

CV 4 Braking Rate

This determines how quickly the locomotive will decelerate. It works in exactly the same way as CV 3 Acceleration Rate (above), but can have a different value. It normally takes longer to stop a train than to get it going.

CV 5 Top Speed

This is used to limit the top speed of the locomotive. Most model locomotives can go much faster than the real thing. By setting CV5, so that the locomotive is travelling at a slower top speed, you not only make operations more realistic but enable the speed steps to have more effect.

The default value is the maximum of 255 and allows the full voltage to reach the motor. Decreasing this value reduces the maximum voltage reaching the motor. For OO gauge, the DCC track power is normally 14 to 16 Volts. Once this has been converted from AC to DC by the decoder, the maximum voltage available to the motor will be in the region 11 to 13 Volts. Typically, for every 10 you subtract from CV5 you will reduce the maximum voltage by about 0.5V.

CV 6 Speed Curve Modifier

This is used to set the motor voltage at the middle of the range of speed steps. This allows you to tailor the voltage output to suit the locomotive's motor. Setting a low value means that the low speed steps will be closely spaced, whilst the high ones are farther apart. Setting a high value has the opposite effect. The combination of CV 2 (Start Voltage), CV 5 (Top Speed) and CV 6 give great flexibility in determining how a locomotive will respond to the range of speed steps.

The default value of 0 indicates that the Speed Curve Modifier is not being used. Setting it to the mid-range value of 128 will have the same effect. For OO gauge decoders, the motor voltage at the middle speed step is typically 6V. For every 10 that you add or subtract from 128, you will increase or decrease the mid-point voltage by about 0.5V.

CV 7 Manufacturer Version Number

You cannot change this value. It is set by the manufacturer and indicates the version of the decoder that you have. It has no effect on the performance of the locomotive.

CV 8 Manufacturer ID Number

You cannot change this value. It is set by the manufacturer and indicates the identification number issued to the manufacturer by the NMRA. It has no effect on the performance of the locomotive.

Most decoders also offer the facility to reset all the CV values to their default setting by writing a specific value to CV8. Their value varies from decoder to decoder so it is necessary to check the manual to establish what it is. A reset is useful if a decoder starts to misbehave, which can be caused by a power fluctuation which has resulted in some of the CVs being corrupted.

CV 9 Total PWM Period

If the decoder uses Pulse Width Modulation (PWM) for the motor output, then this CV sets the length of the pulses. If your decoder uses PWM, then you should consult the decoder's documentation to establish suitable settings. A value of 0 indicates that PWM is either not available on the decoder or is not in use.

CV 10 EMF Feedback Cutout

If the decoder uses back-EMF to regulate the motor speed, then this CV allows you to set the speed step above which it is no longer used. Back-EMF is a way of measuring how fast a motor is running. This can be used to establish if the motor needs more or less voltage to maintain the desired speed. It ensures that trains do not slow down when climbing hills or run away when descending them. It is also of great help in getting motors to run slowly for shunting operations. Many analogue controllers have similar features usually labelled 'feedback'. A value of 0 indicates that EMF feedback is either not available on the decoder or is not being used.

CV 11 Packet Timeout

Gives the maximum period of time that the decoder will maintain its current speed without receiving a valid message from the command station.

CV 12 Power Source Conversion

Defines how the locomotive is powered if the decoder address (CV 1) is set to zero. This is chiefly provided for compatibility with older command control systems such as Hornby's Zero-1 and you are unlikely to need to amend it.

CV 13 Alternate Mode Function Status

Defines which functions (F1 – F8) can be controlled if the decoder is operating on a different command control system (as set by CV 12). You are unlikely to need to amend this value.

CV 14 Alternate Mode Function 2 Status

Defines which functions (F9 – F12 and FL) can be controlled if the decoder is operating on a different command control system (as set by CV 12). You are unlikely to need to amend this value.

CV 17/18 Extended Address

When a locomotive decoder is set up to use extended (4-digit) addressing, these two variables contain the address. (To establish if extended addressing is in use, you need to check bit 5 of CV 29.) CV17 is the first byte of the address and CV18 the second. CV17 must have a binary value between 11000000 and 11100111 inclusive to be valid.

CV 19 Consist Address

Where the locomotive is in a consist, this CV indicates the consist's address. Bit 7 indicates the relative direction within the consist (0 indicates normal operation, 1 indicates that the locomotive is in reverse when the consist is moving forwards). Bits 6 to 0 indicate the consist's address. A value of zero indicates that the unit is not part of a consist.

CV 21 Consist Address Active for F1 – F8

Where the locomotive is in a consist, this CV defines whether functions F1 through to F8 will respond to instructions sent to both the locomotive and the consist or just the locomotive. Each bit is used to control a function. A value of 0 indicates that the function will only respond to instructions sent to the locomotive's address. A value of 1 indicates that the function will respond to instructions sent to both the locomotive's and consist's addresses. F1 is controlled by bit 0, F2 by bit 1, F3 by bit 4 and so on up to F8, which is controlled by bit 7. Using CV21 and 22 enable you to select which functions are applied to the consist as a whole or individual locomotives within it, such as headlights on the front locomotive and tail lights on the rear one.

CV 22 Consist Address Active for F9 – F12 and FL

Where the locomotive is in a consist, this CV defines whether functions F9 through to F12 and FL will respond to instructions sent to both the locomotive and the consist, or just the locomotive. Each bit is used to control a function. A value of 0 indicates that the function will only respond to instructions sent to the locomotive's address. A value of 1 indicates that the function will respond to instructions sent to both the locomotive's and consist's addresses. FL in the forward direction is controlled by bit 0, FL in reverse by bit 1, F9 by bit 4 and so on up to F12, which is controlled by bit 5.

CV 23 Acceleration Adjustment

This value affects the normal acceleration rate for the locomotive set in CV 3, 'Acceleration Rate'. The intended use is to enable you to change the momentum of the train to simulate differing loads, while retaining the normal value unchanged. Thus the adjustment could be 0 for a light engine and 100 for a long mineral train.

The value can range from 0 to 127 set by bits 0 to 6, with the adjustment being either positive or negative depending on the value set in bit 7 (0=positive,

1=negative). The adjusted acceleration rate is calculated as: CV 23 * 0.896/Number of speed steps in use.

CV 24 Deceleration Adjustment
This value affects the normal deceleration rate for the locomotive set in CV 3, 'Acceleration Rate'. The intended use is to enable you to change the momentum of the train to simulate differing loads whilst retaining the normal value unchanged. Thus the adjustment could be 0 for a light engine and 100 for a long mineral train.

The value can range from 0 to 127 set by bits 0 to 6, with the adjustment being either positive or negative depending on the value set in bit 7 (0=positive, 1=negative). The adjusted acceleration rate is calculated as: CV 23 * 0.896/Number of speed steps in use.

CV 25 Speed Table / Mid-Range Speed Step
This value is used either to indicate which preset speed table is to be used or the particular speed step that will produce the mid-range motor speed. A value of 0 or 1 indicates that the CV is not being used or is not available on the decoder. A value of 2 indicates a linear curve. The motor speed will increase by an equal amount for each speed step. A value between 3 and 127 indicates which of the built-in speed tables will be used. A value between 128 and 154 defines which of the 28 speed steps will make the motor run at half-speed. 128 is equivalent to step 1, 129 to step 2, 130 to step 3, through to 154 for position 26. It is not possible to set the mid-range speed step to steps 0 or 27. If the decoder operates with 14 speed steps then the value will be divided by two.

CV 27 Automatic Stopping Configuration
This CV is under re-evaluation by the NMRA and may be amended. It is used to define the conditions that will cause the decoder to automatically stop the locomotive.

Bit 0 – Enable/disable automatic stopping in the presence of an asymmetrical DCC signal which is more positive on the right rail (when facing forwards). A value of 0 indicates 'disabled' or that the function is not available on the decoder, a value of 1 'enabled'.

Bit 1 – Enable/disable automatic stopping in the presence of an asymmetrical DCC signal, which is more positive on the left rail (when facing forwards). A value of 0 indicates 'disabled' or that the function is not available on the decoder, a value of 1 'enabled'.

An asymmetrical DCC signal is one that reaches a higher positive voltage than negative, or vice versa. It is used to create sections of track that automatically slow a train to a halt, for example in front of signals or on dead-end sidings.

Bit 2 – Enable/disable automatic stopping in the presence of a signal-controlled cut-out signal. A value of 0 indicates 'disabled' or that the function is not available on the decoder, a value of 1 'enabled'. This is a special DCC signal that tells all locomotives that receive it to slow to a stop. Like asymmetrical DCC signals, it is normally used to stop trains overrunning red signals.

Bit 3 – Not currently used.

Bit 4 Enable/disable automatic stopping in the presence of forward polarity DC. A value of 0 indicates 'disabled' or that the function is not available on the decoder, a value of 1 'enabled'. This is used to override the decoder's normal behaviour if it finds itself on a DC-powered track section. Normally, if the DC voltage will cause the locomotive to move forwards it will adjust its speed to match the DC voltage. If this bit is set to 1 then, instead of changing speed, the locomotive will stop.

Bits 6 and 7 – Not currently used.

CV 28 Bi-directional Communication Configuration
This CV is under re-evaluation by the NMRA and may be amended. It is used to define the way that the decoder handles bi-directional (RailCom) communications.

Bit 0 – Enable/disable unsolicited decoder-initiated transmissions. A value of 0 indicates 'disabled' or that the function is not available on the decoder, a value of 1 'enabled'. Setting the value to 1 indicates that the decoder can start communications rather than waiting for something to ask it for information.

Bit 1 – Enable/disable initiated broadcast transmissions using asymmetrical DCC signal. A value of 0 indicates 'disabled' or that the function is not available on the decoder, a value of 1 'enabled'.

Bit 2 – Enable/disable initiated broadcast transmissions using a signal-controlled signal. A value of 0 indicates 'disabled' or that the function is not available on the decoder, a value of 1 'enabled'.

Bits 3, 4, 5, 6 and 7 – Not currently used

CV 29 Basic Configuration Register
This variable contains a number of different settings that do not justify their own unique CV.

Bit 0 Direction of Travel Set to 0 = Normal. Locomotive moves forward when controller is set to forward.

Set to 1 = Reversed. Locomotive has either been wired incorrectly or it is required to operate this locomotive in reverse. For example, the tail locomotive of a pair of BR Class 20 diesels.

Bit 1 Speed Steps
Set to 0 = Operates with 14 or 27 speed steps. Used when the decoder can support 28/128 steps but the Command Station cannot.
Set to 1 = Operates with 28 or 128 speed steps.

Bit 2 Analogue Mode
Set to 0 = Locomotive will only respond to DCC signals. It will not operate on analogue layouts.
Set to 1 = Locomotive can be operated on both DCC and analogue layouts.

Bit 3 Bi-directional Communications
Set to '0' if bi-directional communications are not in use or the decoder is not designed to use them. Set to '1' if bi-directional communications are in use.

Bit 4 Speed Table
Set to 0 = Uses default speed table (set in CV2 and CV5).
Set to 1 = Uses special speed table set in CV66 to 95.

Bit 5 Address System
Set to 0 = Uses base address (set in CV1).
Set to 1 = Uses extended address (set in CV17 and CV18).

Bit 6 No current use.

Bit 7 Decoder type.
Set to '0' for multi-function decoder (motor and function outputs).
Set to '1' for accessory decoder (no motor control).

To set or decode the values see the notes on Binary/Hex Conversion on pages 152-4.

CV 30 Error Information
You cannot change this value. It is set by the decoder if there is a problem or error. Apart from a zero value indicating 'no error', the values are specified by the decoder manufacturer. Refer to the decoder's documentation to establish what any codes mean. It has no effect on the performance of the locomotive.

CV 31 Decoder Sub-Address
This CV is under re-evaluation by the NMRA and may be amended. It is used to differentiate different decoders in the same locomotive or multiple unit. For example, you might have a decoder in each car of a multiple unit to control lighting, or you might have two decoders in a locomotive to provide extra function outputs. Each decoder will respond to the same locomotive address. The sub-address is used when the settings on a particular decoder need to be changed in isolation from the other decoders.

Bits 0-3 contain the decoder's sub address. If the value is 0 then the decoder has no sub-address. The maximum number of decoders that can be operated individually on one address using sub-addresses is 7.

Bits 4-7 Not currently used.

CV 32 Decoder Sub-address Flag
This CV is under re-evaluation by the NMRA and may be amended. It is used to indicate which of the sub-decoders respond to queries from other DCC accessories.

Bit 0 Used to designate the decoder which will respond to bi-directional communication requests. If the value is 1 then the decoder will process bi-directional communications. If the value is set to 0 it will not. Only one decoder in the locomotive or multiple unit should have this bit set to 1.

Bit 1 Used to designate the decoder which will respond to long-form CV access instructions. If the value is set to 1 then the decoder will respond to these instructions, if the value is set to 0 it will not. Only one decoder in the locomotive or multiple unit should have this bit set to 1.

Bits 2-7 Not currently used

CV 33-46 Function Output Locations
These CVs allow you to allocate which function on your cab controls a specific function output on the decoder. This allows you to reallocate the function outputs to suit your installation. For example, if you have installed 2 x 4-function decoders in a locomotive you can specify that decoder 1's outputs respond to FL(f) (forward lights), F1, F12 and F2, while decoder 2's outputs respond to FL(r) (reverse lights), F3, F11 and F2. In addition, you can make a single function key control more than one function output on the decoder, which is useful if you need to operate something that draws too high a current for a single output.

Each CV configures a different function. The CV value indicates which outputs the function will control. Each bit corresponds to one potential output.

Bit 0 – FL(f), Bit 1 – FL(r), Bit 2 – F1, Bit 3 – F2 and so on up to Bit 14 – F12. Bits 15 and 16 are not used.

CV	Function	Default Value
CV33	FL(f) Forward headlight	0000000000000001
CV34	FL(r) Reverse headlight	0000000000000010
CV35	F1	0000000000000100
CV36	F2	0000000000001000
CV37	F3	0000000000010000
CV38	F4	0000000000100000
CV39	F5	0000000001000000
CV40	F6	0000000010000000
CV41	F7	0000000100000000
CV42	F8	0000001000000000
CV43	F9	0000010000000000
CV44	F10	0000100000000000
CV45	F11	0001000000000000
CV46	F12	0010000000000000

So to change the normal F1 output on a decoder to respond to F5, you would need to make the following changes:

CV35 F1 key – change from the default value of 0000000000000100 (operates F1 output) to 0000000000000000 (operates no output)

CV39 F5 key – change from the default value of 0000000001000000 (operates F5 output) to 0000000000000100 (operates F1 output).

To change a decoder so that the F1 and F2 outputs both responded to the F1 key, you would need to make the following changes:

CV35 F1 key – change from the default value of 0000000000000100 (operates F1 output) to 0000000000001100 (operates F2 and F1outputs).

CV36 F2 key – change from the default value of 0000000000001000 (operates F2 output) to 0000000000000000 (operates no output).

CV 65 Kick Start

Specifies the extra voltage kick that will be supplied to the motor when moving from stop to the first speed step. This is used to overcome the mechanical resistance that many older motors have when starting to turn. The extra voltage jolts them into motion and is then removed so that they run at the specified speed.

CV 66 Forward Trim

Specifies a factor to be applied to the voltage level when the locomotive is moving forwards. This is used to make the locomotive travel faster (or slower) when going forwards than it would normally for any given speed step. If the value is 0 then no forward trim is applied. For values between 1 and 255 the adjustment is calculated as Normal Speed * (CV66/128). So a value of 128 would cause the forward and normal speeds to be the same. A value less than 128 would cause the forward speed to be less than the normal speed and a value greater than 128 would cause the forward speed to be greater than the normal speed.

This CV is of great use when running locomotives double-headed as it allows you to adjust their individual speeds to match without having to overwrite the normal decoder settings.

CV 67-94 Special Speed Table

Allows you to tailor the speed of the locomotive at each speed step to suit your requirements. As not all motors perform in the same way, you can use the speed table to make them perform consistently. Some motors require larger changes in voltage at slow speeds. By changing the output for each speed step, you can optimise each decoder's performance to suit the motor to which it is connected.

CV 95 Reverse Trim

Specifies a factor to be applied to the voltage level when the locomotive is moving backwards. This is used to make the locomotive travel faster (or slower) when going backwards than it would normally for any given speed step. If the value is 0 then no reverse trim is applied. For values between 1 and 255 the adjustment is calculated as Normal Speed * (CV95 / 128). So a value of 128 would cause the backward and normal speeds to be the same. A value less than 128 would cause the backward speed to be less than the normal speed and a value greater than 128 would cause the backward speed to be greater than the normal speed. This CV is of great use when running locomotives double-headed, as it allows you to adjust their individual speeds to match without having to overwrite the normal decoder settings.

CV 105 & 106 User Identification

These CVs are reserved for the locomotive's owner to store identification information. In the US, the recommendation is to use your NMRA membership number. There is no equivalent in the UK, but selecting a random value to use for all your locomotives might enable you to prove ownership if it were ever necessary.

Appendix C

Binary/Hexadecimal/Decimal Conversion

Where a number of variables are combined in one CV, the DCC system uses a binary number system. Depending on which system you use, you may need to enter the values as binary, hexadecimal or decimal numbers.

Binary Entry

This is simply the value (1 or 0) for each value in turn, starting from bit 7 and running to bit 0. For example suppose you wish to enter the following setting:
Bit 0 = 0, Bit 1= 1, Bit 2 = 1, Bit 3 = 0, Bit 4 = 0, Bit 5 = 0, Bit 6 = 0, Bit 7 = 0.
First you would reverse the order:
Bit 7 = 0, Bit 6 = 0, Bit 5 = 0, Bit 4 = 0, Bit 3 = 0, Bit 2 = 1, Bit 1 = 1, Bit 0 = 0.
Then you would enter 00000110 on the keypad.

Hexadecimal Entry

Some systems require the binary entry to be converted to hexadecimal. This is a number system based on 0-15 instead of 0-9.
An 8-bit binary number converts to two hexadecimal digits

Binary	Hexadecimal
0000	0
0001	1
0010	2
0011	3
0100	4
0101	5
0110	6
0111	7
1000	8
1001	9
1010	A
1011	B
1100	C
1101	D
1110	E
1111	F

Thus our binary number of 0000 0110 would be entered as 06. A binary number of 1101 0011 would be entered as D3.

Decimal Entry

Some systems require a decimal entry. In this case, the 8-digit binary number converts to a number between 0 and 255. The value can be calculated as follows:

Bit 7 x 128 + Bit 6 x 64 + Bit 5 x 32 + Bit 4 x 16 + Bit 3 x 8 + Bit 2 x 4 + Bit 1 x 2 + Bit 0.

The final value will never be greater than 255. Using our binary number of 00000110 we would calculate:

128 x 0 + 64 x 0 + 32 x 0 + 16 x 0 + 8 x 0 + 4 x 1 + 2 x 1 + 0 = 6.

So the value would be entered as 6.

As you can see from the table below, it is very important to know which type of number your system wants, as 10 is very different in binary, hexadecimal and decimal. The table makes a very handy conversion tool from one number system to another.

Binary	Hexadecimal	Decimal	Binary	Hexadecimal	Decimal	Binary	Hexadecimal	Decimal
00000000	00	0	00101101	2D	45	01011010	5A	90
00000001	01	1	00101110	2E	46	01011011	5B	91
00000010	02	2	00101111	2F	47	01011100	5C	92
00000011	03	3	00110000	30	48	01011101	5D	93
00000100	04	4	00110001	31	49	01011110	5E	94
00000101	05	5	00110010	32	50	01011111	5F	95
00000110	06	6	00110011	33	51	01100000	60	96
00000111	07	7	00110100	34	52	01100001	61	97
00001000	08	8	00110101	35	53	01100010	62	98
00001001	09	9	00110110	36	54	01100011	63	99
00001010	0A	10	00110111	37	55	01100100	64	100
00001011	0B	11	00111000	38	56	01100101	65	101
00001100	0C	12	00111001	39	57	01100110	66	102
00001101	0D	13	00111010	3A	58	01100111	67	103
00001110	0E	14	00111011	3B	59	01101000	68	104
00001111	0F	15	00111100	3C	60	01101001	69	105
00010000	10	16	00111101	3D	61	01101010	6A	106
00010001	11	17	00111110	3E	62	01101011	6B	107
00010010	12	18	00111111	3F	63	01101100	6C	108
00010011	13	19	01000000	40	64	01101101	6D	109
00010100	14	20	01000001	41	65	01101110	6E	110
00010101	15	21	01000010	42	66	01101111	6F	111
00010110	16	22	01000011	43	67	01110000	70	112
00010111	17	23	01000100	44	68	01110001	71	113
00011000	18	24	01000101	45	69	01110010	72	114
00011001	19	25	01000110	46	70	01110011	73	115
00011010	1A	26	01000111	47	71	01110100	74	116
00011011	1B	27	01001000	48	72	01110101	75	117
00011100	1C	28	01001001	49	73	01110110	76	118
00011101	1D	29	01001010	4A	74	01110111	77	119
00011110	1E	30	01001011	4B	75	01111000	78	120
00011111	1F	31	01001100	4C	76	01111001	79	121
00100000	20	32	01001101	4D	77	01111010	7A	122
00100001	21	33	01001110	4E	78	01111011	7B	123
00100010	22	34	01001111	4F	79	01111100	7C	124
00100011	23	35	01010000	50	80	01111101	7D	125
00100100	24	36	01010001	51	81	01111110	7E	126
00100101	25	37	01010010	52	82	01111111	7F	127
00100110	26	38	01010011	53	83	10000000	80	128
00100111	27	39	01010100	54	84	10000001	81	129
00101000	28	40	01010101	55	85	10000010	82	130
00101001	29	41	01010110	56	86	10000011	83	131
00101010	2A	42	01010111	57	87	10000100	84	132
00101011	2B	43	01011000	58	88	10000101	85	133
00101100	2C	44	01011001	59	89	10000110	86	134

Binary	Hexadecimal	Decimal
10000111	87	135
10001000	88	136
10001001	89	137
10001010	8A	138
10001011	8B	139
10001100	8C	140
10001101	8D	141
10001110	8E	142
10001111	8F	143
10010000	90	144
10010001	91	145
10010010	92	146
10010011	93	147
10010100	94	148
10010101	95	149
10010110	96	150
10010111	97	151
10011000	98	152
10011001	99	153
10011010	9A	154
10011011	9B	155
10011100	9C	156
10011101	9D	157
10011110	9E	158
10011111	9F	159
10100000	A0	160
10100001	A1	161
10100010	A2	162
10100011	A3	163
10100100	A4	164
10100101	A5	165
10100110	A6	166
10100111	A7	167
10101000	A8	168
10101001	A9	169
10101010	AA	170
10101011	AB	171
10101100	AC	172
10101101	AD	173
10101110	AE	174
10101111	AF	175
10110000	B0	176
10110001	B1	177
10110010	B2	178
10110011	B3	179
10110100	B4	180
10110101	B5	181
10110110	B6	182
10110111	B7	183
10111000	B8	184
10111001	B9	185
10111010	BA	186
10111011	BB	187
10111100	BC	188
10111101	BD	189
10111110	BE	190
10111111	BF	191
11000000	C0	192
11000001	C1	193
11000010	C2	194
11000011	C3	195
11000100	C4	196
11000101	C5	197
11000110	C6	198
11000111	C7	199
11001000	C8	200
11001001	C9	201
11001010	CA	202
11001011	CB	203
11001100	CC	204
11001101	CD	205
11001110	CE	206
11001111	CF	207
11010000	D0	208
11010001	D1	209
11010010	D2	210
11010011	D3	211
11010100	D4	212
11010101	D5	213
11010110	D6	214
11010111	D7	215
11011000	D8	216
11011001	D9	217
11011010	DA	218
11011011	DB	219
11011100	DC	220
11011101	DD	221
11011110	DE	222
11011111	DF	223
11100000	E0	224
11100001	E1	225
11100010	E2	226
11100011	E3	227
11100100	E4	228
11100101	E5	229
11100110	E6	230
11100111	E7	231
11101000	E8	232
11101001	E9	233
1110101	EA	234
11101011	EB	235
11101100	EC	236
11101101	ED	237
11101110	EE	238
11101111	EF	239
11110000	F0	240
11110001	F1	241
11110010	F2	242
11110011	F3	243
11110100	F4	244
11110101	F5	245
11110110	F6	246
11110111	F7	247
11111000	F8	248
11111001	F9	249
11111010	FA	250
11111011	FB	251
11111100	FC	252
11111101	FD	253
11111110	FE	254
11111111	FF	255

DCC Locomotive Record Card

Locomotive type:	
Number:	
DCC address:	
Type of decoder:	

CV	Value	Comments:

Notes:

Glossary

A (Amp)
A measure of electric current.

AC (Alternating current)
Electric current that constantly changes direction.

Accessory Decoder
A decoder that operates accessories such as points and signals rather than a locomotive.

Address
The number of a locomotive, comparable to a telephone number.

Amp
Unit of electrical current. The more Amps that a booster can supply, the more locomotives and accessories you can have operating on your layout.

Analogue controller
Standard 12V DC controller, not capable of generating DCC commands.

Analogue locomotive
Standard 12V DC locomotive, not fitted with a DCC decoder.

Back EMF
When an electric motor runs it generates a voltage across its terminals. Some locomotive decoders measure this and use it to keep the motor running at a constant speed.

Binary Number
A number made up of bits. Values count up in twos rather than 10s. So 1 represents 1, 10 represents 2, 100 represents 4, 1000 represents 8, and so on.

Bit
Short for BINARY DIGIT. A single value of 0 or 1. A single bit can be used to indicate if something is off or on. A number of bits can be used to make a binary number.

Booster
Takes the low-power digital signal from the command station and amplifies it so that it has enough power to operate locomotives and accessories. A layout may have a number of boosters in order to provide sufficient power.

Bus Wires
Used to distribute power and/or information around the layout.

Byte
A group of 8 bits giving a value between 0 and 255.

Cab
Allows you to set the speed and direction of a locomotive. May also provide other facilities such as control of functions and programming. The cab sends commands to the command station.

Cab bus
A set of wires that run around the layout connecting cabs to the command station.

Circuit Breaker
Device that will shut off power to part of the layout if a short circuit is detected.

Command Station
The 'brains' of the system. Takes information from the cabs, formats it for DCC operation and passes it as a digital signal to the booster.

Configuration Variable (CV)
Address, starting voltage, acceleration rate and deceleration rate are examples of features which can be customised within the locomotive decoder.

Consist
Method of controlling several locomotives at the same time with a common address.

DC (Direct current)
Electric current that runs continuously in one direction.

DCC
Abbreviation for Digital Command Control.

Decoder
A device that receives DCC commands and acts on them; for example, to turn on a light or increase motor speed.

Extended Address/Extended Addressing
Not supported by all command stations or decoders. This is a method that allows locomotive addresses from 128 to 9999 to be used.

Function
A decoder controlled switch that can be used to operate lights and other accessories.

Locomotive address see Address

NMRA (National Model Railroad Association)
North American model railroaders organisation who control the DCC standards.

Operations Mode
The ability to set Configuration Variables of decoders whilst on the layout. Also known as Programming on the main.

Power Bus
Wires that provide power (usually 16V AC) to accessory decoders.

Power District
An electrically isolated section of the layout. A short circuit or overload within the section will not cause the rest of the layout to shut down.

Programming
The process of setting the Configuration Variables of a decoder.

Programming on the main
The ability to set Configuration Variables of decoders whilst on the layout. Also known as Operations Mode Programming.

Programming track
A section of track, electrically isolated from the layout, used for setting and reading the Configuration Variables of a decoder. Programming using this track is called Service Mode programming.

Railcom
Bi-directional communication system that allows locomotive decoders to transmit information as well as receive it.

Service Mode Programming
Programming the Configuration Variables of a decoder using the Programming track.

Speed steps
The number of increments that a decoder uses to change from stop to full speed.

Stealing
Taking control of a locomotive that is currently being operated by another cab.

Track Bus
Wires that connect the command station to the rails and accessory decoders.

Walkaround controller
A handheld cab that allows the operator to move around with the locomotive that they are operating.

Index